The Story of Food
in the Human Past

The Story of Food in the Human Past

How What We Ate Made Us Who We Are

ROBYN E. CUTRIGHT

The University of Alabama Press | Tuscaloosa

The University of Alabama Press
Tuscaloosa, Alabama 35487-0380
uapress.ua.edu

Typeface: Minion Pro

Cover design: Lori Lynch

Cataloging-in-Publication data is available from the Library of Congress.
ISBN: 978-0-8173-2082-9 (cloth)
ISBN: 978-0-8173-5985-0 (paper)
E-ISBN: 978-0-8173-9338-0

CONTENTS

ILLUSTRATIONS

PREFACE

In my first year of graduate school at the University of Pittsburgh, I took a course called Paleokitchen taught by my advisor, Marc Bermann. The course inspired me to analyze food remains from a set of ceramic pots placed in the burials that I excavated under the watchful eye of my mentor Carol Mackey in Peru the next summer. I wrote a master's thesis on this analysis, but I still wanted to learn more about ancient foodways. My doctoral thesis took a culinary approach to understanding imperial conquest, and I later taught several iterations of my own version of the Paleokitchen course as a professor at Centre College.

Over the past few decades, archaeologists, paleoanthropologists, and cultural anthropologists have become intensely interested in studying food. While food has always played a central role in big questions about human evolution and the origins of agriculture, recent studies have considered food in the context of everything from political feasts that shored up imperial power to daily kitchen tasks in rural villages. Cutting-edge scientific methods have allowed archaeologists to use highly technical lines of evidence such as bone chemistry and microscopic pollen embedded in ancient lake cores to ask and answer new questions. New findings and key theories are published and debated in countless scholarly monographs, edited volumes, and journal articles.

This book synthesizes the extensive archaeological and paleoanthropological literature on food. It explores how the quest for food has shaped us as humans, and how human biology and culture have in turn shaped what we eat. As when I teach the Paleokitchen course to undergraduate students, my goal in this book is to communicate some of the most interesting anthropological approaches to food in the human past and to summarize some of the key findings of this work for readers new to archaeology, or those who are curious about what people ate in the past.

I discuss my own archaeological research in Peru in this book, but I also rely on global case studies drawn from the research of many colleagues. The case studies I choose to highlight do not constitute an exhaustive look at food in the past. It would be impossible to provide full coverage of all the fascinating and high-quality anthropological research on food in one book. My goal is to give readers a sense of what we know about food in the human past and how we know it. I am indebted to my colleagues who produced the wide-ranging research discussed in this book, and I apologize for any errors in reporting or interpreting their work.

ACKNOWLEDGMENTS

Many colleagues offered specific advice, support, and resources during this project. Michael Twitty shared his bibliography on United States food history. Jerry Moore wrote a book (*The Prehistory of Home*) that inspired the approach I take here and encouraged me to write books connected to what I teach. Many colleagues, including Anna Guengerich and Lauren Herckis, shared resources, ideas from their specific areas, and feedback based on their own similar courses. My editor at the University of Alabama Press, Wendi Schnaufer, and the anonymous reviewers contributed important critiques, suggestions, and comments that strengthened the final product immensely.

I am grateful for the support of Centre College during the writing process. Various parts of this process were funded by sabbatical support, the Faculty Development Committee, the Charles T. Hazelrigg Chair enabling funds, and other Centre College funds. Especially important was support from my colleagues in the Anthropology and Sociology and Latin American Studies programs. Three Centre students provided special assistance. Jimmy Robinson served as a research assistant during initial stages of writing. Jessica Hale wrote a paper that contributed useful sources on Viking funerary feasts in chapter 7. Kate Himick's detail-oriented copyediting was essential during a later stage of manuscript development. Former Centre student and artist Isabelle Ballard drew several figures.

I am honored to be part of a group of scholars at Centre who encouraged and supported me as I proposed, researched, wrote, and edited this book. Core members of what started as a writing accountability group and has become a group of close friends and mentors include Eva Cadavid, Mary Daniels, Sara Egge, Jennifer Goetz, Danielle La Londe, Stacey Peebles, Shayna Sheinfeld, KatieAnn Skogsberg, and Kaelyn Wiles.

My love of food has been nourished by Annie Krieg, Kate Redmond,

Laurel Cutright, and the many other friends and family members who have participated in endless conversations about food; cohosted Anthropology Family Thanksgivings, potlucks, and dinners; and shared recipes, starters, homebrews, and cultures. My husband Drew Meadows has listened to me rehearse this material for four separate classes (so far) and one book and still asks interesting and helpful questions.

This book is dedicated to my father, Dr. Noel Cutright. As a conservationist, ecologist, and birder, he taught people about the natural world around them and inspired them to protect it. He tirelessly communicated science to the public and shared his passion for birds with local clubs, public radio audiences, state officials, business owners, utility industry executives, the ornithological community, his family, and basically anyone who would listen. He is my role model and the inspiration for this book.

The Story of Food
in the Human Past

INTRODUCTION

Food for Thought

A group of Neandertals sits around a fire under a rock overhang as evening falls. It is 46,000 years ago at Shanidar Cave, Iraq. All day, the group has foraged through the rugged landscape of the Zagros Mountains, and now they gather in the warmth and relative safety of shelter to cook and eat. The menu includes a porridge of wild barley, legumes, dates, and wild goat cooked using hot stones from the fire. Starch grains from this meal, and a lifetime of others like it, leave a residue on one individual's teeth. Millennia later, scientists will scrape off this hardened residue and identify the fossilized remains of the meal.[1]

⚶

Not far away in northeastern Jordan, 30,000 years later, Natufian villagers gather at a basalt hearth in the center of a solidly built house. Despite living in permanent homes, the villagers do not tend farms. Instead, they gather wild cereals, plants, and tubers and hunt gazelles and hares in the surrounding landscape. Using grinding stones, a cook has carefully ground and sifted wild wheat into flour, added the roots of a wild sedge plant, and formed the resulting dough into flat baked loaves. As household members eat and talk, crumbs of bread fall into the fire. Much later these charred crumbs will be found during an archaeological excavation and identified by archaeobotanists as the world's oldest bread.[2]

⚶

Workers at Amarna village in the New Kingdom period of ancient Egypt are involved in an ambitious royal project. After Akhenaten became pharaoh in the fourteenth century BC, he changed the state religion and moved the capital. In addition to laborers, the construction of a new capital city requires engineers, masonry experts, and other craftsmen, who live in the Amarna village. After a day working on buildings destined to be abandoned after Akhenaten's death, the workers come home to a tightly packed village to cool off on the roofs of their homes and catch up with their neighbors. In exchange for their work, the state provides them with grain rations—farmed grain from fields, now, not the wild grains of the previous scenes. Grain is transformed to bread at the grinding stones and shared ovens of the village. Archaeologists will use the locations of ovens and grinding stones to reconstruct social organization in the village.[3]

⚷

Members of the Maynard extended family sit down for a dinner of pork chops and fresh garden tomatoes at the mahogany table in the side room of their Annapolis, Maryland, home. As an African American family in the mid-eighteenth century, the Maynards have to find their way in a society in which discrimination and violence are common and their freedom is contingent and tenuous. The family prefers pork enough to brave the discomfort of dealing with white shopkeepers to obtain it. At the same time, they grow food in their backyard and fish in local waterways to maintain a certain amount of autonomy within white-dominated food systems. Archaeologists will recover evidence of sixty years of meals like this one from their yard and root cellar. They will interpret the menu as a reflection of the Maynards' participation in and resistance to dominant society, a way to stake out their own community and individual identities.[4]

⚷

A group of dusty archaeologists gathers on the side of a mountain in northern Peru to take a break. We have been digging through the remains of eight-hundred-year-old houses for hours: scraping and brushing away the sand, sifting it through screens to recover pieces of pottery, seeds, bones of guinea pigs and dogs, copper needles, and other household detritus, labeling plastic bags to preserve the context of each artifact, and recording the work with notes, photos, and measurements. As my colleagues and I lean against the mountainside or relax on piles of sifted dirt, I pass around a bag of store-bought bread rolls and mandarin oranges. William, a member of the local community, passes around a bag of Andean gooseberries his cousin brought home from a weekend trip, and we gossip and joke until it is time to start working again.

Each of these meals took place in a different part of the world, at a different historical moment over thousands of years. Each was the product of very different social structures, relationships with the environment, economies, and food preparation technologies. The individuals who ate these meals led dramatically different lives and understood their worlds in very different ways. Yet these very different meals also share a few essential characteristics.

First, all these meals sat at the interface of biology and culture. They consisted of the plants and animals available in their specific environments, and they responded to the nutritional needs and physical structure of the human body. Each meal was also a product of culture, a term that refers to the behaviors, beliefs, worldviews, and objects shared by a group of people, learned through enculturation into that group. Each meal reflected the technologies, from fire to refrigeration, developed and sustained by that particular society. Ingredients were shared, exchanged, or purchased according to each society's economic system, and meals were prepared according to each society's division of labor. The combinations and flavors of each meal revealed cultural ideas of what an appropriate meal looked like and how it should be eaten. These meals were one way that individuals and communities made meaning of their worlds and, in a small way, expressed what it meant to be human. Thus, the meals described here provide a powerful window onto all these diverse dimensions of life.

We humans are incredibly flexible in what we eat, within the constraints imposed by our bodies, environments, and cultures. Culture might help us adapt to our surroundings, our particular ecological and economic conditions, but our surroundings do not exist outside culture. Rather, our surroundings are a product of culture. For instance, when Europeans arrived in eastern North America, the "untouched" forests they saw had been carefully shaped by intentional fires and other methods by Native Americans for millennia.[5]

Culture is more than an adaptive mechanism. It is a system of beliefs, values, and ideals about how things work, what things mean, and how we should behave. Culture shapes how we understand ourselves, our connection to the world and others, and our experience. What it means to be a woman or man, what a traditional family looks like, how humans relate to the natural and the supernatural, and what foods are appropriate in which context are all shaped by culture rather than fixed by instinct. What we eat is implicated in our individual identities but also in how we navigate larger structures of power and meaning. This book is about how food has shaped us as humans, how we have shaped and reshaped cuisine through our long history as a species, and how this history has made us who we are.

A second shared characteristic of these meals is that they are visible to us through archaeological research into past societies. Archaeologists use material remains—buildings, hearths, pots, seeds, burials—to study past human societies and cultures. This book is as much a story about archaeologists as it is a story about the past.

Many archaeologists use food as a line of evidence to reconstruct other aspects of ancient social organization, economy, politics, gender relations, and so on. In this sense, figuring out what people ate helps us answer big social questions about the past. Other archaeologists study food itself. What did preparing and eating certain meals mean in specific cultural contexts? How was food used to maintain structures of power or to resist, to make meaning of the world and of individual experiences, or to express identity? Each set of archaeologists is interested in knowing something different about the past, but they use similar methods and data to draw their conclusions.

Archaeological techniques for recovering and analyzing evidence have improved, allowing us to better answer old questions and generate new kinds of data. New theoretical approaches have also asked new questions and reevaluated earlier models. By looking at archaeological research on food, we can see the process of scientific inquiry at work, asking questions, laying out hypotheses, gathering data, and then either rejecting or refining those hypotheses. As with any science, archaeologists' own societies and identities shape the kinds of questions they ask and the kinds of explanations they prefer.

This book synthesizes how research on food has contributed to key debates and new questions about the human past. These questions include the role of particular resources in human evolution, the time depth of some fundamental human social behaviors like gendered divisions of labor and domesticity, the causes and effects of a worldwide transition to agriculture, and the emergence of hierarchical forms of social organization. Specialists in archaeology, paleoanthropology, and related fields have debated these questions for decades in highly technical journal articles and conference presentations, aimed at an audience of other specialists. In this book, I draw on the work of these specialists along with my own archaeological research to speak to a more general audience. My goal is to tell the story of what humans ate in the past, and how archaeologists have used food to understand what it meant to be human in different times, places, and social positions.

HUMANS: OMNIVORES WITH CULTURE

Humans eat at the complex intersection of biology and culture; we eat to survive, but we also eat as cultural beings. Anthropologists who study food distinguish *diet* and *cuisine*. *Diet* refers to the food we eat on a daily basis. Diets should, but do not always, provide the macronutrients (proteins, carbohydrates, and fats) that fuel our bodies as well as micronutrients such as vitamins and minerals that keep us healthy. Like our close relatives, chimpanzees, humans are omnivores. Our teeth and digestive system are equipped to process a wide variety of plant and animal products. We are not specialists like the koala, which eats only eucalyptus, or the lynx, which eats mostly snowshoe hare. Lynxes and koalas never wonder what to eat or figure out whether a particular food will be healthy or poisonous. Natural selection has done this work for them, leaving them to figure out simply where the next leaf or hare will come from.

For humans, and other omnivores like pigs, bears, raccoons, and rats, the question is more complicated. If we can eat a wide range of foods, what should we eat? Food writer Michael Pollan has notably written about this so-called omnivore's dilemma.[6] Not all potential foods are equally nutritious, available, or safe to eat, but instinct alone does not tell us omnivores which to choose. Omnivores need to balance experimentation with caution; we need to be curious about new foods but also wary of the unknown. We need to be able to connect feeling bad now with foods we tried earlier, to avoid making the same mistake again. Rats very easily learn to avoid foods that make them sick, and humans too become averse to foods that have negative effects. However, humans have another tool to solve the omnivore's dilemma—culture.

If diet is the food we actually consume, *cuisine* is the set of cultural rules, ideals, and behaviors that shape what is appropriate to eat, when, with whom, and in what preparations. Our cuisine helps us, as omnivores, decide what is appropriate to eat, and how we should eat it. Different cuisines have different rules for what to eat, how, and when. Peanuts are part of the diet in the United States, Senegal, and Vietnam, but they are incorporated into different dishes (peanut butter and jelly sandwiches, spicy stews, or green papaya salad, for instance). Each of these different peanut dishes occupies a different place in its specific society and cuisine.

Culture and cuisine also define what is food and what is not food, from within the broad range of substances humans might safely eat. No human society regularly eats everything edible in its environment, because culture does not distinguish food from not-food solely based on toxicity. Insects like grasshoppers and ant larvae are considered food in cuisines of Mexico but not Spain; the French ate horse but the British did not; guinea pigs are party food in Ecuador and Peru but pets in the United States, and so on.

Is there any consistency across cultures in what is considered food and what is not? There might seem to be a simple biological answer to this question: some plants and animals are simply poisonous or inedible to humans. Even so, people in some societies have found ways to process and transform products into food, through cuisine. Bitter manioc or cassava, a starchy root that grows in the Amazon, can cause cyanide poisoning unless it is peeled, grated, soaked, fermented, and thoroughly cooked, but it is regularly eaten.[7] Even "sweet" varieties of cassava must be cooked to neutralize their lower quantities of cyanide, yet these varieties are commonly consumed around the world in dishes like fried yuca, mofongo, or tapioca. Another example of a culinary transformation of an inedible food is dairy. The ability to digest milk as an adult is rare in many human populations, but cuisine has responded by using fermentation to digest problematic milk sugars and make products like cheese, yogurt, and kefir.[8] These examples show that biology alone cannot completely answer the question of why we eat what we do.

Psychobiologist Paul Rozin suggests that there are some universal human behaviors when it comes to food choice.[9] Sensory effects in the mouth, appearance, anticipated consequences of consumption, ideational factors, and the nature or origin of the substance itself all affect whether we reject or accept particular foods. Rozin suggests that association with nausea is especially powerful in shaping food aversions, which makes good sense considering that paying attention to foods that make us feel sick would have helped us avoid toxic or dangerous food in the past. Another powerful and fairly universal reaction to food is disgust, when we connect a substance with feces, insects, or rot. Yet in some societies mealworms, fermented kimchi, or mold-covered blue cheese are considered entirely appropriate for consumption and are even highly desired, so even deeply seated aversions and reactions are conditioned by culture.

Food preferences in humans are shaped by a few genetic predispositions, such as a preference for sweet flavors, an avoidance of bitter tastes, and an interest in but fear of new foods. However, these evolved preferences cannot fully explain our choices, according to Rozin. We consume, and even crave, a lot of natural irritants and bitter substances. Coffee, tea, and dark chocolate are all bitter, while alcohol, tobacco, and some spices are all irritants. These substances are highly desired by many people, and even occasional negative reactions like nausea do not necessarily keep us from consuming them.

Rozin studied how people come to enjoy eating spicy chili peppers through a complex cultural, physiological, and psychological process. Children who grow up with a cultural preference for spicy foods, such as the Mexican children Rozin studied, learn to like spicy chilies as they observe adults enjoying them and perceive that they are valued. Exposure tends to increase liking, so over time emulation becomes enjoyment. In addition to social factors, psychobiological factors may help explain why people come to like spice. It may be that pain associated with a spicy chili pepper becomes pleasant as people realize the pain is not really harmful. Eating chilies might be seen as a way to engage in controlled risk-taking. The pain might also cause the body to produce opiates, spurring a pleasant and addictive aftereffect to a hot meal.

Chilies and other spices might also help us add unfamiliar foods to our diets by providing a familiar flavor profile. Flavorings do not contribute much to diet in terms of calories, but they are essential to cuisine. You are probably already familiar with some common flavor profiles that make different cuisines distinctive: chilies and lime in Mexican cuisine; soy sauce, ginger, and rice wine in Chinese cuisine; Indian curries made with coriander, fenugreek, cumin, and chilies; and so on. Rozin believes that these distinctive flavorings reduce fear about new foods by making them taste familiar, in the same way that putting ketchup on a new food might make a picky American five-year-old eat it. From this perspective, cuisine might be adaptive in that it helps us incorporate new foods into our diets.

If there are some psychological regularities in the way humans react to food and incorporate it into cuisine, then the human diet must be, at least to some extent, the product of evolution. Many scholars have considered whether there might be a specific diet to which humans are evolutionarily suited. Chapters 1 and 2 explore this question in more detail, but in general an evolutionary perspective shows humans are generalists in the sense that we thrive within a wide range of diets, systems of social organization, family structures, climates, and so on. Much of our behavior as a species is so flexible that the ability to live and eat in variable ways must have proved successful for our ancestors.

While all people must consume enough calories and certain vitamins and minerals to avoid starvation and deficiency-based illness, these parameters are wide. A brief survey of the diets of modern human societies emphasizes this incredible variation.[10] The traditional Inuit diet consists mostly of fatty marine meat and fish, while the traditional diet of central Mexico emphasizes vegetable cornerstones of corn, beans, squash, chilies, and greens plus eggs, insects, and meat. Diets in the Andes are starch-heavy, based on potatoes, quinoa, fava beans, and other high-altitude tubers and grains, while forager diets in Tanzania rely heavily on nuts and honey in addition to game and tubers.[11] While scarcity and malnutrition occasionally occur in all these settings, these diets have stood the test of time and thus must be able to support relatively healthy human populations.

WHY DO WE EAT WHAT WE DO?

For humans, then, eating involves choosing a set of foods to eat out of a range of possibly edible foods. Nutritional requirements and other aspects of human biology shape those decisions, and probably push humans toward a broad generalist diet. The environment shapes the foods that are available, but humans reshape our environments as we grow or forage food. Cultural understandings of the world also influence our decisions, by defining what is food in the first place, how these foods should be prepared, and what is appropriate to eat in particular contexts.

Every cuisine has its own shape, and its own answer to what and how we should eat. But what is cuisine? Is it an adaptive mechanism that helps societies live within the basic parameters of their ecosystems? A cognitive and symbolic system that responds to universal cultural structures, or specific cultural contexts? A set of preferences and behaviors shaped by power, politics, and social identity? All these answers have been proposed by anthropologists and social theorists working from different theoretical standpoints. A quick review of some of the most influential approaches reveals widely divergent views on why we eat what we do.

The Meal as Unconscious Structure

One answer to the question of why do we eat the way we do, views cuisine as just one arena of human society that betrays the deep structures of culture.

The most famous proponent of this structuralist approach is anthropologist Claude Lévi-Strauss. Lévi-Strauss has suggested that we choose to eat certain species not because they are "good to eat" but because they are "good to think."[12] He wrote, "the cooking of a society is a language in which it unconsciously translates its structure—or else resigns itself, still unconsciously, to revealing its contradictions."[13] In other words, food choices are one of the ways we as humans think about and structure our world. The goal of the anthropologist in studying food is to uncover that structure.

For Lévi-Strauss, everything was defined in opposition to something else. I am a woman because I am not a man. My pug is a dog because she is not a cat, or a horse. Culture draws a line around every concept by opposing it to other concepts. By looking at how sets of oppositions are structured and used to define the world, we can understand the cultural mind. Lévi-Strauss's most famous discussion of food focuses on what he called the culinary triangle (figure I.1).[14]

The triangle starts with the opposed categories of *raw* and *cooked*. Double oppositions form a triangle, in which each term is both linked and opposed to the others. In the case of food, the three points of the triangle are the raw, the cooked, and the rotten. Raw food is unmarked, untransformed, conceptually linked to nature. Both rotten and cooked foods are transformed, but rotten food is transformed by nature and cooked food by culture. There are really two oppositions at work, nature/culture and transformed/untransformed.

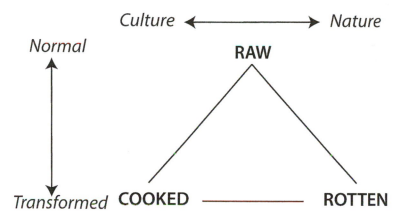

FIGURE I.1. Lévi-Strauss's culinary triangle. (Redrawn from Lévi-Strass, "The Culinary Triangle," p. 34, Robyn Cutright)

This triangle plays out through different modes of cooking too. According to Lévi-Strauss, many cuisines make a central contrast between roasted and boiled food. Both are cooked, but roasted food is directly exposed to fire, while boiled food is mediated by first covering it in water and then heating in a pot. This distinction comes down, again, to the opposition between nature and culture, where roasted food is closer to nature, raw (or at least not always uniformly cooked, and often bloody), and unmediated. By contrast boiled food is mediated and transformed. Boiled food matches up with the category of the rotten because it is mediated and transformed, because of its consistency, and because many languages connect the two (for instance, the term *potpourri* actually refers to rotten food). Boiled food is what Lévi-Strauss called an *endo-cuisine*, prepared for home use by a small group, while roasted food is *exo-cuisine*, offered to guests outside the family group. The opposed categories of female/male can be mapped onto boiled/roasted, since men are more likely to grill or roast meat for company, while women are more likely to prepare the daily meal.

Lévi-Strauss built a complex web of oppositions and transformations to show how we structure and conceptualize food. As evidence for the pervasiveness of this structure, he cited myths, practices, and terms from a huge range of societies and languages, yet it often seems to me that he just picked examples that fit his framework. He needed to stretch the incredible diversity of human languages and cultures to show that they all respond to the same internal logical structures, and I am not fully convinced. However, I think Lévi-Strauss's approach is useful in the way it sees cuisine as deeply embedded in and connected to other aspects of culture. In this holistic view, cuisine is one of the grammars through which people make meaning of our worlds.

The Meal as Social Grammar

Unlike Lévi-Strauss, British sociologist Mary Douglas does not think that universal structures exist.[15] She does think that food encodes messages about the pattern of social relationships, though, and that categories are defined through opposition. In her view, the mind works with cuisine in the same way it operates with language and other cultural systems. It distinguishes order, draws a line around it, and separates it from disorder. There are a limited number of these structures, which are repeated across different domains and at different scales. Repetition enhances the meaning of each category and opposition.

Distinguishing order, bounding it, and separating it from disorder is how we understand and make meaning of the world, in Douglas's view.[16] For Douglas, dirt is simply matter out of place—there is nothing inherent about the dirt that makes it impure, only the fact that it is not where (or what) it should be. She uses this idea to explain the dietary restrictions laid out in Old Testament Leviticus, which notably prohibit observant Jews from eating pork and shellfish, among other foods. Douglas argues that the prohibitions are based on the way animals are classified. Pigs have cloven hooves, but do not chew cud, so they fall outside the classification system. In fact, the pig pollutes in several ways at once—it falls outside of the classification system, it eats carrion, and it is eaten by outsiders. To simplify Douglas's logic, the pig falls outside the rules of the meal, and in so doing it endangers the ordered systems of the meal and more broadly the society.

Mary Douglas uses the British meal as an example of how structure helps distinguish between appropriate and inappropriate meals. What, Douglas asks, is the difference between a bunch of snacks and a proper meal? It is not necessarily calories or nutrients, it is that a meal has a specific "grammatical" structure. A conglomeration of food that does not follow that structure might satisfy our bodies, but not our minds. We might not feel that we have had a "proper meal," even if we have eaten sufficient calories.

All human societies have language. Linguists have debated whether all languages share a universal grammar at some level, but clearly all languages have a structure and a grammar. There are ways to put words together that make sense, and ways that do not. For Douglas, cuisine is the same. All cuisines have a grammar, but not the same grammar.

For the British cuisine Douglas knows best (and I would argue for some parts of American cuisine as well) this structure can be given as an equation: A + 2B. Douglas suggests that each meal has one stressed element (A) and two unstressed elements (B). A basic meal in this structure might consist of roast chicken (A) with potatoes and broccoli (2B). We know that chicken is the stressed element because, if we are asked to describe the meal we might just say "roast chicken" but we probably would not just say "broccoli." Vegetarians or vegans are familiar with how this grammar shapes our expectations for a meal. At a family Thanksgiving meal in the United States, where vegetarians avoid eating turkey but fill their plates with vegetables, rolls, salads, and cranberry sauce, they might be asked: *What are you going to eat, just sides?* They are missing the stressed element, which is often meat in American and British cuisine, and so what they eat does not "count" as a satisfying meal to everyone. However, a vegetarian meal of spaghetti (A) with garlic bread and salad (2B) might satisfy a prying relative because it has the correct structure.

What is interesting is that this A + 2B structure is repeated at different scales throughout British (and American) cuisine. You might eat chicken with potatoes and broccoli at dinner, but dinner itself might consist of a main dish (A) with appetizer and dessert (2B). During a day, you might eat a large meal at dinner (A), and two smaller ones at breakfast and lunch (2B). Even within one dish, you might see the A + 2B equation repeated at a smaller scale. You might have a baked potato (A) with sour cream and chives (2B). After dinner, you might have coffee (A) with cream and sugar (2B). At each of these scales, the repeated structure assures us that we are having a complete, satisfying meal.

Other cuisines have a very different grammar. For instance, a Chinese student in my class once pointed out that a meal for her consists of a grain accompanied by a variety of small dishes. She expressed frustration that American students can be satisfied by a meal of just one dish. For Douglas, the point is that we recognize what is appropriate and satisfying to eat because it follows the culinary structure we are accustomed to. The meaning of a meal lies in its analogy to other meals, the way it fits within the larger structure. Yet Douglas does not give us a framework to account for why different cultures have different culinary grammars. Nor does she account for how grammars change, something that anthropologist Mary Weismantel has addressed in the context of highland Ecuadorean cuisine.

The Meal as Sign and Symbol

For Mary Weismantel, cuisine is a system of signs, a symbolic conversation, and a form of household production.[17] Weismantel studied the cuisine of Zumbagua, a mountain farming community in Ecuador, in the early 1980s. The region was struggling with development and change stemming from greater access to the national economy, and Weismantel found cuisine to be one of the places where conversations about change took place, in part because of the richness of food as sign, symbol, and product. I focus first on the first two properties of food in Weismantel's theory: sign and symbol.

When anthropologists write about food (or anything else) as a sign, they are drawing on the field of semiotics. Semiotics tries to understand how people create and communicate meaning through language and other systems of signs. A sign is anything that stands for something else. As Weismantel explains, it can be hard to think of a food, like a potato, as a sign. A potato is a physical object, so how can it be a representation of something? The reason for this confusing terminology is that we experience and understand the physical world through our social construction of it. According to semiotics, we cannot experience the potato as a physical object separate from our social understanding of it. Instead, we always relate the physical object in front of us to the categories that exist to describe it, which are formed by language and culture.

Weismantel uses the potato as an example because it is central to Zumbaguan cuisine but also important in other culinary systems, where it carries very different meanings. Consider the meaning of the potato in nineteenth-century Ireland, where it was a basic staple in a cuisine impoverished by centuries of economic exploitation, or in twenty-first-century Kentucky, where it appears everywhere from Thanksgiving dinner to a fast food meal. From this perspective, "potato" does not have a meaning independent from our social construction of the world.

Like a language, then, a cuisine is a system of signs based on a shared understanding of meaning, in which signs might be defined through opposition to other signs. Just as we might think of day and night, or cat and dog, as signs in opposition, so residents of Zumbagua understand meals in opposition to special treats; raw, sharp, masculine flavors like spicy chilies or salt in contrast to cooked, feminine sweets; or a daily bowl of soup in contrast to a celebratory plate of food.

In addition to being signs in a system of meanings, foods can be metaphors in a conversation about the world. Weismantel gives the example of breakfast foods in Zumbagua. For Zumbaguans of mixed Spanish and indigenous descent, those who do not consider themselves primarily indigenous but rather part of the white middle class, breakfast typically consists of hot water, into which white sugar and instant coffee are added, and two bread rolls. Indigenous Zumbaguans also refer to breakfast as "*café*," or coffee, but it can consist of hot water to which brown sugar and barley meal are added.

Bread, once traditionally considered a luxury good and eaten as a special treat by indigenous Zumbaguans, became a point of conflict in the 1980s as children wanted to eat it for breakfast instead of barley meal porridge. Bread was desired because it symbolized white, middle-class luxury; it had to be purchased, which meant that the family had to be engaged in the cash economy. Toasted barley flour symbolized a rural, indigenous identity that had been stigmatized since the Spanish colonized South America, but also tradition and homey comfort; it could be produced locally on a family's land so it did not require cash. In dealing with children's demand for bread at breakfast, Zumbaguan mothers were responding to a symbolic pressure to develop and assimilate. Weismantel also reports instances when people defined themselves as "barley-eaters" in explicit resistance against the modern world.

Weismantel describes the complex systems that underlie how people think about food, yet food is not just a symbol in her work. It also has a material reality, linked to relationships of household production. Food, as both a symbol and a physical substance that must be procured, cooked, and consumed every day, takes part in complicated conversations about identity, modernization, and change.

The Meal as Ecological Adaptation

In a sense, from a structural perspective, cuisine is all in our heads because food is good to think. We study food to understand more about ourselves as cultural beings. But as Weismantel's work points out, food is also a product of certain forms of household production. Food is not just in our heads, after all, it is a material and biological necessity. Cultural ecologists argue that cuisine, like culture more broadly, helps us adapt to the specific set of resources available to us and the environment that produces them. We eat what we do, argue cultural ecologists, because it helps us adapt to our environment.

The well-known anthropologist Marvin Harris has looked specifically at food taboos to identify their deeper ecological logic and show how cuisine might be adaptive.[18] He argues that the Torah and the Koran both ban consumption of pork because raising pigs does not make ecological sense in the Middle East. Pigs do not eat grass, like cud-chewing goats and cows, so they compete with humans for food. They need a lot of water to drink and to keep cool, which make them expensive to support in arid environments. They do not offer secondary products like wool or milk, so they are less economically versatile than sheep, goats, or cows. They do not thrive with a nomadic lifestyle. All these factors make pigs ill-suited for desert herders and nomads in the Middle East, especially after the population grew and forests declined in the region after 5000 BC.

Yet pigs are delicious, and people want to eat them. It turns out that we humans are not always very good at putting long-term ecological sustainability before our own short-term desires. Harris argues that the societies that persisted in the Middle East were the ones that encoded ecologically sound behavior into religious belief. In this case, the religious taboo against eating pork became a strong part of religious belief and identity, such that it even persists in Jewish and Muslim populations that live in places where pigs are ecologically viable.

Harris's argument about pigs relies on the general assumption that the material aspects of life, like ecology and economy, come first, and that beliefs and culture develop later to ensure that a society maintains a sustainable approach. Those societies with beliefs and cultures that did not help them remain sustainable would not have endured. This perspective does help explain why different societies have different cuisines, which was a problem with Lévi-Strauss's approach. Like Lévi-Strauss and Douglas, however, Harris is better at describing static stable systems than accounting for change.

Rather than using linguistic or structural analysis, cultural ecologists use quantitative data to argue that cuisine serves an adaptive purpose. Anthropologist Roy Rappaport also studied pigs, this time in a small-scale society in Papua New Guinea. Rappaport's classic book, *Pigs for the Ancestors*, argues that the complex annual ritual cycle of the Tsembaga people in Papua New Guinea works to regulate people's interaction with their forest environment.[19]

Rappaport carefully measured how much food the Tsembaga grew using a slash and burn gardening technique and how much they gathered, how much of each different food they ate, and how much they fed their pigs and other animals. Pigs were semidomesticated. People gave them substandard or leftover sweet potatoes but did not keep pigs in pens, and pigs also foraged for trash and sometimes raided the gardens. The Tsembaga liked having pigs around, but too many pigs became a strain on their gardens and their labor. When pigs got too numerous, the Tsembaga hosted an elaborate feast where 85 percent of the pigs were eaten. This feast released taboos against warfare with neighboring communities. Warfare was cyclical, since it was caused by the desire to get even for past attacks, and would go on until a defeat or truce placed a new taboo on warfare. Men returned to the gardens, the pig population began to grow, and the cycle repeated itself.

Rappaport's measurements and calculations allowed him to argue that this ritual cycle regulated the balance between the community, its neighbors, the pig population, and the gardens, even if the Tsembaga themselves did not explain it that way. From the perspective of cultural ecology, the meaning of the ritual to believers is separate from the objective impact it has on their behavior. This is one of the weaknesses of the cultural ecology approach. The emphasis on how human and nonhuman actors interact in a broader ecosystem makes sense, but the emic, or insider's, view of the Tsembaga is too important to just cast aside as a superficial epiphenomenon that dupes people into acting in an adaptive way. This view also ignores the many cases in which human societies do not maintain ecological balance with their surroundings.

The Meal as Political Negotiation

Humans are political animals. Power, authority, and resistance are important social dynamics that can be expressed through cuisine. Returning to the case of pigs in the Near East, Mary Douglas's structural perspective emphasized categories and the inherent impurity of that which is neither one thing nor the other. For Marvin Harris, the prohibition represented a way to ensure adaptation to a harsh environment by enshrining ecologically responsible behavior in religious belief. A political perspective offers a different explanation.

Archaeologist Steven Falconer's research at a Bronze Age village in Jordan does not explicitly address the question of the taboo against pigs,[20] but it does offer some insight into the political economy of pigs. The Bronze Age was a period of increasing urbanization, and Falconer was curious to see how villagers responded to growing urban markets and the increasing demands of urban elites. Urban elites would have been interested in incorporating a rural village into economic and political networks to extract taxes. Falconer studied the economic production of a village called Tell el-Hayyat during this period. He found that over time, people increased their production of economically useful goods, especially wine, olive oil, and sheep/goats, which could be traded with growing urban centers. The temple, a central economic institution of Near Eastern communities, played a role in this production. However, households also invested in pigs.

Unlike wool, olive oil, and wine, pig meat is not easy to store and transport to a market located a week's walk across a desert. Unlike sheep and goats, it is not easy to march a herd of pigs to market in a distant city. Pigs are, however, an extremely efficient way to transform household scraps and surplus grain into protein, which can be stored alive until needed. By adding a pig to their household repertoire, Tell el-Hayyat families gave themselves access to meat that was essentially untaxable. Falconer suggests that rural villages engaged in urban networks but also developed hedges against taxation. From this perspective, we might see a prohibition against pork as a way for urban elites to fight back against rural tax evasion. The case of Tell el-Hayyat suggests that we should not discount politics, power, and other social dynamics in trying to understand why people eat the way they do.

Archaeologist Monica Smith has studied the long history of food preference and food politics in South Asia, and specifically the preference for rice in India and Sri Lanka.[21] Food preference refers to the way individuals choose from among available options on the basis of multiple factors—economic, biological, nutritional, cultural—within a complex social context.

Even though individuals express their preferences through the foods they choose to eat, Smith argues, food preference is not solely individual but also social. Food is a basic way we express our identification with a group. It both reveals and helps build social relations.

In South Asia, rice was a basic staple, but it was also highly desirable and strongly preferred. This preference, in Smith's argument, led to policies favoring increased rice production, including large-scale irrigation projects organized by the state. It also inspired labor input by rural villagers, who wanted to be able to eat more rice. Smith suggests that elites were able to build consensus around these projects because the strong preference for more rice made the benefits easily visible to the population. The cultural ideals and belief systems of the people, in this case their culinary preference for rice, sustained the political projects of ancient South Asian leaders.

While some political perspectives emphasize consensus and others conflict, all agree that politics is deeply embedded in why we eat what we do. It is possible to look at our own contemporary American diet from this perspective as well. Michael Pollan suggests that agricultural subsidies have dramatically shaped the US diet by promoting the intensive production of a few commodity agricultural products like corn and soy.[22] Because these were cheap to produce and protected by government policies, farmers produced more, and agricultural companies sought new ways to process and use these products. Ultimately, this means that almost everything we buy at the grocery store, from soda to salad dressing, has some form of corn in it. In contrast, fresh fruits and vegetables are labeled "specialty crops" and have historically received much less support from US agricultural policies. Political support of some kinds of farming over others shapes prices in the grocery stores, where processed food made of corn and soy is often much cheaper than unprocessed fruits and vegetables, and prices ultimately affect the choices we make as consumers.

Economics, politics, and power play central roles in what we eat, as do the dynamics of food preference that Smith describes. My archaeological research investigates how these dynamics play out on an everyday basis in ancient households, and how cuisine relates to social continuity and social change. It resonates with archaeologist Cynthia Robin's stance that "everyday life matters,"[23] because cooks in kitchens must translate large-scale processes of conquest, cultural change, migration, and economic production as they prepare daily meals for their families.

In this book, I am interested in examining how what we ate in the past connects to broad questions of human evolution and prehistoric social organization—how food has shaped us as humans, and how we have shaped and reshaped cuisine through our long history as a species. I often tend to emphasize the material as opposed to the symbolic or structural in explaining why we eat the way we do. However, I also know that food is not just calories and nutrients; it is also a way in which people make meaning and tell themselves who they are.

UNCOVERING THE MEAL

Anthropologists have thought about food from many different perspectives, with different views on the interplays between ecology and culture, and between universal structures and particular histories. In this book, I synthesize a wide range of theoretical perspectives and archaeological case studies, focusing on two related questions about what people ate in the past.

The first question is, "*How did food shape us as humans?*" To answer this question, I focus on the work of paleoanthropologists, primatologists, paleoclimatologists, and evolutionary biologists. Paleoanthropologists study human evolution by excavating fossilized remains of ancient human ancestors along with the tools they made and the environments they modified. They study the shape of the fossilized bones and teeth to understand how particular features like brain size, gait, and diet changed through time, and to reconstruct the relationships between different species. They use bone chemistry as evidence of what these individuals ate and look at the other animals found alongside them to understand what the environment was like. Remains of stone tools and animal bones that show marks from cutting and chopping also provide clues about these ancient ancestors and what they ate.

To help flesh out the record of fossilized bones, I explore contributions from primatologists, who study our close primate ancestors. Looking at what we share with modern chimpanzees, and how we differ from them, alerts us to key features of what it means to be human. I also draw on evolutionary biology, which focuses on how natural selection has shaped our behavior and bodies, for insights into the kinds of pressures our ancestors had to face to survive. Finally, since food represents one point where we are tightly connected to our environment, I use reconstructions of ancient environments drawn by paleoclimatologists on the basis of records preserved on sea floors and in glacial ice to tell the story of environmental shifts over millions of years of human evolution.

Part I of this book explores the role of food in human evolution, placing more emphasis on biological adaptation but still considering the role of culture. In chapter 1, I consider the deep evolutionary past of human diet. By comparing humans to our closest living relatives, chimpanzees, I highlight some key aspects of human eating behavior. Humans transform our food, we eat meals rather than graze throughout the day, and we eat with strangers. These behaviors must have emerged since our ancestors diverged from the ancestors of modern chimpanzees millions of years ago. Over the first several million years of this distinct human lineage, a few key traits emerged. Walking on two legs, living at least part time on the ground, and making tools emerged as brain size was only beginning to grow. How did diet, and especially meat eating, play a role in the evolution of these traits? And can looking at meat and other resources in the evolutionary past help us figure out what to eat today?

Chapter 2 looks at how human ancestors began to control fire and use it to cook. One theory has it that cooking was the key invention that allowed human ancestors to finally leave the trees for good and cook food, grow bigger brains, and begin forming social groups oriented around a pair bond. A contrasting theory explains the trajectory of human evolution one to two million years ago by giving roasted tubers and female social bonds central priority. In either case, chapter 2 suggest that cooking over a fire today means recalling a legacy that began long before *Homo sapiens* appeared on the scene.

In chapter 3, I investigate the origins of cuisine as culture and adaptation. I focus on two highly complex, intelligent species: *Homo sapiens* and Neandertals. New research increasingly paints Neandertals as intelligent, well adapted to the environment of Ice Age Europe, and capable of complex cultural behavior like burying their dead. How did *Homo sapiens* survive to populate the world, while Neandertals and other closely related species died out? Chapter 3 considers the debate about what modern humans and Neandertals ate, and whether food had anything to do with Neandertal extinction and human survival. Chapter 3 ends with a description of human foraging societies that eventually spread to every continent apart from Antarctica, setting the scene for the next dramatic culinary transformation, described in the second section of the book.

The second central question of this book is, "*What role did food play in past societies?*" This question asks how the quest for food shaped societies, and how social and political structures shaped cuisine. To answer this question, part II of this book uses archaeology to explore how culture and cuisine were intertwined in the past.

To reconstruct what people in the past ate, archaeologists use multiple lines of evidence. We survey landscapes to find remnants of human occupation, called sites, which can tell us how past societies used the environment to find or grow food. We carefully map and excavate sites, documenting everything we uncover and sifting the soil to find small artifacts discarded as trash or left behind when people abandoned the site. Remains of plants and animals in household trash or in the remains of ancient hearths show us the resources people used (figure I.2). Broken pottery can tell us how food was stored, cooked, and served, and chemical residues preserved on the inside walls of pots can help us see what exactly they were cooking. Microscopic pollen and plant parts found by sifting through the sediments of ancient communities can tell us more about what people were eating and about the environments where they lived.

Some of our evidence for what people ate in the past comes from the human body itself. The chemistry of our bones preserves a record of what we ate. Tooth wear can provide insights into the broad characteristics of diet, and physical wear on the body can suggest the kinds of work that were important. If archaeologists get very lucky, sometimes we find the actual food itself, as pollen grains stuck in plaque on teeth, preserved stomach contents, or preserved feces known as coprolites.

Other evidence comes from more indirect sources. Sometimes people recorded images of what they ate or the social contexts of food consumption in art. Other times, the tools people developed to capture, grow, or process food can tell us about their priorities and constraints. Even the location

FIGURE I.2. Excavated plant parts being sorted and analyzed. (Robyn Cutright)

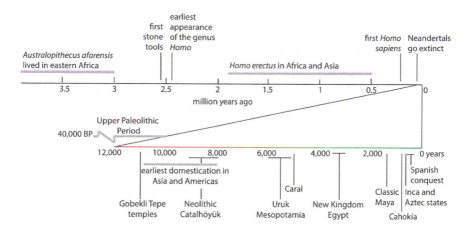

FIGURE I.3. Timeline of some key events and periods. (Robyn Cutright)

of communities and other infrastructure, like canals, on the landscape can hint at how people were interacting with their environment to obtain food. Because the material record is patchy and often frustratingly incomplete, archaeologists usually draw together as many lines of evidence as possible, including historical or modern examples of similar contexts, in order to draw conclusions about the reciprocal relationships between food and culture in the past (figure I.3).

Around 10,000 years ago, some human groups began to interact with the plants and animals in their environments in a fundamentally new way. Chapter 4 explores some explanations for how and why people domesticated plants and animals and adopted a farming lifestyle. By comparing the independent development of agriculture in the Near East and Mexico, and the subsequent spread of farming from these centers to Europe and North America, I investigate how farming fundamentally transformed human societies, human health, and the relationship between humans and the environment. Many of the processes tied to the origins of farming, such as population growth, specialization and social differentiation, reliance on just a few staple crops, and human impact on the landscape have continued to intensify in the modern era.

Chapter 5 focuses on large celebratory meals or feasts. While we like to think of these big meals as purely social, in fact they can be intensely political. Once archaeologists started to look for feasts in the past, we found them everywhere, in part because feasts leave behind such unmistakable, visible material traces. In chapter 5, I sketch out arguments that feasts played an important role in the first farming, in the origins of inequality, and in the construction of the pyramids and other ancient public works, among other important social dynamics.

Chapter 6 looks at how class shapes cuisine. I lay out some defining characteristics of high-class cuisine and look at some examples from the past. Food is a powerful symbol of class and reflects (and transmits) relations of inequality and even exploitation, as I show by looking at the case of enslaved African Americans on antebellum plantations. Even broad, violent processes such as conquest and colonialism can play out at the dinner table, as I show through my archaeological investigations in Peru.

Chapter 7 focuses on the role of food in ritual. From the ritual consumption of sacred foods (including human flesh) to funeral feasts, food is an essential component of many religious and social rituals. Some special foods even alter or heighten our perception of these events, and many foods gain meaning from their association with sacred or special meals.

While they may not be as exciting as a feast or ritual meal, in chapter 8 I argue that daily meals are equally meaningful. I use my work in Peru and case studies such as early farming in Turkey and the Russian fur trade in California to investigate how daily meals can tell us about family, gender, and identity in the past. Ultimately, chapter 8 focuses attention on how people use food to tell ourselves and others who we are.

We all eat, but it is not so clear why we eat the way that we do. As omnivores and generalists, we are not driven solely by instinct. We are forced to decide what to eat, and biology, ecology, culture, and politics contribute to the decisions we make. All animals have a diet, but only humans have a cuisine. We play with our food, think through our food, give meaning to food. Throughout this book, I tell the story of food in the human past and how it is intimately intertwined with what it means to be human in both a biological and a cultural sense. I also tell the story of how archaeologists have studied food, and how a focus on food has shifted our understanding of the human past. In exploring how past humans and contemporary archaeologists have used food to make meaning and sense of their worlds, I hope that you will ultimately consider your food preferences and choices as part of this story.

Part I

HOW DID FOOD SHAPE US AS HUMANS?

Food in Human Evolution

1

HUNTERS AND SCAVENGERS

The True "Caveman" Diet

When I teach classes on food and human evolution, I ask my students to follow the Paleo diet, also known as the "Caveman Diet,"[1] for a few days. The Paleo diet was popularized by nutrition expert Loren Cordain in the early 2000s,[2] though the idea that we should eat like our Paleolithic ancestors has been around much longer. By cutting out any foods added to our diet by the agricultural or industrial revolution, such as grains, legumes, dairy, and processed sugar, the Paleo diet claims to improve health by focusing on foods that have been with humans since deep in our evolutionary past—meat, eggs, tubers, vegetables, fruit, and nuts. The logic goes that because humans evolved to eat these foods, our bodies should thrive on them. By eating Paleo, proponents say, we can avoid the negative health consequences of the modern diet such as obesity, diabetes, and heart disease.

Most of my students struggle to eat Paleo on campus. Food available in the cafeteria and nearby convenience stores centers on starchy staples such as rice, pasta, and bread. Dairy, especially cheese, is everywhere. Most foods are highly processed, making it hard to select options with only Paleo ingredients. And for vegetarians or vegans, the protein selection is limited. Most students report needing to eat many more fruits and vegetables than they expect and still feeling hungry all the time. The papers they write often question how humans in the past could even survive on what they perceive as a limited diet that lacks carbohydrates.

⚶

The challenges of "eating Paleo" in the contemporary United States go deeper than just the range of student choices at the cafeteria. There is a reason that food service focuses on rice, bread, cheese, and processed foods—these are

FIGURE 1.1. Map showing locations of key sites from chapter 1. 1 = Daphne Major, Galápagos; 2 = Hadar, Ethiopia; 3 = Gombe reserve, Tanzania; 4 = Olduvai Gorge, Tanzania; 5 = Taung, South Africa. (Robyn Cutright)

much cheaper than meat and fresh fruit in American grocery stores. Our agricultural system is set up to produce grains and meat, not the variety of nuts, root vegetables, and natural sweeteners like honey that would have been available to our ancestors millions of years ago on the African savanna. In later chapters, I focus on our agricultural landscape in greater detail. Here, I examine the anthropology behind the Paleo diet.

The Paleo diet claims to work because it emphasizes the foods humans adapted to eat over our long evolutionary trajectory. But how do we know what those human ancestors ate? Mostly meat? Mostly veggies? When we look at societies across the globe today, we see a huge range of traditional diets, from mostly vegetables and grains in places like India, to mostly meat in northern latitudes, to mostly fruit and roots in Polynesia, to corn and beans in Central America.[3] Did this variety exist during the long span of human evolution? Did we evolve to eat only some foods, and if so, which ones?

Answering these questions helps us critically evaluate the claims of the Paleo diet, but they are also part of a broader investigation into the pathway of human evolution, and the factors and pressures that made us human. Diet has played a big role in anthropological theories about evolution. Anthropologists have thought of it as a response to changing climates, a driver of behaviors like cooperation and communication, or a way to support a growing, energy-hungry brain. Many of these theories begin by considering what is unique about our human diet and extrapolating from there about what forces might have shaped or supported these differences, along with other notable characteristics of modern humans such as our big brains, our preference for walking on our hind legs, and our complex cultures and languages.

This chapter explores what sets the human diet apart from that of other primates in the context of classic theories about human evolution and new scientific evidence. Ultimately, this evidence for human diet and evolution helps us to think not just about key turning points over the last several million years, but also how we should eat today.

WHAT IS UNIQUE ABOUT HUMAN DIET?

To figure out what our ancestors ate during the past four to six million years, anthropologists use two broad categories of evidence. We look at the fossil evidence itself—the mineralized bones and teeth of ancient human ancestors and the animals with which they shared their habitats—along with archaeological finds of stone tools, fire rings, and living spaces. It can be hard to visualize the full range of behavior from a few fragments of bone, though.

One way to flesh out the fossil record is to observe the closest living relatives of ancient human ancestors, and this is the second broad category of evidence anthropologists use to understand ancient diets. We, *Homo sapiens*, are the closest living relatives of Paleolithic humans. Archaeologists consider the Paleolithic to begin when humans first started making stone tools, about 2.5 million years ago (the word Paleolithic means "old stone" age), and to end with the invention of farming about 10,000 years ago. So we can compare ancient human ancestors to ourselves, and especially to modern groups that live by hunting and gathering in similar environments to the ones our ancient ancestors inhabited. We can also use living primates as an analogy. Chimpanzees, both the common chimp (*Pan troglodytes*) and the bonobo, or pygmy chimpanzee (*Pan paniscus*) are our closest living relatives. By comparing the way humans and other great apes like chimpanzees eat, we can see what, exactly, is unique to humans, and can speculate about how and when these unique characteristics evolved.

Like other primates, humans are omnivores and generalists. We have teeth for grinding and for tearing. We can subsist on a wide variety of diets. Many primate species, from bush babies to chimpanzees, eat from a variety of ecosystems and occupy territories that include different kinds of habitats. Humans have taken this to the extreme—we eat from a global network of ecosystems and consume food thousands of miles away from where it grew.

Like other primates such as gorillas and chimpanzees, we do not eat every potentially edible food in our environments. Gorillas rely on just a few preferred kinds of leaves and stems, and chimpanzees prefer to eat fruit even if it is not very abundant nearby. When is the last time you ate squirrel, or acorns, or dandelion leaves? These are fairly common edible species in cities and towns across the United States, but you probably do not consider them a regular part of your diet. Your culture helps you make this decision—in other societies those plants and animals would be considered food without question. Interestingly, chimpanzees also learn from their social group what is good to eat and what is not.

Primate researchers have documented the varied diets of different chimpanzee groups by observing them and collecting feeding remains and feces. In some cases, this variation is due to the availability of different resources, but in other cases chimps in similar environments choose to eat different things. For instance, western chimpanzees in Mali and Senegal smash baobab fruits and eat tree bark. Senegalese chimps eat six insect species, but even though all six are also present in Mali, chimps there eat only two insect species.[4] This finding supports other evidence of cultural variation among chimpanzees.[5] If culture is a set of learned, shared ideas and behaviors, then differences in tool use and food preferences could be described as cultural differences, even if chimpanzee culture seems to be much less symbolic and complex than human culture. And there are other similarities in the way humans and chimpanzees eat.

For humans and other social primates, finding food and eating it are social experiences. Students find their friends before walking to the campus cafeteria, friends meet over drinks or coffee, and spider monkey troops forage under the direction of a dominant female or break into small groups to search out small patches of fruit in the tropical rain forest. Hierarchies, power, and dominance play a role in these social interactions. Of course, mothers share food freely with their offspring, but food is also shared among unrelated individuals. Primate researchers have observed female chimps offering sex in exchange for some of the meat just killed by a male chimpanzee hunting group.[6] Immature male bonobos might beg by positioning themselves next to adults and staring from inches away as they eat, but one study found that subordinates had only a 25 percent success rate.[7] In contrast, dominant individuals more successfully pressure subordinates to share. The researchers who conducted these studies believe that sharing reinforces social bonds but also allows the beggar to assess their social relationships with other members of the group. While social dominance also plays a role in human food sharing, for example when the patriarch of the family sits at the head of the Thanksgiving table and carves the roast turkey, subordinates are not usually forced to beg overtly or fear that they will not be served.

There are other differences. We humans eat with our social groups, but unlike chimpanzees we also eat among strangers without stress.[8] We may graze on snacks all day, as foraging gorillas do, but we are probably more likely to gather foods together at home, prepare them in a kitchen, and eat them together with family or friends. Chimpanzees may use twigs to fish termites out of a mound, or crack open nuts with stone hammers, or sop up water with a sponge of leaves. Humans, in contrast, use tools like toasters, woks, blenders, and microwaves to fix elaborate dishes that include ingredients from different ecosystems, mixed together in ways that we consider to be appropriate and tasty. While we eat some ingredients raw and unprocessed (think of lettuce or strawberries), we process others until the original plant or animal is no longer readily apparent, make elaborate combinations that require multiple steps (balsamic vinaigrette or ranch dressing for that lettuce, whipped cream or shortcake for those strawberries), and use a variety of cooking techniques to transform ingredients into dishes.

Anthropologist Richard Wrangham believes that cooking may have played a key role in setting humans on a different evolutionary trajectory from our primate cousins. In his book, *Catching Fire*, Wrangham points out that people do not thrive on a raw food diet, despite many fad diet books that claim the opposite.[9] In cases where shipwreck survivors, members of expeditions lost in the jungle, or raw food dieters eat only raw foods, Wrangham finds that they do not thrive. They generally lose weight, even when they eat large quantities of raw food. Compared to chimpanzees, humans have smaller guts, smaller mouths, smaller teeth, weaker jaw muscles, and greater susceptibility to toxins and microorganisms.[10] We are not well suited to surviving in the wild without tools to break down, cut up, or cook food. We need our grinding stones, cooking pots, and microwaves to predigest our food, in effect. This is a key difference between humans and our closest relatives. But when and how did this behavior emerge? Could this be a key to understanding what set humans on our particular evolutionary pathway?

Evolution through Natural Selection

When we ask questions about how and when key human traits emerged, we are asking about human evolution. Evolution, and especially human evolution, has been a cultural flashpoint in the United States. While there are many different perspectives from which to explore the origins of humanity and what it means to be human, anthropologists view humans in an evolutionary framework. This means that we view humans as a biological species shaped by natural selection and other evolutionary processes.

Natural selection is a central mechanism of evolution. First proposed by Charles Darwin and Alfred Wallace in the 1850s, natural selection works when different members of a population have different traits, such as beak size or eye color, and these traits are passed down from parent to child. Darwin did not understand exactly how this happened, as genes and DNA were unknown in his time, but he could see by studying pigeon breeding that traits were indeed inherited by offspring. In Darwin's conception of natural selection, more individuals are born in each generation than can be supported by the available resources. This creates a struggle for survival that only some individuals can win. To the extent that a particular expression of a trait makes it easier for an individual to survive and reproduce, it will be passed down more frequently to the next generation than others. If individuals with blue eyes are more successful at finding food or attracting a mate than individuals with brown eyes, the logic goes, more children in the next generation will have blue eyes than brown. If the conditions favorable to blue eyes persist over enough generations, blue eyes will become much more common than brown eyes.

Darwin's model hung together logically and did a good job describing and suggesting a mechanism to explain the variation that scientists at the time could see in the natural world. However, the actual process of natural selection itself could not be seen. Only the end result, the existence of different species with different characteristics, could be recorded. Many proponents assumed that natural selection worked so slowly and incrementally that it could never actually be seen to happen. It was not until the 1970s that scientists were able to convincingly document natural selection at work.

In their highly regarded study of natural selection, Peter and Rosemary Grant studied finches on the barren, isolated island of Daphne Major, in the harsh but beautiful Galápagos.[11] They measured the size and shape of the beaks of the medium ground finch each year and combined that data with meticulous records of rainfall, temperature, the availability of different resources, the number of offspring each pair of finches produced, and how many of those offspring survived to reproduce themselves. The result was a magnificent, detailed picture of evolution in action.

One year near the beginning of their study, little rain fell for the whole season. Resources dried up and became rare, finches died, and the finch population dropped. The next year, the average beak size in the population had increased substantially—birds with large beaks were more likely to survive and reproduce, and their offspring had bigger beaks too. Bigger beaks made it easier to crack open large hard seeds, some of the last resources available in the drought. In this case, different members of the finch population had different-sized beaks. They passed the genes for beak size down to their children. Not all finches lived to reproduce, and the ones with bigger beaks in this case were more likely to reproduce than smaller-beaked finches. So the average beak size increased over the course of a generation, because birds with bigger beaks were better adapted to environmental conditions.

The story of the big-beaked finches provides us with some important concepts for thinking about the role of food in human evolution. Natural selection acted on the inherited traits of early humans, so the characteristics that persisted or emerged were those that increased the likelihood that an individual would survive to reproduce. Key behaviors, such as the ability to cook and process food, to make tools, or to share food, can be understood as adaptations to a particular social and natural environment, just like bigger beaks were adaptations to a dry environment in the Grants' study. The important question to ask is, when do we see particular traits emerge, and how were they adaptive in a particular environment? This means that we need to look not just at the characteristics of early ancestors of modern humans, but the environment and climate where they lived in eastern and southern Africa, between two and four million years ago.

WHO WERE OUR EARLIEST ANCESTORS?

By comparing the accumulation of mutations in the modern human and chimpanzee genetic codes, scientists suggest that these two species last shared a common ancestor six to eight million years ago.[12] From that shared ancestor, one lineage led to modern chimpanzees, and another ultimately to modern humans. Anthropologists use the term *hominin* to refer to the members of that latter line—human ancestors who were more closely related to modern *Homo sapiens* than to any other living species but had brains, bodies, and behavior different enough from humans to be categorized as different species.

The earliest of these hominins spent a good amount of time in trees, an adaptation they share with modern chimpanzees and bonobos. While chimps can and do walk on the ground, they are much more comfortable spending time in trees than are humans. Likewise, while chimps can walk on their hind limbs, they are much more comfortable than humans walking on all fours. The skeletons of chimps and humans attest to this difference. Chimps' heads project forward from their bodies, with the spinal cord entering through a hole called the foramen magnum at the back of the skull, while modern humans' skulls balance on top of our bodies with the foramen magnum located underneath. Chimps' pelvic bones are long and narrow, their arms are relatively longer compared to their legs, and their fingers and toes are long and curved.

These contrasts between the skeletons of ground-dwelling humans who walk on two legs (terrestrial bipeds) and tree-adapted chimpanzees who are most comfortable on all fours (arboreal quadrupeds) give us two ends of a spectrum along which we can organize the fossil skeletons of different hominins. We can place ancient hominins along this spectrum to identify the earliest appearance of bipedalism and other human traits, such as large brains, less difference in size between males and females (or less sexual dimorphism), and smaller teeth. In order to understand what was happening around the time when we think behaviors uniquely associated with human food behavior began, we need to look at three main groups of hominins: the gracile australopiths, the robust australopiths, and early *Homo*.

Lucy and Friends: The Gracile Australopiths

In 1974, paleoanthropologist Donald Johanson and Tom Gray, a member of Johanson's team of researchers from the Institute of Human Origins, were searching for hominins in the Middle Awash Valley of Ethiopia, at a site called Hadar. Millions of years ago, Hadar was at the edge of a large lake surrounded by marshes and a mix of grassland and forest that fluctuated through time. This region is arid and rocky today, which incidentally makes it perfect for prospecting for fossil bones. Fossils are not obscured by vegetation, and the active geology of the Rift Valley has lifted and exposed the sediments where hominins were buried.

After riding out in a jeep to map a new part of the site, Johanson and Gray decided to take a different route back to camp. Driving through a wash, they spotted fossilized bones. After excavating over the next few weeks, they had hundreds of fragments of fossil bone that added up to 40 percent of one individual's skeleton. The team named this remarkably complete hominin female individual "Lucy," after the Beatles song that was playing during their celebration. While Lucy has captured our imagination, she is just one of at least thirty-five members of the species *Australopithecus afarensis* found at Hadar, where they lived around 3.2 million years ago.[13] Decades earlier, in a South African limestone quarry, paleoanthropologist Raymond Dart had uncovered the fossil of a young individual from a similar species we now classify as *Australopithecus africanus*.[14] We now know that several related species of these small-bodied "australopiths" lived in the mixed woodland and savanna grasslands of eastern and southern Africa between about four and two million years ago.

Australopiths were shorter than most modern humans. They had much smaller brains than *Homo sapiens*, and proportionally bigger teeth (figure 1.2). Their arms were longer in proportion to their legs compared to modern humans, and their fingers were longer and more curved, though not as much as those of modern chimpanzees. However, they were much more comfortable on two legs than chimpanzees, and had hips, knee joints, and feet adapted to efficient bipedal walking. One of the ways we know this is that a remarkable set of footprints left by several australopith individuals walking on two legs was preserved in volcanic ash that fell 3.6 million years ago.[15]

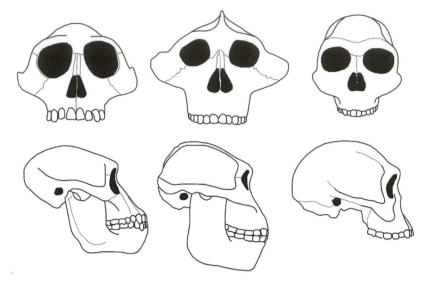

FIGURE 1.2. Skulls of a gracile australopith (*Australopithecus afarensis*), left, a robust australopith (*Paranthropus boisei*), center, and early *Homo* (*Homo habilis*), right. (Redrawn and modified from Carol Ember, Melvin Ember, and Peter Peregrine, *Physical Anthropology and Archaeology*, 2nd ed. [New York: Pearson, 2007], 260–61, Robyn Cutright)

This evidence indicates that some aspect of australopith survival or reproduction benefited from more efficient bipedal walking (or the genetic mutations responsible for these traits would not have spread through the population). Walking on two legs might allow individuals to see greater distances in a treeless landscape, which means that taller individuals would be able to see food or danger from farther away. An upright posture might cool the body more efficiently in hot environments. Bipedal individuals can more easily get from tree to tree where wooded areas are sparse, increasing their access to resources, territory, and mates. Bipedalism frees up the hands to carry things like tools or food, for instance, which could relate to behavior such as accumulating food at a central place, sharing food, and provisioning mates and children with food foraged from a wider landscape.[16]

Anthropologists are unsure whether one or all of these possibilities played a role in selecting for bipedalism. Notably, however, a number of these ideas make sense in the context of a landscape where grasslands were increasingly more common than forests. This is the exact trend we see in East Africa at the time. Global climate records indicate swings between cooler/drier and warmer/wetter phases, and local fossil records of the plants and animals that shared the landscape with hominins suggest that East Africa saw a slow shift from forest to dry open grassland between 3.5 and 1.5 million years ago.[17]

A changing environment would mean changes to the availability of different foods. While it is challenging to interpret all the different evidence for ancient diet, and understandably there was a good deal of variation across Africa and through time, we do have some idea of what australopiths ate between four and two million years ago—a true Paleo(lithic) diet. Australopiths, like most primates, had a generalized set of teeth that could grind plants but also tear meat and crack seeds. Australopith incisors were more similar to gorillas (which eat leaves and shoots) than to chimps (which eat a lot of fruit with thick husks). Their molars and chewing muscles were large and their tooth enamel thick, suggesting they were adapted to eat hard, brittle, and abrasive foods like roots or grass.

While tooth shape (like finch beak size) indicates the forces of natural selection that drive fitness, tooth wear reflects what individuals actually ate. A summary of recent research on different fossils from different sites shows that australopiths had tooth wear patterns consistent with a diet of soft plant foods, which suggests that hard brittle foods were not preferred or were not commonly consumed by australopiths even though they had the ability to eat them.[18] This might be like the case of big-beaked finches, whose ability to eat large seeds can make the difference between life and death in dry years (thus passing along those big beak genes) but who happily eat small and medium seeds when these are available.

What we eat shapes our bone chemistry, because the minerals we eat are used to build our bones. Grasses, sedges, roots, nuts, berries, and leafy plants have different types of metabolisms, which means they make slightly different versions, or isotopes, of carbon.[19] As individuals eat from these different categories, their bones and teeth absorb the carbon isotopes and come to reflect the isotopic signatures of the plants that made up their diet. By looking at these signatures, researchers have suggested that *Australopithecus africanus* ate a mix of fruits, leaves, and grasses (or the animals that ate these foods, which could range from grazing herbivores to termites) and spent a good amount of time in a grassland environment.[20] Australopiths, in other words, were probably dietary generalists who ate a range of foods from an environment in transition from forest to grassland.[21] But the australopiths I have discussed so far were not the only ones on the ancient grasslands.

Big Kids on the Block: Robust Australopiths

Paleoanthropologists can detect several new australopith species on the scene beginning about 2.5 million years ago, including *Paranthropus robustus* in

South Africa and *Paranthropus boisei* in eastern Africa. Because they had much larger teeth and large, flat faces with huge jaw muscles (see figure 1.2), this group is referred to as robust australopithecines to distinguish them from the more delicate or gracile australopiths I discussed previously. Their faces, teeth, and skulls are so different that many researchers place them in a separate genus (*Paranthropus*) from *afarensis* and *africanus*. I sidestep the technical debate about classification here, but it is clear that the robust australopiths had teeth and jaws that look very different from those of the gracile australopithecines, suggesting that something about their diet, habitat, and behavior was different. Robust australopiths did not go extinct until perhaps 1.5 million years ago, meaning that they had to adapt to an increasingly arid open savanna environment.

Many researchers have suggested that the large teeth with thick enamel and heavy chewing muscles of robust australopithecines indicate a very specialized diet of hard, brittle foods like nuts or very fibrous ones such as roots or grasses. This classic view of robust australopiths as nutcrackers or grazers has been questioned more recently by bone chemistry and tooth wear studies. Bone chemistry studies have indicated that what *P. robustus* ate varied seasonally,[22] so it could not have been that much of a specialist. Other studies have supported a more generalist diet for robust australopiths that included a mix of tubers, leaves, nuts, and grasses and also possibly grass-eating animals or insects.

However, the ability to withstand the stress of chewing fibrous or hard foods is not likely to have emerged in multiple species, in different parts of Africa, unless it conferred some advantage. Individuals with larger teeth and stronger jaws must have been more likely to survive and reproduce than individuals with smaller ones, and so again it could be that although they generally preferred a more varied, omnivorous diet, robust australopiths needed the ability to fall back on fibrous, tough, hard-to-chew foods when times got, well, tough.

The Earliest Members of the Genus *Homo*

Between 2.5 and 2 million years ago, another member of our family tree was also living on the increasingly open grasslands of eastern Africa: *Homo habilis*. This species displayed so many features that are similar to the modern human line, compared to australopiths, that it is placed in our genus, *Homo*, rather than in the genus *Australopithecus*. While paleoanthropologists debate the precise ancestry and species designation of these early *Homo* fossils,

I am most interested in how early *Homo*'s diet and adaptation contrasts to the other hominins it overlapped with in time and space.

Early *Homo* had a larger brain and a smaller face than gracile and robust australopiths, though it still would have looked very different from modern humans (see figure 1.2). It had larger incisors, which gave it more shearing power, and smaller teeth overall compared to australopiths. It was bipedal, but still had long powerful hands reminiscent of australopiths and was still much smaller than modern humans at three to five feet tall. It was not the first hominin to use stone tools—the earliest evidence of stone tool cutmarks on animal bone arguably dates back to 3.3 million years ago, and stone chopping tools from two million years ago are associated with robust australopiths as well as early *Homo*. But stone tools and evidence that they were being used to break down animal carcasses becomes much more common after two million years ago.[23]

In terms of diet, early *Homo* still had the teeth of a generalist, and isotopic studies have found overlap between the diet of early *Homo* and robust australopiths in the same regions. Some researchers believe that early *Homo*'s diet was wider and more varied than that of australopiths, and that dietary flexibility and expansion represented important evolutionary strategies in the face of climatic variation.[24] However, the diet of early *Homo*, and to a lesser extent robust and gracile australopiths, has been caught up in questions not just about the Paleo diet, but in some fundamental debates about what it means to be human.

WHAT WAS ON THE MENU TWO MILLION YEARS AGO?

We have some tantalizing clues from bones and teeth, but is it possible to more precisely identify some key foods that may have supported or spurred the development of behaviors like walking on two legs and making stone tools? Can we trace back some of the characteristics of human eating behavior to this distant moment in human evolution? Even before Donald Johanson found Lucy in 1974, anthropologists have been trying to answer such questions, initially focusing on the role of meat.[25]

"Man the Hunter"

One day more than fifty years ago,[26] a young researcher named Jane Goodall watched a chimpanzee she had named David Greybeard strip leaves off a twig, dip the twig into a termite mound, and scoop termites into his mouth.

When Goodall reported this observation, of a chimpanzee making and using a tool, to her mentor, paleoanthropologist Louis Leakey, he famously exclaimed, "Now we must redefine man, redefine tools, or accept chimpanzees as humans."[27] Goodall's patient observations of chimpanzees at the Gombe reserve in Tanzania shattered many long-held notions about our close primate cousins, showing the gulf between us to be much narrower than scientists had previously believed.

Goodall observed her chimps hunting as well as using tools. Prior to the 1960s, most anthropologists thought of primate diet as largely vegetarian and imagined that the earliest human ancestors would have eaten a largely vegetarian diet too. What Goodall observed must be an aberration, researchers figured, because meat could not be a natural part of chimpanzee diet. But by the 1970s, Goodall had published documentation of chimpanzees hunting for small monkeys and other mammals, and the scientific community could no longer deny it.[28]

Even though it is now clear that chimpanzees hunt, we also know that meat never makes up a large portion of their diet. Hunting success rates are low, and prey animals are small, so after they are divided up among hunters and other members of the group, they do not provide much actual nutrition. For these reasons, researchers like Craig Stanford believe that hunting is more important for chimpanzee male bonding and status competition than as a contribution to the diet.[29]

For paleoanthropologists writing in the 1950s and '60s, the main question to answer was how a bipedal, tool-using hunter evolved from an arboreal, vegetarian ancestor. Paleoanthropologists Sherwood Washburn and Virginia Avis proposed in 1958 that one of the main differences between humans and the living apes is that humans are much more carnivorous. Humans hunt and kill animals much larger than we are and, consequently, we are feared as predators by other animals. Many people today enjoy hunting and hunt as a hobby even if they do not need the meat to survive. Washburn and Avis believe that these dynamics have shaped us as a species. They state, "Our whole conception of wild and tame is a reflection of the human hunting attitude."[30] In their view, using tools and hunting helped to select for greater intelligence and social cooperation, including working as a team and sharing food with dependent members of the social group. As brain size increased, hominins developed even more complex technology and communication, including spoken language. In turn, growing technological and social skills allowed these human ancestors to hunt larger territories and live in larger social groups. As the quote suggests, hunting behavior plays a fundamental role in our modern human cultural conception of the natural world.

Other paleoanthropologists joined Washburn in seeing hunting as the key development driving hominin evolution toward what they saw as classically human behaviors. Members of this "man the hunter" school believed that hunting selected for the mental and physical qualities needed to produce more technologically complex tools. Hunters would have been more successful if they were good at cooperating and communicating with others, and if they were able to put together a successful plan. Forethought, planning, communication, and social cooperation would favor the development of bigger brains and more analytical and social intelligence; this development would be fostered by the availability of high-quality meat in a hunting diet. Paleoanthropologist Raymond Dart even suggested that human ancestors distinguished themselves from other primates principally by being aggressive hunters.[31] Deadly hunting skills, along with a propensity for aggression and competition, made these "killer apes" successful in competing with other savanna predators for game.

The "man the hunter" model was developed largely by comparing modern humans with other primates because archaeological evidence was still limited. It focused explicitly on what researchers considered to be male hunting activities aimed at provisioning dependent females and infants, taking a male perspective that was common in the scientific literature of the time. Even the name of the model focused attention on early "man." Thanks to the efforts of teams of paleoanthropologists toiling under the hot sun of eastern and southern Africa through the 1960s and '70s, archaeological evidence slowly began to accumulate. Would it support this hunting-centric view of human evolution? At the same time, a feminist revolution was underway in the United States and would eventually draw attention to the implicit biases and assumptions of man the hunter.[32]

Challenges to Man the Hunter

In the late 1970s a team of paleoanthropologists led by Henry Bunn and Glynn Isaac set out to excavate in a place called Koobi Fora, in northern Kenya.[33] At these sites, they uncovered curious clusters of worked stone and bone artifacts that began to hint at a picture of hominin activity 1.5 million years ago. Isaac thought these clustered artifacts could be home bases where hominins (probably early *Homo* although *Paranthropus boisei* fossils were also found in the same area) could make stone tools and bring food to be processed and eaten.[34] At home bases, hominins could congregate in the shade, and their larger group size would serve as protection against predators.

In this scenario, even though animals were hunted and eaten, the centrally important dynamic was not meat itself, but the act of eating it together. The social interactions that took place at home bases, and the sexual division of labor that allowed males to hunt, females to gather, and both to share these resources with the social group, represented some of the central characteristics of *human* eating behavior. In this context, bipedalism could have helped individuals carry food to a central place where it would be shared. While this model maintained a focus on a nuclear family with a sexual division of labor easily accepted by Western readers at the time, it did emphasize sociality and interaction among all individuals, rather than bloodthirsty hunting undertaken only by males, as the essential hominin adaptations.

This idea soon came under fire. Archaeologist Lewis Binford decided to use his observations of living hunters and gatherers to question assumptions about what had happened at Koobi Fora and elsewhere. He wondered whether those home bases were just accumulations of debris deposited by carnivores, scavengers, flowing water, and the occasional early hominin. On an open savanna, any area with shade and water would be a common amenity shared by hunters and scavengers, including hominins, and bones and tools would build up there over time to eventually look just like the home bases Isaac identified (figure 1.3).

To Binford, Isaac's story about two-million-year-old homes stocked with plentiful meat just seemed unlikely.[35] Instead, he proposed that if early humans ate meat, it would have been accidental at best. How could puny, three-foot-tall, naked apes without claws or large canines and only rudimentary tools compete with big cats, hyenas, and other powerful predators and scavengers on the African savanna? It seemed more likely to Binford that early humans occasionally came upon a mostly eaten carcass that they could finish off, but that they would have been confined to the end of the scavenging line.

Paleoanthropologists in the 1980s had a challenge. They had several different scenarios for the role of hunting and home bases for hominins two million years ago. Some had argued hominins were mighty hunters of the savanna. Others viewed them as marginal scavengers at best. Paleoanthropologists had to identify elements of the fossil record that could help them distinguish between these two ends of the spectrum. Luckily, the fossil record does preserve some good evidence for whether early humans were

FIGURE 1.3. Activities that might contribute to artifact clusters at Koobi Fora. (Original art by Isabelle Ballard, Robyn Cutright)

carnivorous, and whether they were the ones doing the hunting, or whether they were only getting the tail end of others' kills.

It can be hard to interpret the dietary record preserved in bone chemistry. Earlier, I explained how the ratios of different carbon isotopes in bones reflects dietary emphasis on different categories of plants. However, a certain ratio might represent a diet rich in grasses, or in antelope that had eaten C_4 grasses themselves, or in grass-eating termites, even though each of these diets would support very different models for the role of meat and hunting in human evolution. While the isotopic picture is blurry, researchers see evidence that robust australopiths and early *Homo* were almost certainly eating some meat.[36] Because of their interpretive challenges, isotopes alone could not provide the answer; more evidence was needed to really see what the diet was like at Koobi Fora and the Zinj floor.

In response, some archaeologists began to look more carefully at the animal bones themselves. They discovered that it was possible to see cut marks from stone tools on some fossilized bones. They could also see gnaw marks from carnivores and scavengers on the bones. With the right forensic knowledge, these two kinds of marks can be distinguished from each other. Gnaw marks are rounder in profile, like the gouges your dog makes as she chews on a bone, while cut marks look more like a *V* in cross section. By looking at where these marks occur on the bones, and which ones came first, analysts can reconstruct the sequence of events that occurred after the animal died. It turns out that the patterns are messy and somewhat conflicting, but there is clear evidence that at least some early humans had regular access to meaty carcasses, at least of smaller prey.

According to recent research, hominins two million years ago had something in common with zombies—they loved brains.[37] Anthropologist Joseph Ferraro and a team of researchers recently looked at a collection of animal bones from a few layers of occupation at Kanjera South in Kenya. The pattern of cutmarks suggested to them that early humans were regularly bringing back, to a central place, small animal carcasses with plenty of meat on them. They chose not to carry back the full carcasses of medium-sized animals, though; instead, they preferred to bring back only the meaty limbs . . . and heads. The level of fracturing to the heads indicates that they were being cracked open with stone tools so that early humans could access the fat- and vitamin-rich brains.

Coincidentally, the first stone tools, dating back to 2.6 million years ago, tend to be choppers. Choppers have round bases that nestle into the palm and sharp points and edges that effectively crack animal skulls and bones to

extract brains and marrow hidden within. Only hyenas, of all savanna animals, have strong enough jaws to crack open marrow bones, so early humans may have found the perfect niche to exploit—and the perfect way to
supplement a fibrous, vegetarian diet with high-quality fat and protein.

But did hominins need to hunt to have "regular access to meaty carcasses?" Are there other ways besides hunting to get early access to animal
carcasses that still had a lot of meat on them? Paleoanthropologist Robert
Blumenschine doubts that hominins had early access to carcasses.[38] After
all, hominins were small, not very fast, and not very well armed two million years ago.

To evaluate the hunting hypothesis, Blumenschine and his team members observed the behavior of hunters, scavengers, and prey in eastern Africa today. They reasoned that observing modern animal behavior in a similar ecological setting—woodlands along rivers and grassy savannas—would
help them understand how hominins would have fit in. They also observed
animal carcasses to see how various predators and scavengers, including lions, hyenas, and vultures, break the carcass down. By comparing the stages
of breakdown to the locations of stone tool cutmarks on fossil remains, they
hoped to determine which elements of the carcass were still available when
hominins butchered it. This would tell them whether hominins had early
access to meaty carcasses or were scavenging bits of flesh and marrow from
picked-over skeletons.

Blumenschine's work led to a few key observations. One is that even on
picked-over carcasses, rich fatty marrow would still be available to hominins
with stone choppers. Even as latecomers to a lion kill, hominins would have
been able to extract substantial nutrition from the remains. The work also
identified some strategies hominins could have used to gain early access to
smaller carcasses. In the wooded areas along rivers, nocturnal leopards often stash their kills in trees during the day. Protected from other scavengers,
like vultures and hyenas, these smaller carcasses would have been vulnerable to theft by tree-climbing hominins during the day while the leopards
slept. This niche could have been exploited by hominins to give them access
to meat that would supplement foraged plants and the occasional scavenged
marrow and brains from larger carcasses.

For researchers like Blumenschine, scavenging makes a lot of sense as an
early hominin strategy. The richly diverse life on the savanna would provide plenty of opportunity to scavenge, and the success rate would be much
greater than hunting (as carcasses rarely outrun their pursuers). The earliest
stone tools look more like carcass-processing choppers than hunting tools

(figure 1.4), though of course tools made of wood or bone would be invisible to archaeologists after so much time. The coexistence of cut marks and tooth marks on bones shows that hominins shared access to carcasses with other animals. Blumenschine even identifies a common pattern, in which the carnivores often had first access, followed by hominins, who left the carcass for other scavengers to pick over after they finished.

Blumenschine and other proponents of a scavenging model argue that scavenging would require many of the same kinds of behaviors as hunting. Hominins who used tools and cooperated with a social group would be more successful scavengers. Contemporary Maasai warriors can scare lions away from their kills by working in a group. While ancient hominins were less than half the size and nowhere near as dangerous to lions as modern hunters, it is possible to imagine a band of hominins communicating and cooperating to steal and scavenge carcasses. Scavenging also requires complex mental maps of the landscape to locate carcasses, and the ability to reason from observations (more vultures than usual are circling over that water hole) to conclusions (something possibly edible is dead).

Perhaps one of the reasons that a scavenging model has been slow to catch on is that it radically re-envisions the place of our ancestors on the ancient savanna. Rather than aggressive, dangerous predators, it sees hominins as small, fairly smart but relatively unimpressive players in the ecosystem, grabbing the scraps of hyena leftovers. Certainly, this is a much less majestic view of our past. It also just seems unappetizing and possibly dangerous to eat raw meat left on animals that have died of natural causes or been killed and left for hours in the sun. Blumenschine's observations suggest that disease transmission would have been unlikely as most animals die from

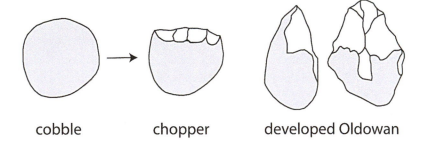

cobble   chopper   developed Oldowan

FIGURE 1.4. Earliest stone tools. On the left is a simple chopper made from a round cobble. On the right is a more complex Oldowan tool. (Redrawn and modified from Ember, Ember, and Peregrine, *Physical Anthropology and Archaeology*, 330–32, Robyn Cutright)

starvation or age. Modern chimpanzees eat raw meat all the time, and scavenged leopard kills would be relatively fresh when hominins stole them. Even though we might not think of it as particularly appetizing, scavenged meat would probably have been a viable option for hominins.

Currently, Robert Blumenschine is locked in debate with another paleoanthropologist, Manuel Domínguez-Rodrigo, over whether hominins regularly had early access to carcasses.[39] Unlike Blumenschine, Domínguez-Rodrigo thinks that the material evidence clearly shows that hominins had regular early access to carcasses, such that they had to be actively involved in hunting or at least scaring the initial hunters away from the kill early on. No one doubts that hominins would have cracked open bones and eaten marrow when they came across a carcass. The question is whether early access or "power" scavenging, in which hominins confronted carnivores like lions and chased them away from kills, was really that common, and whether hunting is even still on the table. Only continued detailed analysis of the evidence will end the debate. While the role of males and females in different types of scavenging has not been a focus of as much discussion, I will discuss the issue of gender bias in models of human evolution a bit further in chapter 2.

WHAT DIET DID WE EVOLVE TO EAT?

In this chapter, I have shown how the scientific community arrived at the current understanding of the diet of some of the earliest members of the evolutionary line leading to humans. I have argued that diet was intertwined with a changing environment, and with the evolution of other human characteristics such as bipedal walking and big brains that are good at designing tools, reasoning, and communicating with a large social group.

Hominins had teeth that provided a tool kit for a varied diet. The ability to eat a wide variety of resources allowed hominins to survive in a landscape that varied seasonally, spatially across the wide range of ecosystems that hominins occupied through eastern and southern Africa, and over the span of several million years. For this reason, it is probably not useful to calculate the exact contributions of resources to the "Hominin diet," since such a diet would average together so much variation across time and space.

The research is clear that even four million years ago, meat was on the menu for many hominins. In some ways, it does not necessarily matter for reconstructions of ancient diet whether hominins primarily hunted or scavenged, because we know they were eating meat at least occasionally in combination with other foraged resources. Meat was likely more important for australopiths and early *Homo* species, which had larger bodies and perhaps better technology, than for earlier hominins. Evidence for processing carcasses certainly seems to become more common with the earliest members of the genus *Homo*, beginning about 2.5 million years ago. However, the research does not support the view that hominins were mainly meat eaters to the exclusion of other foods.

Ultimately, it is less interesting to calculate the specific dietary contributions of meat versus plants or to settle once and for all the proportion of hunted to scavenged meat in the hominin diet than to consider the social behaviors shaped by what human ancestors ate in the past. Hunting and scavenging can both help account for a movement toward greater social cooperation and communication. They both might serve as selective pressures for increased technological capacity and intelligence including reasoning and planning, all of which are important in the story of human evolution.

Also interesting is how anthropologists have told this story in different ways using different evidence. Much of the debate over hunting versus scavenging as it has developed over the past sixty years has to do with how we think about ourselves as humans. Are we master predators sitting at the top of the food chain, or are we subject to predation ourselves, at the mercy of a harsh ecosystem in which we are merely players?

I believe that it is increasingly necessary to view humans as only one part of what anthropologist Anna Tsing would call an assemblage of human and nonhuman actors.[40] In Tsing's account, fungi, trees, and microbes coproduce the mushrooms that humans around the world buy and sell in a global market. More broadly, humans affect ecosystems and harvest resources, but even today, our survival relies on complex and often largely unseen multispecies partnerships.

The Paleo diet is where many people first come across the idea that our ancient ancestors ate very differently from the average westerner. It might even be their only source of information about diet in the human evolutionary past. Since the Paleo diet purports to reflect hominin diets, I end this chapter by looking critically at how it stacks up to the paleoanthropological evidence. The Paleo diet recommends foods like roots, leaves, berries, nuts, eggs, fish, meat, and honey. This list seems true to the range of foods available to our ancestors, even though it leaves out other foods that human ancestors definitely would have eaten, like marrow, brains, insects, and grass seeds. The diet does not, however, account for the way humans, plants, and animals have evolved since the dawn of agriculture, described in more detail in chapter 4. Our hominin ancestors were not eating grain-fed meat, which is fattier and contains antibiotics, and is often highly processed in contemporary Western diets. Nor did they eat meat every day. While some Paleo dieters take an extra step toward authenticity by eating grass-fed or wild meat such as bison and ostrich, they probably still eat more meat than our early ancestors.

Overall, I think the Paleo diet is probably a healthy one, but not because it perfectly matches the blueprint provided by an imagined environment of evolutionary adaptedness, a generic African savanna at some point in the deep past. Rather, I think eating Paleo is just one of several possible diets that help consumers who are lucky to have access to an abundance of calories avoid eating too much sugar, refined flour, food processed with preservatives, and other high-calorie, high-sodium foods that were not readily available even one hundred years ago, much less to our hominin ancestors. All the scientific evidence suggests that there was not just one way to eat in the deep human past.

The social cooperation and communication that could have been fostered by hunting and scavenging became increasingly important around 1.8 million years ago, when the fossil record records the emergence of a new species, *Homo erectus*. *Homo erectus* was larger-bodied, bigger-brained, truly terrestrial, and made it out of Africa and all the way to China. As we will see in chapter 2, it may be that *Homo erectus* was the first hominin to use fire, live in pair-bonded social groups, and cook food, all of which continue to be a part of the human experience today.

2

LITTLE HOUSE ON THE SAVANNA

Fire, Grandmothers, and Homo erectus

Almost two million years ago, a young boy died in Nariokotome, in present-day Kenya. An infection in his tooth may have spread through his body and killed him. Nariokotome Boy, as he is called today, was tall (he would likely have reached six feet as an adult), with a lanky frame, long legs, and the speed and endurance to make a living in the hot, dry grasslands of the Rift Valley. He was probably born relatively helpless and grew up being cared for by his mother, siblings, and other relatives, sleeping uneasily through nights populated by nocturnal predators and waking to forage, hunt, make tools, and socialize.[1] Nariokotome Boy was not human. His brain was smaller than a human boy's and his face projected out from a low forehead and heavy brow ridges. Yet he looked and moved more like a human than any other species had to this point.

This species, *Homo erectus*, would leave Africa and survive in landscapes as diverse as Indonesia and China. It would use a relatively large brain to make the most complex and symmetrical stone tools in history up to that point and even, perhaps, tame fire as an essential form of defense. In this chapter, I sketch an outline of *Homo erectus* body and behavior in what we know of its evolutionary context. I then explore several influential anthropological models that invoke fire, new foods, and new social (and perhaps even cultural) behaviors as intimately intertwined with *Homo erectus* evolution.

⚖

In chapter 1, I described the earliest members of our *Homo* genus as in some ways not too different from earlier australopiths, with a generalized diet, a bipedal gait (but still fairly long arms and strong hands and feet for grasping

Figure 2.1. Map showing locations of key sites from chapter 2. 1 = Hadza territory, Tanzania; 2 = Lake Turkana, Kenya; 3 = Dmanisi, Georgia; 4 = Zhoukoudian, China; 5 = Java, Indonesia. (Robyn Cutright)

branches), and a fairly small body. Early *Homo* had a proportionally bigger brain, smaller teeth, and less projecting face than australopiths and made and used stone chopping tools to break down carcasses. The earliest *Homo erectus* fossils, which date to about 1.8 million years ago, reveal that these established trends continued. But in other ways, *Homo erectus* represented something completely new.[2]

Unlike the shorter, smaller-brained australopiths and even early *Homo*, *Homo erectus* was about the size of modern humans, five to six feet tall. Even more significantly, as the description of Nariokotome Boy hints, it

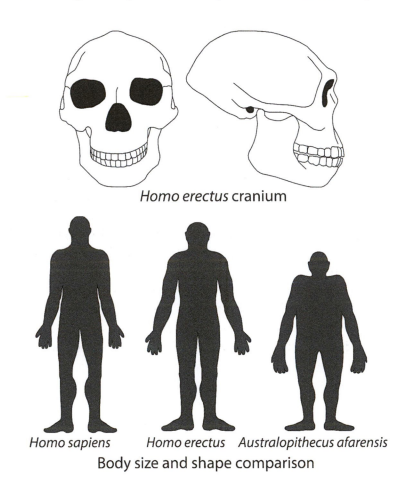

Homo erectus cranium

Homo sapiens   Homo erectus   Australopithecus afarensis
Body size and shape comparison

FIGURE 2.2. *Homo erectus* skull (*top*) and comparison between body size and shape in gracile australopiths, *Homo erectus*, and modern humans (*bottom*). (Redrawn and modified from Ember, Ember, and Peregrine, *Physical Anthropology and Archaeology*, 404–5, and www.internetlooks.com/humanorigins.html, Robyn Cutright)

had modern human body proportions, with relatively longer legs, shorter arms, and shorter less curved fingers (figure 2.2). *Homo erectus* was no better suited to tree living than contemporary humans.

The skull also looks different, again in a continuation of trends toward a larger brain that we can trace back to earlier hominins and even further back in the evolution of all the great apes. *Homo erectus* had a much bigger brain than previous hominins (an average of 900 cubic centimeters, compared to 680 cubic centimeters in earlier members of the *Homo* genus). This is still smaller than the modern human brain, which averages 1,200 cubic centimeters. Though there is no direct relationship between brain size and intelligence, the fact that *Homo erectus* had a bigger brain than previous hominins does probably signal that it had greater cognitive abilities, and there is some archaeological evidence to support this.

Homo erectus had a long, low braincase compared to humans, and a low, receding forehead (see figure 2.2). Its skull was more robust, with thicker bone, a noticeable brow ridge, and lots of bony buttresses. The skull is so thick and well-protected that some paleoanthropologists have suggested it was selected for as a defense against violent attack, by prey, predators, or other *H. erectus* individuals. Though *H. erectus* had a brain much closer in size to modern humans than earlier hominins, the difference in shape probably means that it thought differently than do modern humans.

Homo erectus may have been the first hominin to lack significant body hair. Anthropologists are not sure exactly why less body hair would have given individuals an advantage—perhaps it allowed for more efficient cooling in hominins walking on two legs, while hair on the head would still protect from the sun?[3] The sun might also be responsible for another trait that sets humans apart from our close primate cousins: our wide range of skin colors. Modern chimpanzees have relatively light skin, which is protected from the sun by thick body hair. Dark skin pigmentation in hominins could have been an adaptation to exposure to bright sun and the damaging effects of solar radiation near the equator in the context of a lack of thick body hair.[4] Studies of the DNA of modern humans with African ancestry have suggested that genes for dark skin pigmentation became widespread 1.2 million years ago.[5] There is circumstantial evidence, at least, to suggest that *Homo erectus* probably looked a lot more like humans than did earlier hominins.

Homo erectus was the first hominin to colonize new continents, following the expansion of savanna grasslands across central Europe, Indonesia, and China. Some fossils from places like Dmanisi, Georgia, in central Europe, are almost as old as *H. erectus* fossils from East Africa and look very primitive, with some features that place them close to the root of *Homo erectus* development.[6] This means expansion happened early in the history of the species (or that we are missing some even older fossils in Africa, which could easily be true). *Homo erectus* populations successfully adapted to these different environments, so much so that they persisted in East Asia for a million years, up until about 300,000 years ago.

To extend its range so far, *Homo erectus* had to adapt to many different environments. One of the ways it could have done this is to control fire. Another way would be to manufacture more technologically sophisticated tools than earlier hominins. *Homo erectus* populations are known for a new kind of stone tool called an Acheulean hand ax (figure 2.3). Hand axes are much more complex than the first stone tools, which were made by knocking a few flakes off a hand-size stone cobble to make an edge or point for chopping and hacking. Acheulean hand axes were teardrop shaped, hand-sized tools with stone flakes removed symmetrically from all faces. (Archaeologists call this kind of tool a biface.)

Anthropologists who study how the brain worked in the past have suggested that crafting bifacial Acheulean hand axes would require much more advanced foresight, planning, and motor control than earlier tools.[7] They

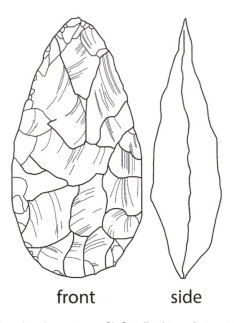

front   side

FIGURE 2.3. Acheulean hand ax, a type of bifacially chipped stone tool associated with *Homo erectus*. (Redrawn and modified from Ember, Ember, and Peregrine, *Physical Anthropology and Archaeology*, 404–5, Robyn Cutright)

would have been used as a sort of all-purpose Leatherman or Swiss Army knife tool, for chopping, sawing, and slicing. Some archaeologists have even speculated that females might choose mates who were better at making beautiful, symmetrical hand axes, allowing them to function almost like a male peacock's tail in expressing health and good genes to potential mates.[8]

Acheulean hand axes were produced using a very similar mental template for a million years. Modern humans tend to restlessly alter the style and look of material culture like tools, clothing, and jewelry, even when the function or use stays the same. Even a couple thousand years of technological stability is remarkable for us. The slow rate of change of hand ax style is one clue that we should not think of *Homo erectus* as just a duller version of modern humans. Instead, they may have thought and acted very differently from us.

In other ways, though, *Homo erectus* behavior would have been recognizably human. One of the skulls found in Dmanisi, Georgia, belonged to an old male with no teeth.[9] He had lost all his teeth, and bone had regrown over the sockets. This means that he lived for years after losing his teeth, which in turn suggests he must have been cared for by the other members of his group. The size and shape of the *Homo erectus* female pelvis, taken together with the growing size of the brain, indicates that children would have been born relatively helpless and required parental care for years. For *Homo erectus*, family social bonds would have been central to survival in a way that is not so unfamiliar to us.

WHAT DID *HOMO ERECTUS* EAT?

It is reasonable to think that the visible changes in the fossil record must have accompanied other, less visible changes to behavior, social organization, and, especially relevant for this book, diet. So, what does the fossil record tell us about *Homo erectus*'s diet and social behaviors related to eating? First, as we did with earlier hominins, we can look at the teeth for clues about diet. *Homo erectus* had smaller teeth than earlier hominins, but they were still very robust compared to ours. Researchers observe a lot of variation in microwear patterns on *Homo erectus* teeth, which suggests that diet was variable and did include some hard or tough foods.[10] At an *H. erectus* site called Zhoukoudian in China, archaeologists have found remains of walnut, hazelnut, pine, elm, rambler rose, Chinese hackberry, horse, rhinoceros, wild boar, and deer, illustrating the potential for dietary diversity in one location.[11]

One *Homo erectus* skeleton from Koobi Fora in Kenya provides possible evidence for diet-based disease. This individual had coarse woven bone growth, possibly a symptom of too much Vitamin A. Where could *Homo erectus* get too much Vitamin A? One way would be eating toxic amounts of carnivore liver.[12] Another way would be eating bee brood (eggs and larvae) along with honey.[13] For modern foragers in Tanzania, honey is a huge source of calories during some seasons of the year.[14] *Homo erectus* would have found honey to be the densest concentration of calories from sugar on the savanna, worth the danger of stealing it from bees. Either possibility offers an intriguing window into the wide range of foods foraged by *Homo erectus*.

Eating a broad spectrum of resources was important for *Homo erectus*. It had to adapt to many different environmental conditions across its range and to climates with a lot of seasonal variation. Reconstructions of the ancient environment show not only a long-term drying and cooling trend that expanded East African grasslands but also a period of greater variability and more rapid swings in climate after about 2.5 million years ago.[15] As with early *Homo*, and even with the gracile australopiths, the trend seems to be toward a generalized diet, capable of adjusting to different ecosystems and periods of climatic change,[16] rather than a narrow, specialized diet. This means that it may be more useful to talk about the *kinds* of resources that *Homo erectus* would need, rather than list specific foods they ate.

The fossil record preserves other more circumstantial but also more theoretically interesting clues about *Homo erectus*'s diet, in its body size and configuration. One notable feature that *Homo erectus* shares with humans is a big brain. Brains consume a lot of energy; biologists would say that they are energetically expensive. One way to support the growth of a bigger brain is to increase the overall metabolism and take in more energy. Another way is to make metabolic trade-offs—shrink some organs to support the growth of others. Which way did *Homo erectus* go?

Anthropologists Leslie Aiello and Peter Wheeler developed the expensive tissue hypothesis to address this question.[17] They start by observing that modern humans have much bigger brains compared to body size than do modern chimpanzees. Aiello and Wheeler argue that humans do not support big, energy-hungry brains with supercharged metabolisms, but by making trade-offs.[18] When they compare other organs in relation to body size, Aiello and Wheeler find that other organs hold steady, but humans have much smaller digestive tracts than chimpanzees. We seem to have shrunk our guts while growing our brains.

Part of this difference in gut size is related to walking on two legs. Quadrupeds that walk on all fours have long narrow pelvises and a gut that hangs down, suspended from the spine. Bipeds like humans walk upright. The human pelvis is broad and short and curves up to support the gut tucked under the ribs. Thus a smaller gut may simply work better mechanically for bipeds. Hominins had been spending time on two legs since at least six million years ago, but *Homo erectus* looks like the first obligate biped. That is, it is the first of the hominins to be tied to walking on two legs, no longer able to easily transition back to the trees. Or, to put it in more positive terms, *Homo erectus* was the first hominin with an efficient two-legged stride that allowed it to walk or run all day.[19] The shape of *Homo erectus*'s pelvic girdle suggests that, like us, it carried its guts tucked in above its pelvis.[20]

Your digestive system breaks down the food you eat into the energy you need to power your body. A smaller gut has less surface area, less volume to use to break down and absorb nutrients from your food. But *Homo erectus* had a big brain to power, and its smaller gut still needed to provide the same amount of energy. To extract enough energy to power its hungry brain, *Homo erectus* needed a source of high-quality food, with lots of nutrients by weight.

This relationship, between body size, gut size, and diet, has a broad pattern across all kinds of animals, not just apes and hominins. Large animals, like elephants, tend to have large guts and can take in a lot of food. That food must be common, but it does not have to be high in nutrients—something like grass, say—because the animal can just keep eating. In contrast, a small animal, like a bat, has a small gut that fits less food. The food needs to be higher quality, like insects for example, but it does not have to be as common because the animal needs less. This relationship is called the Jarman-Bell principle, and it can allow scientists to make guesses about the diets of animals based on their size.[21]

If *Homo erectus* had a smaller gut compared to earlier hominins, but the same energy needs relative to its body size, it needed a higher quality, more nutritious food source. Grasses and sedges might have been fine for robust australopiths, but they would not suffice for *Homo erectus*. We have now arrived at a question that intimately intertwines the evolution of *Homo erectus* and the role of food—what was this high-quality resource? Hominins had been eating meat for at least a million years before *Homo erectus* came on the scene, so meat alone cannot be the answer. So, was *Homo erectus* simply a better hunter? Or could other resources or technologies have come into play that would support a bigger brain and a new gut configuration? Paleo-anthropologists have floated some very interesting answers to that question, answers that connect food to social relationships, sex, and life courses that set humans apart from other primates.

PAIR-BONDED COOKS

Anthropologist Richard Wrangham believes that fire and cooking set *Homo erectus* on this new path.[22] Cooking makes calories more available in food. This is why many dieticians recommend that you eat a lot of raw fruits and vegetables if you want to lose weight, by the way. During most of human prehistory, the goal was not to cut back on calories but to get as much nutrition as possible out of whatever food was available. Cooking softens fibrous, hard foods, making them easier to chew. Large teeth that grind and shear are not as necessary for a diet of soft cooked foods, and individuals do not have to spend most of their day chewing to take in enough nutrients. The gut can process cooked food more efficiently because cooking starts the process of breaking down foods.

Cooking is not the only way to increase the amount of available nutrients and decrease chewing time of food. Researchers have shown that mechanical processing (grinding, chopping, grating) can be almost as effective as chemical processing (cooking) in making food easier to break down.[23] Other forms of chemical processing, like soaking, sprouting, or using microorganisms to make fermented food such as sauerkraut, kimchi, sour pickles, and yogurt, can also essentially "predigest" food for us. But cooking has the potential to be faster and easier than these methods.

Wrangham argues that humans are physically adapted to cooked food. Not only do we have smaller guts and smaller teeth than chimpanzees, but we are more susceptible to plant toxins. We have developed various processing methods, including cooking, fermenting, and leaching, that allow us to eat foods that are dangerous to us raw. The benefits of cooking are seen especially in fibrous, starchy foods like tubers, the underground storage organs of plants. Cooking softens the tuber, converts starch to sugar, and helps decrease the toxins that plants use to protect these large stores of water and calories.[24] Tubers are a common resource in savanna environments today, and hominins would have benefited from being able to "unlock" the nutritional potential of this food and convert a relatively low-quality resource to a delicious, high-quality roasted tuber.

Of course, cooking also makes food more delicious. It converts starches to sugars, caramelizes, sears, brings out flavors and smells that make food appetizing. Humans may be the only ones who make fires to cook food for fun (figure 2.4), but we are not the only ones who find cooked food more appealing. Wrangham and his colleagues have set up experiments to show that chimpanzees prefer to eat cooked food and are willing to wait for it even if raw food is available.[25] He reports that when one researcher asked Koko the gorilla, via the sign language researchers had taught her, why she preferred cooked food, she signed back that it was more delicious. Wrangham uses this evidence to suggest that once the cooking breakthrough occurred, hominins would immediately have preferred cooked food to raw.

Wrangham admits that there is one problem with the idea that cooking opened the door to *Homo erectus*'s development—a lack of archaeological evidence. Some paleoanthropologists have identified hearths as far back as 1.4 to 1.6 million years ago in East Africa.[26] Other researchers think control over fire and its use to cook food on an everyday basis did not happen until much later, perhaps as late as 500,000 years ago, long after the unique characteristics of *Homo erectus* developed.[27] Archaeologist Martin Jones believes the first clear evidence of fire comes even more recently, from 180,000 years ago in Africa. This coincides roughly with the first anatomically modern humans there.[28] Paleoanthropologist C. Loring Brace thinks that cooking sparked a reduction in tooth size and sees the biggest changes in tooth size

FIGURE 2.4. Cooking over an open fire, Jequetepeque Valley, Peru. (Robyn Cutright)

(and thus evidence that cooking had become a common practice) around 100,000 years ago in cold northern climates.[29]

Wrangham, however, believes *Homo erectus* must have had regular access to fire, perhaps even as early as 1.8 million years ago. Cooking would explain so much of what we can observe of *Homo erectus* physiology, and fire itself would explain additional *H. erectus* characteristics. Wrangham points out that even for people today, the savanna can be a tough place to get a safe night's sleep. Without fire, he suggests, it would have been hard for *Homo erectus* to fully transition out of the trees. Sleeping around a campfire would provide a measure of security and allow hominins to more safely sleep on the ground. Likewise, it would be hard for *Homo erectus* to live in cooler climates like the Republic of Georgia or China without fire. Archaeological evidence of fire naturally becomes increasingly harder to find the further back we go, but despite the lack of concrete evidence for fire, Wrangham sees no other way to explain the suite of characteristics we observe in *Homo erectus*.

Wrangham's model goes beyond the role of cooking in providing the necessary food and protection for a big-brained, terrestrial hominin. He suggests that cooking was part of a broader social adaptation in which social groups were based on cooperating, monogamous pairs consisting of a male and a female. His logic runs like this: once a preference for cooked food and the ability to cook were in place, it would have made sense to collect food and bring it back to a home base rather than stopping to cook and eat throughout the day. However, a pile of cooked food sitting in a central location would be a target of theft by larger, socially dominant members of the group. Females who cooked would need protection from other males in the group if cooking was going to be worth it. By offering a male access to cooked food, a female could rely on his protection from other males. The resulting division of labor would expand the range of food that could be brought in by freeing up the male's time to hunt. A male hunter could risk a failed hunt if he knew he would still be able eat the food the female foraged. Successful hunts, even if they were only occasional, would reward both male and female with a periodic abundance of calories and protein.

Sexual dimorphism refers to differences in body size and shape between males and females of the same species. Wrangham notes that *Homo erectus* was less sexually dimorphic than earlier hominins as well as other primates, like gorillas, that do not practice monogamous pair bonding. Male gorillas defend harems of several females and can be twice as heavy as female gorillas. While human males are on average bigger and stronger than human females, the good deal of overlap in male and female ranges means that we are not very sexually dimorphic. *Homo erectus* seems to fall somewhere in between modern humans and gorillas.[30]

Wrangham also notes a feature of human sex that sets us apart from our closest relatives. Human females do not go into estrus, a period when female behavior and bodies signal externally that they are fertile. While human females are most fertile during a short period in the menstrual cycle, we do not overtly signal this through genital swelling (like female chimps) or sexual receptivity.[31] It is thus not immediately obvious to everyone in the group when a woman is fertile. Unlike other mammals, human females are receptive to sex throughout our cycles. Wrangham suggests that sexual receptivity, hidden estrus, and a reduced gap between male and female body sizes were all selected for by the pair-bonding logic of the earliest cooks.

Wrangham's model has males hunting and females cooking. The fossil record does not preserve much evidence of what tasks males and females did, so we have to infer based on what we can observe in the modern world. One supporting observation is that hunting tends to be a male activity among chimpanzees.[32] Another observation is that, in almost all societies recorded by anthropologists, women do the majority of the daily cooking, and men are responsible for most of the big game hunting.[33] If these regularities exist across cultures and are shared with our chimpanzee relatives, then Wrangham thinks there is no reason to assume anything different for *Homo erectus*. If there was a sexual division of labor, he believes, then females would most likely have been doing the cooking.

Wrangham builds this complex scenario by linking the timing of certain evolutionary changes to analogies with primates and modern humans. His evidence is largely circumstantial rather than direct, because it is difficult to see social behaviors and family structure in the fossil record. Wrangham emphasizes male-female monogamous bonds as the driving force in the evolution of *Homo erectus*, and by extension modern humans. However, male-female monogamy is only one of the many family arrangements that exist across human societies today. Polygamous families, and especially polygynous families with one husband and multiple wives, are common around the world. Other family forms in contemporary and past human societies include one wife who has more than one husband, partners of the same gender, partners of different genders in societies with nonbinary gender systems (for instance, a third-gender person with a husband), and families based on the maternal line in the absence of marriage. By inserting heterosexual monogamy and associated behaviors—paternal provisioning, male protectiveness, female domesticity and sexual receptiveness—into the

prehuman past, Wrangham seems to be advocating that these specific marriage patterns and gender ideologies are the natural evolved state of humanity. The cross-cultural diversity of past and present families and gender systems stands in counterpoint to this assumption.

Powerful Grandmothers
Wrangham makes a good case that cooking became important after 1.8 million years ago. However, his scenario for male hunting and monogamous
pair bonds is perhaps not equally well-supported. Other models have focused instead on female labor and the social bonds among related females
to provide alternate models for *Homo erectus* family dynamics.

Anthropologists James O'Connell, Kristen Hawkes, and others have drawn
the attention to dynamics of female foraging instead of hunting.[34] Hunting, after all, is not a uniquely human behavior. Chimpanzees hunt and eat
meat, but they do not have a strong sexual division of labor or form monogamous pair bonds. In many present-day foraging societies, meat is a
nice bonus to a daily diet supplied largely by women's foraging. Hunting
seems to play a clearer role in the status game than in feeding the family.[35]
As I discuss in chapter 1, there is clear evidence that hominins had occasional early access to meaty carcasses, but it is unlikely that they ate a diet
heavily reliant on meat.

O'Connell and his team do not simply critique models focused on male
hunting activities. They also shift attention away from monogamous pair
bonds to the family relationship between a woman, her daughter, and her
daughter's children. In other words, they focus on what Kristen Hawkes calls
the *grandmother effect*.[36] This model for the role of provisioning by females,
and especially grandmothers, is based on the kinds of evidence we have already considered, including modern forager behavior, the fossil record, and
modern human biology. These pieces come together not necessarily to completely reject the idea that male provisioning and protection were important
factors in hominin life, but to highlight a complementary and fascinating set
of dynamics on the female side.[37]

O'Connell, Hawkes, and their collaborators developed their grandmother
hypothesis during their research with the Hadza of Tanzania, one of the
few foraging societies left in eastern Africa. The Hadza are *not* primitive
analogs for hominins; rather, they are modern humans with complex language, thought, and culture just like all other contemporary human groups.
They live in the contemporary world and are not some isolated "Stone Age"
tribe. In fact, they show incredible patience in collaborating with scientists

and journalists who want to learn how they hunt and eat, sequence their genes, and even study their gut microbiomes.[38] However, the Hadza are experts in leading a foraging lifestyle in an environment more like the ancient East African savanna than many that exist today, and so it is worth paying attention to how the Hadza live as a potential analogy that can help us understand the challenges and opportunities facing ancient hominins.

Kristen Hawkes noticed that Hadza children have trouble finding enough food in the late dry season, when easily gathered fruit is rare.[39] Children usually accompany their mothers on foraging trips and eat as they go. During the dry season, easy-to-forage resources dwindle and key dry season resources, like large fibrous roots and tubers, are not accessible to children who lack the knowledge and experience to find them and the strength to dig them out. At this time of the year, children are dependent on adults to find food for them. If *Homo erectus* inhabited a cooling, drying savanna environment, tubers may have become increasingly important to them, and their children increasingly dependent on adult help in foraging.[40]

Hawkes found that children's weight varies directly and significantly with the time their mothers spend collecting food. In other words, the more time and energy a mother spends on collecting food, the healthier her children are. When a mother is pregnant or nursing a newborn, however, the health of her older children depends on the labor of older related women—primarily grandmothers. Older women's labor becomes essential to feed children under these circumstances.

To "win" the game of natural selection, the goal is to pass down your genes to as many offspring as possible who live to pass them on to the next generation. The extent to which you are able to get your genes into the next generation is referred to as *fitness*. The most direct way humans can increase their fitness is to ensure that their offspring survive and prosper. In this context, it makes sense that a Hadza (or really any) mother will invest energy in making sure her children are healthy. However, caring for others who are more distantly related to you, say your grandchildren, also helps your genes get passed on. Biologists would say that caring for relatives like grandchildren increases your fitness, but to a less direct extent than helping your children, since your grandchildren also carry a greater proportion of genes that are not yours than your children do.

So it makes sense for women to invest first in their own children. Only after their children are grown does it make sense to invest in other related children, such as their daughters'. If the investment of grandmothers in the past was significant in increasing their fitness, it could explain the development of a curious feature of the human lifecycle: prolonged vigorous lifespan after menopause, and in general the fact that we humans have relatively long lives, delayed maturity, and high fertility for our size.[41]

Following Kristen Hawkes's lead, we might compare life histories of human females, chimpanzees, and other primates.[42] Human females begin to have children and reach menopause at slightly older ages than chimpanzees, but on average both are fertile for about the same number of years. Unlike chimpanzees, however, human women live several decades after their reproductive periods end at menopause and during this time contribute vigorously to their families and communities. In groups like the Hadza, a third of women are over forty-five, so they can make a big impact on overall production.[43] In contrast, chimpanzee females are fertile almost to the ends of their lives, more like human males.

Kristen Hawkes and her team believe that menopause shifts women's focus from nurturing their own children to helping support their daughters' children. In a species moving away from eating fruit, shoots, and termites throughout the day (the chimpanzee model) toward greater reliance on harder-to-obtain resources like tubers that need to be centralized and cooked (the Hadza model), this support would be essential. Elderly women strong and vital enough to give their daughters' children an edge of survival also improve their own reproductive success, ultimately selecting for the vigorous grandmothers we see today (figure 2.5).

The grandmother effect is not the only scenario anthropologists have used to explain longer human lives. In fact, proponents of the idea that meat eating played a central role in making us human have proposed that in adapting to a more meat-centric diet, humans evolved longer lifespans. Caleb Finch and Craig Stanford argue that a longer adolescence might have been selected for in hunting hominins.[44] As culture—learned behaviors, preferences, and practices—became more important to hominin survival, youngsters would need to learn more and more from their parents and elders in general. Hunters with a longer period to learn how to hunt from older group members before reaching sexual maturity and having children would, according to this argument, have higher overall fitness.

A more meat-heavy diet also means a higher intake of fat and cholesterol. It seems that humans are more resistant to cholesterol-related disorders like heart disease than chimpanzees. Finch and Stanford identify several "meat-adaptive" genes that could have increased human life expectancy. Of course, these adaptations could have worked in tandem with the increased fitness of vigorous postmenopausal women.

FIGURE 2.5. Hadza women cook tubers. (Original art by Isabelle Ballard, Robyn Cutright)

The models I have presented here—for cooking, meat eating, and the role of grandmothers—are based on reasoning that links what we observe about humans today to various pieces of evidence about the past. However, it is possible to see the grandmother effect at work much more recently than 1.8 million years ago. Demographers have investigated church records from the Krummhörn region of Germany between 1720 and 1874 to reconstruct family life histories and see if grandparents had any impact on child mortality.[45] After crunching the numbers, researchers found that having a surviving maternal grandmother improved a child's survival by up to 23 percent over the first five years. Having a living grandfather had no effect, but having a surviving *paternal* grandmother actually worsened a child's chances of survival.

Even more interestingly, the effects were more pronounced at different ages. The positive effect of a maternal grandmother was highest between six months and two years—that is, while the mother was nursing and right around when the child was being weaned and the mother could have a new infant. Weaning toddlers might not get enough food, especially without specialized baby foods. It seems that having a maternal grandmother around made a measurable impact on her grandchild's health. The negative effect of a surviving paternal grandmother was most apparent right after birth. The demographers point out that child mortality in the first few months is often attributable to poor health of the mother during pregnancy. This suggests that paternal grandmothers had a negative impact on the health of their pregnant daughters-in-law.

In terms of evolution and fitness, maternal grandmothers can be certain that their daughters' offspring carry their genes, and so investing in the child increases their fitness. A paternal grandmother can never be 100 percent sure that her daughter-in-law is carrying her son's child. Thus, there is an evolutionary logic to why paternal grandmothers might be rough on their daughters-in-law, while investing in the children of their own daughters. This kind of evidence, along with studies of contemporary small-scale societies like the Hadza, convinces me that vigorous grandmothers have a measurable impact on their families.

Hawkes and her team believe that this selection process could have begun with *Homo erectus*.[46] Around 1.8 million years ago, the drying savanna environment would have encouraged the spread of tubers. While tubers do not fossilize, the team used fossils to track the expansion of tuber-eating wild pigs around the region during this same period and figured that the pigs' expanding range could be a response to the spread of their favorite food. Hominins that learned how to dig and cook tubers would unlock a huge source of starchy calories, perfect for feeding a growing brain. Since today, among the Hadza, older women are key tuber foragers, older women's contribution to the diet in the past would also have been especially important in this process.

While this scenario, like Richard Wrangham's, is ultimately speculative, it does fit well with the pieces of fossil and cultural evidence we have. It draws extensively on one cultural model, the Hadza, rather than broad cross-cultural regularities, like the assumption that females cook and males hunt. It focuses more on the resource (tubers) than the technology (cooking). However, the innovation of roasted tubers lies at the core of both scenarios. Unlike Wrangham's model of a *Homo erectus* society based on a core unit of a pair-bonded male and female, Hawkes and O'Connell's model envisions the key social unit as grandmother-mother-child. In reality, both forms of social organization can coexist in the same society.

Both scenarios are really interesting because they focus attention not just on the physical similarities between *Homo erectus* and modern humans but also on the way key aspects of human sociality and human eating might trace their origins back to small groups of *Homo erectus* 1.5 million years ago. Even more interesting are the suggestions that adaptations to certain foods, including tubers and meat, were responsible for many unique aspects of human bodies, brains, and behavior. Yet, as modern humans evolved and expanded across the globe, they encountered different environmental pressures than they had in eastern Africa, and culture played an increasingly prominent role in their responses. In the next chapter, I follow the human story of food even further—to the earliest emergence of humans who thought, spoke, and ate like us.

3

BIG GAME AND SMALL HOUSES
IN THE UPPER PALEOLITHIC

Archaeologists who found a few small bone fragments in Denisova Cave did not expect to revolutionize how we understand hominins at the end of the Pleistocene. They already knew that Neandertals lived in this part of Siberia, and when they sent the tip of a finger bone for DNA analysis, they expected to add to our growing sample of Neandertal genetic codes. However, the results showed that this bone fragment came from a previously unknown extinct hominin species, now known as the Denisovans.[1]

In 2018, the picture got even more interesting. Paleogeneticists focused on one bone fragment that had mitochondrial DNA (DNA that is passed down exclusively from mother to child) that matched Neandertal patterns. The nuclear DNA (passed down from mother and father) of this same fragment was about 40 percent Neandertal and 40 percent Denisovan. This individual was the daughter of a Neandertal mother and a Denisovan father.[2]

We now know that both Denisovans and Neandertals passed down genetic material to humans living today. Denisovans are known only through these few fragments of bone from Siberia, but humans in places like Papua New Guinea today carry some Denisovan genes.[3] Neandertals left behind a clear archaeological record from Spain to Israel to Siberia, and also contributed 1–4 percent of the genes of people who have non-African ancestry.[4] This all tells us that those early humans who migrated out of Africa at some point interbred with the Neandertals and Denisovans they met along the way.

This finding was striking. Neandertals had traditionally been considered a separate species from modern humans, *Homo neandertalensis* to our *Homo sapiens*. Different species are not supposed to be able to interbreed, but this is the only way to account for the presence of Neandertal DNA in modern human genomes. Anthropologists were forced to reconsider the relationship between us and Neandertals (and Denisovans, and between Denisovans and

FIGURE 3.1. Map showing locations of key sites from chapter 3. 1 = Nunamiut territory, United States; 2 = Blombos Cave, South Africa; 3 = Ohalo II, Israel; 4 = Shanidar Cave, Iraq; 5 = Denisova Cave, Russia; 6 = Tiwi Islands and Port Phillip Bay, Aboriginal stories of sea level rise; Australia. (Robyn Cutright)

Neandertals) and have begun to investigate whether our shared DNA might be related to specific adaptations we inherited from them.[5]

If Neandertals, Denisovans, and modern humans were close enough to produce viable offspring, then what does it mean to be human? This chapter explores how humans are (and are not) different from other recent hominins. Neandertals must have been supremely adapted to the cold glacial climates of Eurasia during the last Ice Age. But, if this is so, then how did modern humans end up the only hominin on earth, when for most of the last six million years several different hominin species were alive at any given time?[6] And what, if anything, did food have to do with all of this? In this chapter, I ask what it really means to eat like a human.

WHO WERE NEANDERTALS?

To answer the first, basic question of how humans are different from closely related hominins, I start where chapter 2 left off, with *Homo erectus*. *Homo erectus* lived not only in Africa, like earlier hominins, but also in eastern Europe, China, and Indonesia. Hominin groups in these different regions continued to develop along separate trajectories as the millennia passed. Paleoanthropologists debate many of the details, but by 200,000 years ago we can tell that populations of different hominins around Africa, Europe, and Asia had diverged and adapted to very different selective pressures. In Africa, the current evidence suggests that archaic *Homo sapiens* was present by at least 200,000 years ago, while Neandertals were present in Europe by 300,000 years ago.[7] Selective pressures in hot, dry eastern Africa favored the evolution of a large-brained, tall and lanky human who invented a wide variety of tools, art such as engraved rocks and beads, and language as we know it today.[8] In glacial Europe, natural selection favored cold tolerant, robust Neandertals who used new, technologically advanced stone tools and may also have developed art and language. Figure 3.2 imagines a Neandertal and a human face to face, an encounter that could have occurred at any point after about 100,000 years ago, when humans began to migrate out of Africa. Later in this chapter I return to *Homo sapiens*, but for now I would like to discuss Neandertal life and diet.

Neandertal remains have been found at sites in western Asia and in central and western Europe that date to between 130,000 and 30,000 years ago.[9] During this time, the glacial ice retreated across northern Europe and Asia and gave way to a warmer interglacial period, followed by another glacial advance during the most recent Ice Age.[10] Based on paleoenvironmental

FIGURE 3.2. Artist's visualization of an encounter between a Neandertal and a human. (Original art by Isabelle Ballard, Robyn Cutright)

reconstructions that rely on data from lake cores, ice cores, and archaeological sites, we know that during these glacial periods Europe was much colder and drier than it is now.[11] Ice sheets covered northern Europe, and at their last maximum extent about 25,000 years ago came as far south as Germany and Poland. South of the ice, most of central and southern Europe was tundra or dry steppe grasslands, with only a few pockets of forest remaining in the south. During the warmer interglacial period, this same area was covered in dense forests of pine and spruce or oak and elm, with open tundra farther to the north. Some of the animals available to Pleistocene hunters in Europe are familiar to us, such as wild boar, various kinds of deer, rabbits, ibex, and wild goats. Others, such as forest rhinos, woolly mammoths, cave lions, hyenas, wild horses, and aurochs (wild cattle), are either extinct or no longer live in Europe.

While once we thought of Neandertals as brutish cavemen, the evidence increasingly shows that Neandertals were intelligent and highly adapted to the climate and landscape they lived in. Neandertals had very robust bodies, powerful limbs with pronounced muscle attachments, which indicate well-developed muscles that put a lot of stress on the bones, and a thick trunk. Their faces featured heavy brow ridges, powerful jaws, and large nasal openings (since noses are cartilage, we do not know what their noses actually looked like, but we know they would have been broad).

This physical robustness influenced early stereotypes of Neandertals as brutish troglodytes, but it also probably helped them adapt to the cold climate of glacial Europe. During the coldest periods, west central Europe saw average winter temperatures around 16°F, about 25 degrees lower than today's winter average.[12] Based on archaeological evidence of where Neandertals lived and reconstructions of the climate when they were living there, researchers have suggested that Neandertals could tolerate *average* winter temperatures as low as -4°F.

In modern humans, populations adapted to hot climates over the course of generations tend to have long limbs proportional to their torsos and tend toward a tall thin stature, characteristics that help to disperse heat. Populations living in cold climates tend to have shorter limbs proportional to the torso and tend to be stouter and broader, adaptations that conserve heat.[13] According to this pattern, Neandertal bodies were "hyperpolar." Their wide noses, too, could have helped Neandertals warm and moisten tundra air as they breathed. They probably had higher metabolic rates, like modern humans who live in the Arctic. New genetic research on the Neandertal genes carried by some modern humans suggests that some of those genes might be associated with adaptations to cold such as production of keratin proteins in the skin and hair.[14] All this evidence suggests that Neandertals were extremely well-adapted to their glacial environment.

DNA evidence suggests that Neandertals had light skin and red hair. Light skin is often understood as an adaptation to living in areas, like the northern latitudes, where sunlight is limited. Humans have a love-hate relationship with the sun. Too much of the sun's ultraviolet radiation increases the risk of cancer, among other detrimental effects. Dark skin pigmentation, caused by high levels of melanin production, helps protect against solar radiation's damaging effects. The first *Homo sapiens* in Africa would have had dark skin, and as we saw in chapter 2 dark skin probably evolved in tandem with hairless bodies in hominins over the last million years.

Not enough sun causes other problems. Humans need a certain amount of sunlight to produce vitamin D, and vitamin D deficiency is linked to health problems like rickets and osteoporosis.[15] A lack of sunlight caused by short winter days, cloudy weather, and wearing warm clothes would select for individuals who produce less melanin, and thus block less solar radiation. Today, we can solve this problem through medical technology like vitamin supplements. In the United States, public health campaigns against childhood rickets in the 1930s led to the introduction of vitamin D fortified milk, to combat the effects of urbanization, industrialization, and the Great Migration of African Americans to northern cities.[16] As Neandertals adapted to living in northern latitudes, natural selection favored light skin.

Neandertal skulls were long, low, and robust, with a larger average cranial capacity (and so a larger brain) than modern humans, but their brains probably worked differently from ours. Recent research has suggested that the part of their brain that processes visual images was bigger, so they may have had better (or at least different) eyesight.[17] In contrast, *Homo sapiens*' brains are more dome-shaped, with a larger cerebellum and parietal lobes. These parts of the brain are linked to computational ability, sensory information processing, and social communication.

Artifacts left behind by Neandertals provide evidence of their respectable cognitive abilities.[18] Neandertal stone tools were more varied and complex than those made by earlier hominins. They were able to haft blades onto handles and craft a variety of tools, including scrapers, blades, and points to tip spears. At the very minimum, they would have been capable of complex vocalizations. They may even have made jewelry from bone and ivory, used the mineral manganese as black pigment, made cave art, and buried their dead. Paleoanthropologist Chris Stringer thinks that Neandertals may have

been on a path toward a different form of intelligence and behavioral complexity before they went extinct, and other archaeologists, including Brian
Hayden, question whether Neandertals really were that different from modern humans.[19]

As they spread out from Africa, first north to the Near East and the Ara-
bian Peninsula, and then west to Europe and east to Asia, early modern humans[20] encountered Neandertals, and in some areas coexisted with them for
millennia. What did these interactions look like? They were probably varied: Neandertals may have picked up ideas and goods from early modern
humans. They may have fought and killed each other. They must have interbred and produced at least some offspring that survived.

Interestingly, as geneticists continue to reconstruct ancient genomes and
compare them to modern ones, they have found traces of other species as
well. At the beginning of this chapter, I discussed how contemporary humans from Southeast Asians carry some Denisovan DNA. And there may
have been other archaic groups across Africa, Europe, and Asia who have yet
to be identified, a mosaic of different broadly human populations that likely
encountered one another occasionally.[21] Despite this incredible diversity in
the human line, by the end of the Upper Paleolithic 10,000 years ago, humans
were the only hominin species left. As Chris Stringer has pointed out, this
situation was highly unique; for most of evolutionary history several related
hominin species coexisted and interacted. We are, as he puts it, the Lone Survivors, a somewhat lonely honor.[22] While there are many explanations for the
ultimate success of humans and the extinction of archaic hominins like Neandertals, some researchers have suggested that food played a role in the ultimate persistence of humans at the end of the last Ice Age.

Big Game Hunters?

Just like many cuisines today, Paleolithic diets depended on season and location. There could never have been only one Neandertal diet over the 100,000
years Neandertals lived in Europe, just like Upper Paleolithic human diets
must also have varied. However, the research I discuss in this next section
suggests that stark differences in the basic outline of Neandertal and human
diets had profound implications for the success of each species during the
last Ice Age. As in chapter 1, one of the key factors seems to be meat.

One way to get a broad sense of what Neandertals (and early modern humans) were eating is to look at their bone chemistry, which reflects a summary of diet over the ten years or so before death. As I wrote in earlier

chapters, different kinds of foods (grasses versus roots and fruit, seafood versus land animals) leave different chemical signatures in the bones, which can be detected by measuring the balance of different carbon and nitrogen isotopes. Archaeologists Michael Richards and Erik Trinkaus tested thirteen adult Neandertals and fourteen early modern humans who all lived in Europe, and found some interesting differences.[23] Neandertals from across Europe had dietary isotope values very close to carnivores from the same environments. While Neandertals may have eaten some fish and other kinds of protein, these values suggested that their lifestyle emphasized big-game hunting. Early modern human individuals had a wider range of values, indicating a more varied diet that included plenty of food from oceans and lakes.

The evidence that Neandertals were big-game hunters and top-level predators who focused largely on meat helped overturn previous ideas of Neandertals as sluggish scavengers. Big-game hunting in glacial Europe would have been a dangerous activity. Neandertals used heavy spears that required face-to-face confrontation with large angry animals. By looking at animal bone remains from Neandertal sites, the landscape around kill sites, and the behavior of modern animals, researchers have attempted to understand how Neandertals hunted prey like bison, wild aurochs, or cattle, horse, reindeer, and rhinoceros.[24] They found that Neandertals used various strategies, including driving herds through bottlenecks or into constrained spaces where a mass of animals could be killed at once, and using teamwork to ambush and kill more solitary animals like rhinos. They had to get close enough to big animals to kill them with spears, since it was not until later that Upper Paleolithic humans developed the technology to throw light darts hard enough to pierce the thick hides of these large animals. Bows and arrows appeared far later in the archaeological record, so for Neandertals, hunting meant getting up close and personal with enraged and terrified bulls, buffaloes, and mammoths. These ambush and drive methods would require teamwork among a group of hunters, with some hiding, some driving, and some helping close off routes of escape.

Robust Neandertal skeletons often show evidence of substantial traumatic injury. They frequently have healed breaks to the head and arm, but much more rarely had injured legs. Some researchers have suggested that this pattern matches the injuries sustained by modern rodeo riders.[25] Even though this idea is compelling, it has not stood up well to scrutiny. New evidence shows that Neandertal injury patterns are not that different from later Upper Paleolithic human patterns. Paleoanthropologist Erik Trinkaus suggests that Neandertals who broke their legs simply may not have been able to survive in an environment that demanded constant mobility, and so we do not see individuals with healed breaks because anyone who broke a leg would not have survived for it to heal.[26] While the rodeo rider analogy may not apply perfectly, it is clear that Neandertal life could be rough, hunters had to get up close and personal with their prey, and a successful hunt would have required a team working in a combination of highly planned strategy and skilled reactions in the midst of the final chaos of killing.

If Neandertals were big-game hunters and apex predators who worked effectively in teams, what does this tell us about their social organization? Anthropologists Steven Kuhn and Mary Stiner believe that Neandertals organized themselves in a way that was significantly different from that of Upper Paleolithic humans, and in fact all later human societies as well.[27] Their starting point is the observation that in all known human hunting and gathering societies, men and women do different jobs and focus their efforts on different resources. In almost all cases, men tend to hunt and women tend to gather plants, just as Wrangham argued in the last chapter. Importantly, Kuhn and Stiner point out that these roles might be flexible on a daily or individual basis—a man who has an opportunity to bring back tasty fruit does not ignore it, and individual women develop hunting skills; however, the broad pattern still holds true. Even in places like the Arctic, where plant foods are not very important to the diet, men and women tend to specialize in different areas. In many Arctic societies, women are responsible for making and maintaining the highly technical gear and clothing that allow hunters to survive in such harsh conditions. In this way of thinking, there is no essential link between women and gathering plants or making harpoons. Instead, the key observation is that humans specialize themselves along lines of social identity.

Kuhn and Stiner believe that this division of labor allows different members of the group to develop different expertise and makes provisioning more efficient. Foraged plant foods (not the starchy agricultural staples we have today, like corn, rice, and lentils, but leaves, roots, and fruit) do not generally supply as many calories as meat, but they are more reliable food sources and provide a clear return on investment. Groups able to spare some people to try for uncertain meat while allowing other people to forage for predictable plants would see better returns overall; Wrangham also suggested this idea in his model for *Homo erectus* social organization. If different members of the group—old and young, women and men—developed different areas of expertise, the group as a whole would have a more diverse set of specialized skills.

Kuhn and Stiner wonder if Neandertals used this same efficient division of labor, but acknowledge that the archaeological record is not always very good at telling us this kind of information. Even if we do not have written records, archaeologists still have a few ways to reconstruct the kinds of activities men and women did in the past. Skeletons preserve the bony markers of repetitive activities, allowing us to identify differences in male and female physical labor. Women and men might be buried with different sets of tools, which we could interpret as reflecting their activities in life. Paintings or statues might depict men and women at work on particular tasks. But rarely do these lines of evidence tell a perfectly clear story. For Neandertals, the evidence is much less clear, so Kuhn and Stiner focus on what we know about Neandertal and human diets and artifacts.

Kuhn and Stiner believe that we can safely say that Neandertal diets generally focused on large game animals, not on a broad range of resources including plant foods. They also do not see much evidence that Neandertals crafted highly technical and specialized gear, even though they did wear clothes and make stone tools. In other words, we have a lot of evidence of the kinds of activities that are usually men's tasks in human societies, but not much evidence of women's work. Kuhn and Stiner do not think this is because the evidence of these "female" tasks is simply gone, as we have plenty of evidence for a wide range of foods, technology (harpoons, nets, fishhooks), and tools (needles, awls) at human sites that are almost as old. Instead, they think this evidence tells us that there was a fundamental difference in how Neandertals and early modern humans organized themselves in Paleolithic Europe.

Of course, it is possible that Neandertal women just did not do anything but have babies, but Kuhn and Stiner think it is more likely that both men and women were involved in the difficult, dangerous task of big-game hunting. Female skeletons are similarly powerful and show similar injury patterns and dietary signatures as males. Ambushing animals or driving herds toward chokepoints or traps would require group members to perform different tasks, some of them involving more direct confrontation with the prey than others. Kuhn and Stiner imagine that smaller-bodied women and children participated in less confrontational but still essential parts of the hunt.

When humans arrived in Europe 50,000 years ago, they likely brought a broad-based subsistence system developed in the warmer tropical climates of Africa and the Near East. Following the pattern common to all known human societies, men and women, old and young, would have done different jobs, forming bands of what Kuhn and Stiner call "diverse specialists."

In glacial Europe, they may have adapted this efficient system to access a broader range of plants and animals than the Neandertals. Kuhn and Stiner argue that this system may be one source of the edge modern humans eventually demonstrated over Neandertals, one way that Neandertals were ultimately outcompeted.

Researchers using a wide range of methods to examine Neandertal remains and sites from across Eurasia have started to question the idea that Neandertal diet was narrowly focused on meat, given the broad, flexible diet of earlier hominins. Various studies have begun to find evidence of more breadth and flexibility than initially thought. One study of the wear patterns on Neandertal teeth from Italy showed evidence of a mixed plant and animal diet.[28] Another study of preserved Neandertal feces showed mostly chemical markers from the digestion of meat, but also some evidence of plant consumption.[29] A third study found microfossils from plants, including a range of grass seeds and legumes, stuck in the plaque on Neandertal teeth from caves in Iraq and Belgium.[30] Many of the grass seed starch grains had been altered by heat, showing that Neandertals were not just eating opportunistically as they foraged, but spending time processing and cooking foods before meals. Plaque analysis also showed that Neandertals ate some plants that would not have been useful as food, but may have been medicinal.[31] Finally, analysis of the residues and wear on stone tools used by Neandertals at a site in France showed that they were used to cut and scrape animal hides, but also to work wood and cut up plants and fish.[32]

These creative methods reveal that Neandertals ate a wider range of foods than earlier models proposed. They also question the Paleo diet's assertion, discussed in chapter 1, that cooked grain is a new addition to human diets. Notably, these studies suggest that Neandertals in the southern part of their range, in southern Europe and the Mediterranean, seem to have eaten more diverse diets than Neandertals farther north.

Recent research has also questioned Kuhn and Stiner's view that Neandertal males and females were both involved in hunting to the exclusion of other gender-specific tasks.[33] Again, teeth have proven to offer key insights. A study of tooth wear and damage from Neandertals in France, Spain, and Belgium has shown different patterns in adult male and female teeth.[34] Since the kind of wear and damage the researchers looked at comes from using the mouth as a "third hand"—for instance, to hold tools or materials being worked—they proposed that males and females did different tasks.

To sum up this growing area of research, it seems that while Neandertal bone chemistry and archaeological evidence of tools and animal remains from Neandertal sites suggest heavy reliance on large game, Neandertals certainly also ate plants, fruits, and seafood when available. Since humans ate plants, fruits, seafood, and meat as well, maybe differences between Neandertals and humans are not as sharply drawn as Kuhn and Stiner suggest. Ultimately, Neandertals went extinct after overlapping with early modern human newcomers for some millennia. Could diet (or cuisine) have anything to do with their eventual extinction?

Neandertal Extinction

By about 35,000 years ago, Neandertals were well on the way to extinction, while modern humans were experiencing an explosion of cultural and technological innovation. If Neandertals were so well-adapted to glacial Europe, then why did they die out in the middle of the last Ice Age? One reason could be that Neandertal populations were never very large to begin with. Ecosystems can support far fewer large carnivores than the herbivores they prey on, so predator populations are generally much smaller than prey populations. If Neandertals were primarily big-game hunters, their populations would have remained sparse across glacial Europe. They may even have been prone to periodic regional extinctions or deep population fluctuations as the ice grew and shrank, and in general probably had very low, spotty populations. It would have been hard to support pregnant mothers and infants on an irregular diet of large game, especially if robust Neandertals had higher calorie requirements than modern humans, and so low birth rates may have contributed to low Neandertal populations.[35] Low and fluctuating populations would put a damper on technological innovations and the spread of information and ideas, which may have made it difficult for Neandertals to develop a more complex symbolic culture.

And, of course, the timing of Neandertal extinction is suspiciously aligned with the timing of modern human arrival in Europe. Modern humans and Neandertals overlapped for tens of thousands of years in places like Israel and Iraq (which is where anthropologists hypothesize that interbreeding took place), but in Europe Neandertals went extinct shortly after modern humans arrived, and competition may have played a role. While early modern humans would have been subject to the same fluctuating climate and harsh conditions, it may be that a broader approach to plant and animal resources gave them the flexibility to support larger populations, transmit ideas and innovations, and outcompete Neandertals even in a glacial environment Neandertals had inhabited for millennia.

WHO WERE EARLY MODERN HUMANS?

Anatomically modern humans were present in Africa at least by about 200,000 years ago.[36] These early modern humans were generally similar to us in height, stride, life span, teeth, and motor skills. They were less robust in the upper body than earlier hominins, but their skulls were still thicker, longer, and lower than our average today. Anatomically modern humans made a wide variety of tools, including smaller flake tools, projectiles, and bone tools, and there is evidence for exchange and spread of ideas across growing populations throughout Africa during the Middle Paleolithic.[37] Early beads, art, and the use of red ocher pigment from Blombos Cave in South Africa date to about 70,000 years ago and provide evidence for a growing sense of symbolic communication among these early humans.[38]

Anthropologists debate exactly when to pinpoint the first evidence that early humans not only *looked* like us but also *behaved* like us (and whether this distinction is meaningful at all). Paleoanthropologist Chris Stringer thinks that at a certain point, populations got big enough to sustain and promote the spread of cultural as well as technological innovations;[39] this population growth may or may not have coincided with genetic changes to the way humans think. Modern diversity in African genes and languages preserves the evidence of this long human heritage in Africa.[40] Beginning by

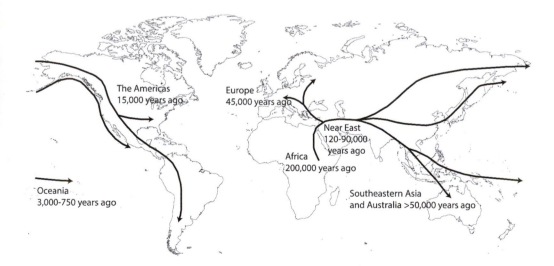

FIGURE 3.3. Expansion of *Homo sapiens* out of Africa. Arrows represent simplified trajectories. (Robyn Cutright)

100,000 years ago, modern humans expanded out of Africa and eventually colonized the rest of the globe, reaching the tip of South America sometime after 15,000 years ago and colonizing the islands of Remote Oceania only 750 years ago (figure 3.3).

Humans carry two different sets of DNA codes. One of these is the DNA in the nucleus of a cell, which we inherit from both father and mother. The other is our mitochondrial DNA, which we get from the initial egg cell contributed by our mothers. Mitochondrial DNA provides a way to trace our maternal ancestry by looking at which populations share mutations that were passed on from mother to child.

Genetic and archaeological evidence currently suggest that *Homo sapiens* had reached the Near East by around 120,000 years ago,[41] where human and Neandertal populations then coexisted for perhaps 50,000 years. By 50,000 years ago, humans had reached the far-flung regions of Southeast Asia, Australia, and Eurasia. *Homo sapiens'* arrival in Europe sparked what paleoanthropologists have traditionally called the Upper Paleolithic Revolution.

In many ways, humans in Upper Paleolithic Europe did what humans everywhere do. They made art and music, had rituals, buried their dead, and invented things. These features appear earlier, perhaps even among Neandertals, who made engravings and seem to have buried their dead intentionally. Some evidence even exists that earlier hominins carved designs that may have been art.[42] Yet in these earlier cases, researchers are still able to debate whether, for instance, Neandertals placed flowers on their dead at Shanidar Cave in Iraq, or whether the flower pollen was brought in later by burrowing animals. Or whether the hashtag scratched into a cave wall in Gibraltar by Neandertals should really be defined as art.[43]

Evidence from 30–40,000 years ago in Europe, and all the way back to 70,000 years ago in Africa, precludes debate as to whether humans were producing art. Anyone who looks at the famous cave paintings in Lascaux, or the female figurines (referred to as "Venuses") carved in ivory, knows that they were intended as symbolic, artistic expression. Anthropologists assume that other kinds of symbolic, abstract thinking, including ritual and complex language as we know it, would also have existed by this time. Did cuisine, or the cultural rules and meanings associated with the food we eat, also emerge around this time?

As Kuhn and Stiner noted, Upper Paleolithic humans used technological and social innovations to obtain a broad diet. One way that Upper Paleolithic humans were different from Neandertals in Europe was their big and diverse tool kit (figure 3.4). Humans made a variety of stone tools and

blades but also developed some seemingly simple but very important technologies. One was the spear-thrower, or atlatl. Essentially, the atlatl is a lever
that increases the speed and force with which a spear is thrown. The base of
a light dart sits against a hook at the end of a handle, and then the handle
is flicked to throw the dart forward. Darts thrown like this could pierce the
hide of a large animal at a distance, eliminating the need for close-quarters
hunting. Recent studies have shown that North American Upper Paleolithic
atlatls could propel a spear at almost eighty miles per hour.[44]

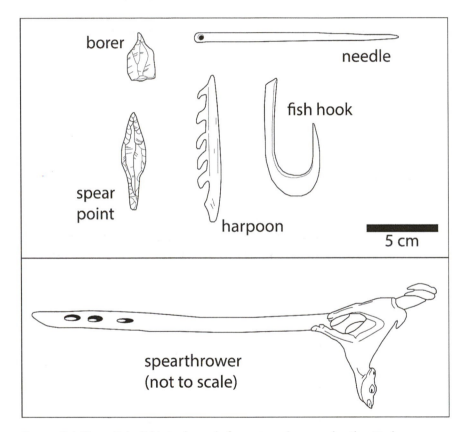

FIGURE 3.4. Upper Paleolithic tools made from stone, bone, and antler. (Redrawn
and modified from original sources by Robyn Cutright. The spearthrower is based
on a Magdalenian period artifact from Mas d'Azil cave in southern France. Dorothy
Garrod, "Palaeolithic Spear-Throwers," *Proceedings of the Prehistoric Society* 21 [July
1956]: figure 3, https://doi.org/10.1017/S0079497X00017370. The fish hook is based on
Dietrich Sahrhage and Johannes Lundbeck, *A History of Fishing* [New York: Springer,
1992], figure 1. The other artifacts are adapted from Paul Pettitt, "The Rise of Modern
Humans," in *The Human Past: World Prehistory and the Development of Human
Societies*, ed. Chris Scarre [New York: Thames and Hudson, 2009], 124–73)

Another technological innovation of the Upper Paleolithic was subtle, but powerful: string. String, made from fibrous grasses, bark, or animal skin and sinew, was organic and thus was not preserved in the archaeological record. However, we know Upper Paleolithic humans had it. Some of the figurines they carved contain depictions of twisted string. They had fishhooks, which would have been useless without string. We know they ate small schooling fish that almost *had* to have been caught in nets, and small animals most easily hunted using traps. The diversity of evidence for string hints at the reason string was so important—it has a wide range of uses. String helped Upper Paleolithic humans clothe themselves, catch fish and small animals, haul back loads of plants in nets, and make jewelry, among many other uses. It fit perfectly in the diverse, broad approach to subsistence that characterized Upper Paleolithic humans.[45]

Another innovation was the relationship between Upper Paleolithic humans and some wolves that began hanging around human camps. Researchers believe that dogs and humans began their long process of coevolution during this time.[46] Wolves who frequented human camps may have gained an advantage over other wolves by feeding on human scraps. Humans would have tolerated friendly and submissive wolves better than individuals who were more aggressive or fearful of humans. If early dogs helped humans hunt, this relationship might also have been beneficial to humans. Early dog domestication is fascinating in its own right but also emphasizes how Upper Paleolithic humans brought a broad range of tools, from string to dogs, and strategies to the quest for food.

UPPER PALEOLITHIC LIVES

Upper Paleolithic humans lived in small bands, and like earlier hominins, their foraging strategies were shaped by the ways in which resources were dispersed across the landscape. In some environments, resources were present in low but even concentrations, in others as dense, widely separated patches, and they always fluctuated with the rapidly changing climate. After the maximum extent of glacial ice in Europe around 24,500 years ago, the ice began to retreat after 18,000 years ago. The last Ice Age was over by around 11,000 years ago. Up until the beginning of the Holocene about 10,000 years ago, the global climate fluctuated more intensely than it has in recent millennia, so ancient foragers had to adapt to broader swings in temperature and rainfall than we tend to experience today.[47]

Archaeologists have shown that foragers' choices about where to live and what to eat are informed by a complex calculus that takes into account the nutritional return of different foods, their reliability, how easy they are to find and how successful each foraging expedition is likely to be, the labor involved in gathering or processing the food, and other such considerations.[48] Foragers tend to practice what anthropologists call residential mobility, which means they move their homes and camps from place to place across the landscape, depending on season, resources, and social considerations. Sometimes, foragers follow a seasonal round, moving with the seasons to forage or hunt. In other cases, they move through a broader landscape on a wider cycle, which might only reoccupy the same territories after decades. This means that many Upper Paleolithic groups in Europe and western Asia left only ephemeral traces of occupation on the landscape, in the form of summer camps, animal kill sites, fall processing camps, and the like.

This reality of mobile forager life means that not every site that dates to the Upper Paleolithic (40,000–10,000 years ago, or BP) and the following Mesolithic (10,000–5,000 BP in parts of Europe and Asia) was a home. Archaeologist Lewis Binford argued that each archaeological site might provide only one piece of a puzzle of Upper Paleolithic lifeways that extended across wide regional landscapes.[49] Binford studied the seasonal round and settlement patterns of modern foragers like the Arctic Nunamiut, to help archaeologists understand the kinds of traces this lifestyle leaves on different landscapes. Unlike Hawkes and O'Connell, who used the Hadza as an analogy for past groups living in a very similar landscape,[50] Binford sought cross-cultural regularities in the forager lifestyle. For instance, he asked Nunamiut foragers where they had lived in previous years and observed and documented how they used different spaces for summer camps, winter camps, seasonal get-togethers, hunting blinds, and caribou butchering sites. Each use left a different set of material remains for future archaeologists to find. Using this data, Binford argued that some of the Upper Paleolithic houses found by previous archaeologists were probably not houses at all, but rather places where people broke down animal carcasses or sheltered out of the wind while on a hunting trip. Even though his argument is limited by the many differences between contemporary Nunamiut and Upper Paleolithic foragers, Binford is likely correct that not every Upper Paleolithic site is a house.

This is why insights from a few, well-preserved houses are so important for understanding cuisine and domestic life in the Upper Paleolithic. A small group of people lived in a foraging and fishing camp on the edge of the Sea of Galilee in Israel 23–22,000 years ago. It consisted of six brush huts with outdoor hearths, and one grave. At some point after the shoreside community was abandoned, the Sea of Galilee rose to flood it and sealed all the remnants of life there under layers of mud. When water levels sank again, in recent decades, archaeologists encountered an incredibly well-preserved window onto Upper Paleolithic life.

Inside one of the huts, at the site archaeologists call Ohalo II, archaeologist Ehud Weiss's team found plant remains clustered around a grinding stone.[51] The archaeologists could even see an empty place in the middle of the scattered plant remains where an individual could have sat to work. The remains included important foods like millet and wild barley, along with a range of other plants, including edible vegetables like holy thistle and mallow, plants with narcotic and medicinal effects, and also the remains of bedding and brushy roofing materials. Flowers were present, which means that people used the floor for the last time in the spring or early summer.

The interior of the hut was arranged according to a plan. Food and medicinal plants were clustered in the northeastern sector around the grinding stone, bedding materials concentrated in the other corner, flowers in the entryway, and roofing materials covering over everything. Someone made stone tools near the entrance, probably facing the light from the door, and left tiny flakes of stone behind. Because plants and stone fragments occurred in two distinct concentrations, Weiss and his colleagues suggested that there may have been a sexual division of labor within the house.[52]

This glimpse into an amazingly preserved 20,000-year-old house shows us some immediately recognizable aspects of domestic life. Food preparation, tool repair, sleeping, and eating all took place in a shared space likely occupied by male and female members of the family. People foraged for wild grass seeds, but also plants with a wide variety of uses, hinting at a full, human life.

A Deep Engagement with Land and Food

The breadth of engagement with the landscape that we see at Ohalo II is echoed at other Upper Paleolithic sites in the Mediterranean region. A long record of resource use from Klissoura Cave in Greece shows that through the Upper Paleolithic and Mesolithic, occupants shifted their focus away from large animals to smaller, faster game, probably as resources around the cave became overexploited.[53] In Spain, the Upper Paleolithic period saw diversification in the range of resources humans were collecting, regional specialization into distinct coastal and inland diets, and intensification.[54]

Intensification means that people were spending more time and energy to collect resources. This could be because the population was growing or because resources with higher returns had become overexploited and thus sparser.

Overall, throughout the Upper Paleolithic and into the Mesolithic, humans in Europe and elsewhere responded to climatic fluctuations and growing regional populations by broadening and intensifying their foraging efforts. Archaeologists call this trend the Broad Spectrum Revolution, and it has extremely interesting implications. In many parts of the world after around 12,000 years ago, humans began a transition from highly mobile, highly focused big-game hunters toward this broader, more intensive foraging strategy that involved collecting and processing more grass seeds. Some archaeologists have thought of this as a period of settling into landscapes that were emerging from glacial fluctuations into a relatively stable environmental period known as the Holocene.[55] It is hard to tell whether populations rose because of this broader spectrum approach or whether the broader spectrum approach was a response to growing populations, but in many parts of the world, populations start to grow slowly in the millennia following the end of the Ice Age.[56]

Archaeologist Martin Jones has pointed out that as humans began to broaden and diversify their diets, they became enmeshed in more and different ecosystems.[57] Rather than focusing solely on big game animals that eat grass, for instance, humans might eat big game, and grass seeds, but also use nets to catch small fish, snares to catch rabbits and other small game, and lines to catch bigger fish, and also dig shellfish and travel to the upland forests for nuts. By involving themselves in more ecosystems, humans avoid the risk that comes from depending on just one small set of resources that could fail. People buffer risk by spreading it across multiple habitats, just like retirement fund managers invest across different financial sectors to protect themselves from a crash in one sector. This strategy increases the connections between the different food webs, which Jones points out increases instability since different ecosystems are now intertwined and subject to one another's fluctuations. In other words, a strategy that buffers risk for a growing human population might lead to a fundamental shift in the way ecosystems are interrelated. Later in the book, I return to the idea that the human food quest affects (and is affected by) ecological instability in complex ways.

A final obvious, but important, point about the residents of Ohalo II and other Upper Paleolithic communities is that these were anatomically and behaviorally modern humans. The people who ground seeds and chipped stone by the Sea of Galilee were humans who thought and acted as much like us as anyone living today. I argued earlier that humans do not just feed, we dine. We have cuisine, a set of cultural rules and beliefs surrounding what we eat and how we prepare it. The residents of Ohalo II and other Upper Paleolithic sites not only had a diet, they also had a cuisine. Probably this was a time when regional cuisines began to diversify and mediate the relationship between people and food in a way we would recognize today. People living on the Sea of Galilee invented dishes like wild barley and fish with savory herbs, while others waiting in southern Spain for the ice to retreat might have built a cuisine around forest resources like red deer, squirrel, and nuts. These culinary traditions would form the backbone of domestic life and, increasingly, cultural identity.

CUISINE AND WHAT IT MEANS TO BE HUMAN

I started this chapter with a challenge to what it means to be human. How can *Homo sapiens* be a unique species if some of us carry Neandertal (and Denisovan) genetic variants? For that matter, how are we unique if Neandertals made art and buried their dead or if chimpanzees also use tools and hunt? In some ways, it makes a lot of sense to consider modern humans from a biological, evolutionary perspective as simply the most recent member of a shared hominin lineage.

Like earlier hominins, we are dietary generalists capable of surviving on an incredibly broad range of diets. This capacity has played an important role in hominin adaptation to a wide range of habitats in Africa and eventually across the world, from Polynesia to Siberia to the Amazon. It was also essential in adapting to a climate that was much more variable over the last several million years than it has been in the last five thousand. In the context of contemporary climate change, we might take some comfort in the fact that hominins are dietary generalists, and that our lineage has adapted to many past climatic fluctuations. This optimism, however, should be tempered by the fact that, even though the lineage persisted, individual species did not always survive these periods of change and instability.

If we share with our hominin ancestors a propensity toward a broad generalist diet and the tendency to use tools and social cooperation to gain an adaptive edge, we are also different from earlier hominins in important ways. As anthropologists and archaeologists like Jones, Stringer, and Kuhn and Stiner argue, each using slightly different terms, modern humans have the habit of innovating in their technology and in their social organization to reach into multiple ecosystems, exploit a wide variety of resources, and affect broad landscapes rather than narrow niches.

Although biologically we are generalist omnivores, culturally humans are rooted in the particular geographies and cuisines that shape our identities. We use culture—art, music, folklore—to pass down knowledge about the right way to interact with plants, animals, and the natural world, and what to do in cases of disaster.[58] For instance, researchers have found in the folktales of contemporary Australian Aboriginal groups references to sea level rise that occurred over 5,000 years ago.[59] While we have not stopped genetically adapting to our environments, much of our adaptation as modern humans is learned and transmitted through culture. Culture has proved to be amazingly flexible and malleable, and today modern humans live as foragers in small bands, and also as software engineers in apartments packed together in global cities of ten million people.

This book is organized around two questions: *how did food shape us as humans? And, what role did food play in past human societies?* This chapter ends the first part of the book, which took up the first question as a lens through which to view human evolution. While *Homo sapiens* has continued to biologically evolve to adapt to changing conditions,[60] archaeologists can speak much more confidently about human social organization and cultural worldviews after the Upper Paleolithic. Archaeological evidence from more recent periods is better preserved, and a growing global population produced more sites for archaeologists to find.

Sociopolitical change and continuity, and the ways in which cuisine and culture are played out in daily life, are easier to discuss in a world populated by modern humans, *Homo sapiens* like us, than in earlier periods. For this reason, the second part of this book abandons a strictly chronological framework. It explores the role of food in different parts of ancient human societies around the world. In chapter 4, I detail the effects of a profound shift in the relationship between humans and food that occurred as some foragers became farmers starting around 10,000 years ago.

Part II

WHAT ROLE DID FOOD PLAY IN PAST HUMAN SOCIETIES?

The Prehistory of Food

4

DOMESTICATING HUMANS

The Origins of the Agricultural Lifestyle

The ancient city of Caral lies a few hours north of present-day Lima, Peru. From the coastal Pan-American Highway, the road to Caral climbs slowly inland, through fields of corn, sugarcane, and fruit trees, into the Andean foothills. Today, Caral seems remote even though it is only a few hours from a city of ten million people. Five thousand years ago, Caral was anything but sleepy and isolated—it was an urban community at the center of a regional exchange system that wove together towns and villages from rich inland valleys down to the Pacific shore.[1]

Caral grew over the course of a thousand years from a small village of reed huts into a city of three thousand people, with pyramid temples, circular plazas, and neighborhoods for elites and commoners (figure 4.2). Every few hundred years, residents rebuilt new facades over the pyramids, which ended up with several layers like Russian nesting dolls. They placed human sacrifices as offerings during construction and made other ritual offerings of burnt food in household hearths, ceremonial altars, and abandoned buildings.

People probably came to Caral from throughout the region to participate in ceremonies and exchange goods. Cotton, gourds, beans, and corn grown in irrigated valley fields were exchanged for abundant anchovies, shellfish, and other marine products. Residents wove cotton into cloth and fishing nets. They cooked their food in baskets and gourds, not pottery, but used clay to make human figurines and musical instruments.

Such an economically and religiously complex regional society was unprecedented on the Peruvian coast. Before Caral, foragers lived in small, temporary communities while they fished on the coast, foraged in the foggy hills, and gathered plants inland along the rivers. During the Preceramic period, people developed irrigation technology that allowed them to grow

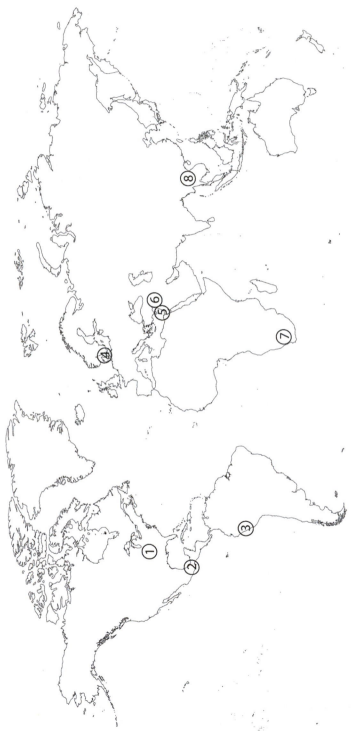

FIGURE 4.1. Map showing locations of key sites from chapter 4. 1= Cahokia, Mississippi Valley, United States; 2 = San José de Mogote, Oaxaca, Mexico; 3 = Caral, Peru; 4 = Mesolithic/Neolithic Denmark; 5 = Natufian pre-pottery Neolithic A (PPNA) Jordan; 6 = Abu Hureyra, Syria; 7 = !Kung territory, Kalahari Desert; 8 = Akha territory, southeast Asia. (Robyn Cutright)

FIGURE 4.2. Caral. (Robyn Cutright)

local plants like cotton as well as newly imported crops like corn. Along with the teeming marine life in the cold Pacific waters, this system was enough to support larger populations, complex trading ties, and cities like Caral.[2]

Caral represented a new way of life for people on the Peruvian coast 5,000 years ago. Its story introduces a revolutionary shift in the way humans related to one another, the environment, and their food that archaeologists see during the first centuries of farming. After about 10,000 years ago, some communities in far-flung parts of the world, including China, Turkey, Papua New Guinea, Mexico, the highland Andes, and Kentucky began to pioneer new kinds of interactions with plants and animals, even as foraging remained an important way of life elsewhere. These experiments ultimately ushered in a dramatically different way of life, first in these scattered pockets, but eventually around the world. Each early farming society focused on a small set of locally domesticated plants and animals, as the map in figure 4.3 summarizes. The story of how this way of life came about, and its implications for human society, health, and diet, is complex, but it can help us better understand how food and human society were interrelated in prehistory, and how these relationships continue to shape our own twenty-first-century lives.

DOMESTICATION, CULTIVATION, AND AGRICULTURE

This chapter surveys the origins of animal and plant domestication and agriculture. Domestication and agriculture are different but connected concepts. Agriculture coincided with radical social, technological, and economic shifts that made a community like Caral possible. Domestication refers to the physical and behavioral changes to plant and animal species that have resulted from human selection. Through the process of natural selection, traits that confer an advantage in survival or reproduction under given circumstances become more common in a population over time. In the case of human or cultural selection, humans decide which traits are desirable or undesirable.

For instance, imagine that people like larger, sweeter tomatoes because they are easier to pick and more delicious. As they collect tomatoes, they are more likely to pick the larger tomatoes and eat them. The seeds from the tomatoes they eat become the basis for next year's crop. Since people chose to eat the biggest and most delicious tomatoes, the genes for large size and deliciousness get reproduced preferentially in the next generation. Over time, these traits become more and more common in the new variety. This happens when farmers choose seeds from the best individuals and plant them, intentionally seeking a better product for the next harvest. It can also happen when foragers preferentially bring fruits with certain characteristics back to camp; these seeds, discarded at the edges of the camp, produce a new generation of fruits more likely to have these characteristics even if the foragers do not have the specific intention to propagate preferred traits.

Domesticates differ from their wild ancestors in some predictable ways. Domesticated plants tend to be larger, more productive, sweeter, and easier to gather than their wild cousins. Domesticated animals tend to be gentler,

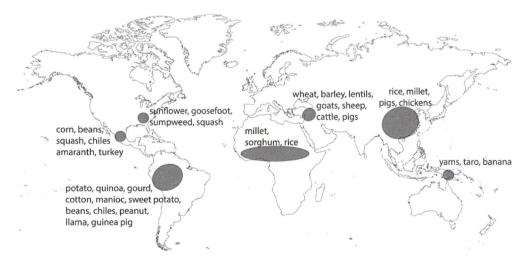

FIGURE 4.3. Some independent centers of early domestication around the world, showing selected plants and animals domesticated in each. (Robyn Cutright)

with smaller males and smaller horns, than their wild counterparts. Other traits are specific to the uses humans have for these plants and animals. For instance, the earliest sheep and goats were hairy, not woolly. Woolliness was selected for over the generations because humans found this kind of coat more useful.[3] Many domesticated plants have split into multiple varieties suited to different habitats, conditions, and uses, as farmers in different regions look for individuals that can survive with less water, at higher altitudes, in shorter growing seasons, store better, and so on. In the Andes, there are more than four thousand varieties of potatoes, each the result of human selection over millennia.[4]

A brief look at wheat and corn helps illustrate the process. Wheat was domesticated in the Near East, where foragers had been gathering abundant wild grasses for thousands of years. As grass seeds ripen, the short stem that connects each grain to the stalk, called a rachis, shatters to allow the seed to fly free. The seeds that land on a welcoming patch of ground become new grasses, so having a brittle rachis that readily releases ripe seeds into the environment is a good strategy for a wild plant. However, this quality is not very helpful to humans, who want to collect a bunch of grass seeds to grind up at home. In ancient wild wheat stands, the trait of rachis brittleness varied among individuals. As human foragers gathered and cut grass stalks with flint blades mounted on curved handles, they ended up with more seeds from mutants with shatter-resistant ears because seeds from stalks with a more brittle rachis had already flown free. If those humans planted some of the seeds they gathered, they would end up with proportionally more of the nonbrittle mutants. Repeat the process over generations and generations of wheat, and you have selected for a new variety of wheat that was more useful to, and dependent on, humans. Domesticated wheat was also physically different from wild wheat, and archaeologists can see these differences in the burnt seeds that fell into hearths and are collected, millennia later, from archaeological sites.[5]

Corn's path to domestication was even more complicated. We now know that corn has a wild cousin called teosinte that grows along field edges in central and southern Mexico, but for a long time scientists were not sure that teosinte was the wild ancestor of corn.[6] While it has similar leaves and stalks, its seeds look more like grass—several stems, or spikes, each hold about a dozen small triangular seeds (figure 4.4). Teosinte does not have kernels in rows on a cob covered with a husk, like corn; instead, each individual seed is separate and covered in its own sheath.

Genetic analyses finally clarified the relationship between maize and teosinte and showed that a few key gene mutations were responsible for the emergence of maize. One of these mutations, to the gene that codes for the hard outer covering of teosinte, made corn kernels more exposed, easier for humans to use, but less protected in the wild. People must have discovered some plants with this mutation and propagated them. This is another example of how the changes associated with domestication often made it harder for a plant or animal to survive in the wild, but that became less important once humans were taking an active role in raising it.

These examples illustrate some key points about domestication. Domesticated varieties are usually physically different from their wild cousins in ways that archaeologists can use to identify them at ancient sites. These physical changes reflect a process of coevolution that took place over generations, in which plants and animals became more dependent on humans to survive and reproduce. You only need to look at how much corn is grown across the world today to see how reliance on humans can be a very successful strategy for a plant.[7] At the same time, foragers who engaged

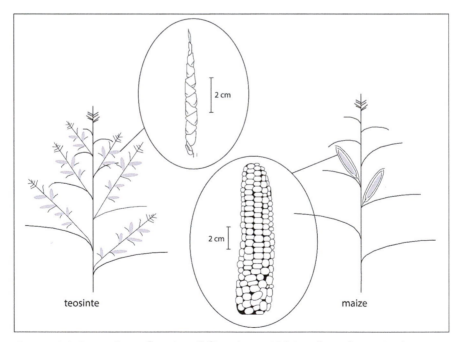

FIGURE 4.4. Comparison of teosinte (*left*) and corn (*right*) stalks and ears. (Redrawn and modified from Nick Lauter and John Doebley, "Genetic Variation for Phenotypically Invariant Traits Detected in Teosinte: Implications for the Evolution of Novel Forms," *Genetics* 160, no. 1 [January 2002]: figure 2, www.genetics.org/content/160/1/333. abstract, Robyn Cutright)

in domestication became increasingly dependent on these few plants and animals.

The process of domestication is intertwined with a complex cultural shift from finding plants and animals out in the world to intentionally cultivating or raising those plants and animals. However, the categories of forager and farmer are not mutually exclusive. Many foraging groups intentionally alter their environments through controlled wildfires, preferential encouragement of useful species, and other means, meaning that foragers might create more productive landscapes without actually planting crops.[8] Some groups pursue intermediate strategies between hunting wild animals and caring for fully dependent domesticated animals. The Gebusi people of Papua New Guinea, for instance, raise semiferal pigs by letting them forage in the rain forest and occasionally rounding them up when they cause too much damage to gardens.[9] Finally, a plant or animal does not have to be domesticated (in the sense of having been shaped genetically by cultural selection) to be planted or raised by humans, even though the process of raising and cultivating often provides the context for the kinds of selection I described earlier. There is a relationship between cultivation and domestication, but not always a clear distinction.

Agriculture refers to a way of life, an economy based on growing plants and raising animals.[10] Farmers might gather the occasional wild plant or go hunting, but the bulk of their food comes from growing domesticated crops and raising animals. While domestication is a process, farming is a way of life that extends beyond just the characteristics of plants and animals. Both domestication and the shift to agriculture are intensely interesting subjects for archaeologists. It is not always clear what prompted farming to be adopted in particular contexts, and not all foragers abandoned their way of life when domesticates became available. Yet, a shift from foraging to farming occurred independently in multiple parts of the world within a few thousand years. For this reason, anthropologists see the transition to agriculture as a cultural process rather than a historical accident.

WHY FARM?

This cultural process did not happen the same way in every part of the world. The specific ways that agriculture developed in different places had a lot to do with particular historical, social, and environmental circumstances. Generations of archaeologists have tried to understand this process. Was agriculture adopted immediately, or did the transition to agriculture take many human generations even after plants and animals were domesticated? Was it intentional—did people mean to become farmers? Or did people proceed down the road to agriculture without a specific agricultural end goal in mind? Were societies *pushed* toward farming as a result of population pressure or climate change, or did the benefits of agriculture *pull* them toward a greater emphasis on farming? Can we account for why societies moved toward domestication and agriculture when they did? In this section, I review some key models developed by archaeologists over the decades. Then, in the next section, I introduce a few case studies with the goal of evaluating these models on the basis of specific archaeological evidence.

In the first half of the twentieth century, the influential archaeologist and prehistorian V. Gordon Childe popularized an approach to the emergence of agriculture as a "Neolithic Revolution."[11] Not only did farming usher in a complete revolution in human society, in this account, but it was also an innovation that appeared and spread rapidly. Childe focused specifically on the Near East region, where a warming, drying trend changed the landscape at the end of the Ice Age. As rainfall decreased, the environment became more hostile, pushing people, plants, and animals together in the areas that remained fertile. In these fertile "oases," people became more intimately aware of plant and animal reproduction and developed a closer, more symbiotic relationship with the plants and animals sharing the oasis. As people began to try to increase the productivity of the most important plants, domestication occurred.

In this "Oasis Theory" model, agriculture emerged in the course of a generation or two—it was a Neolithic *Revolution*—as the result of climate change and human innovation after the last Ice Age. Subsequent research has not supported Childe's view that agriculture emerged quickly, in fertile pockets into which people and plants were pushed; I sum up some of this research later in this chapter. However, archaeologists like Ofer Bar-Yosef continue to argue that climate change played a central role in pushing foragers toward farming.[12]

In contrast to Childe, archaeologist Robert Braidwood argued that agriculture more likely developed in the natural habitats of the wild ancestors of important domesticates.[13] In the Near East, this meant that wheat, barley, goats, and sheep would have been domesticated in their wild range, on the hilly flanks of mountains in Iran, Iraq, and Turkey. Braidwood's model revolved around the role of human cultural innovation rather than external climate change. Ancient people living in the hilly flanks of the Zagros Mountains had to diversify and intensify their food-gathering strategies after effective hunting wiped out larger game. Ultimately, domestication and farming developed out of an intensive focus on gathering wild grain. In this view, agriculture was an innovation that would improve life, discovered by humans after they had observed nature closely enough.

Braidwood's scenario is supported by evidence that foragers in parts of the Near East heavily exploited wild wheat and barley in the millennia prior to domestication and farming.[14] However, not everyone shares Braidwood's optimism about the benefits of agriculture. What if people did not adopt agriculture because they wanted to but because they were forced to by a growing population and increasing pressure on available resources?[15] One proponent of this idea, archaeologist Mark Cohen, argued that at the end of the last Ice Age semi-sedentary foragers living in places like the Near East and perhaps also China had access to so much food that they did not have to be as mobile as before.[16] They began to spend more time living near rich stands of grasses like wheat and millet, which along with plentiful fish and game provided enough resources for semi-sedentary life.

As the pressure to move decreased, so did the pressure to keep the population low. It is hard for mothers to care for several young children at a time while foraging and moving from place to place. Mobile foragers today use cultural methods, including taboos against sex after childbirth, extended nursing periods, abortion, and even infanticide, to make sure they do not have too many children spaced too closely together. A foraging diet that is seasonally low in fat and calories also tends to lower fertility rates.[17]

As foragers became more sedentary, Cohen's argument goes, parents would face less pressure to space births, and so birth rates would rise as taboos against sex after childbirth and other cultural mechanisms relaxed. Diets rich in grass seeds and fatty fish would allow women to build up fat reserves and so increase fertility. Diet would necessarily become broader, as a growing population would require even those resources previously passed over as too hard to forage or process. Ultimately, diversification would not be enough, and people would start to cultivate and select for more productive plants and animals, beginning the process of domestication that ultimately ended in an agricultural economy. In this scenario, the pressure of a growing population pushed foragers toward a farming lifestyle.

Thinking about domestication like this presumes that people had some idea of their end goal when they began the process. Farming becomes an innovation designed to solve a problem, such as a growing population or a changing climate. But the first domesticates were barely more productive than their wild ancestors. How could foragers know that after a hundred or a thousand generations, teosinte would become corn productive enough to feed an empire? Archaeologist Kent Flannery responded to these critiques by suggesting that, to understand the beginnings of domestication, we have to look at it from the point of view of foragers living their lives, not on the basis of the end result.[18]

Flannery's ideas about agricultural origins focus on how foragers try to minimize risk.[19] One of the big risks faced by foragers is that they cannot always rely on plants being where they need them. It is dangerous for foragers to come home empty-handed too often, having spent time and calories on searching for food that they did not find. Foragers want to minimize this risk however they can. One way to minimize risk is to eat a wide variety of resources. That way, they usually find at least something they can use.

Another way to minimize risk is to manipulate the reliability of resources, by moving plants through the landscape, helping to propagate them into new niches, or encouraging them to grow near camps. This is exactly what we see modern-day foragers doing in the examples above. Some plants are extra susceptible to this kind of manipulation, too. For instance, as contemporary gardeners know, some plants are early colonizers of disturbed ground, growing easily from discarded seeds. Pioneer species such as squash and sunflowers were some of the earliest domesticated plants in places like the Americas.

A scenario in which forager lifeways lead toward cultivation and domestication might look like a group of foragers camping under a cave overhang near a stream. They bring food back to the camp each night to cook and eat together, tossing the scraps into the forest at the edge of the camp clearing. When they come back to this good campsite the next year, they find wild gourd vines growing at the edge of the clearing. They may or may not recognize these as growing on last year's trash heap, but they eat the ripe fruits and again toss a few seeds and scraps away. Seeds from preferred plants get selected in this way, beginning the process of domestication.

This same group might also encourage some plants to grow outside their natural ranges or in new habitats, or otherwise manage the productivity of the landscape.[20] Archaeobotanist Dolores Piperno has found some of the earliest domesticated plants in Central and South America alongside evidence for intensified use and even cultivation of plant resources by foragers. This intensification corresponded with environmental shifts at the end of the last Ice Age.[21] Piperno argues that foragers experimented with and manipulated plants in a way that made sense within a forager mindset and helped them meet their dietary needs, but that this manipulation became the first step on the road to domestication.

According to forager-focused models, domesticates might exist for a long time before anyone settles down in a village with a farming economy. Cultivation, which may lead eventually to domestication, might just be part of what foragers do to minimize risk, ensure access to preferred foods, or respond to a changing climate.[22] Various conditions, such as growing populations, political competition, religious movements, or warfare, might underlie decisions to settle down and start making a life around these domesticates centuries later.

But if domestication arises out of core forager behaviors, then why did it not happen everywhere, in every group of foragers around the world? What if domestication was intentional because domesticates were particularly desirable in some specific way, or under specific social conditions? Archaeologist Brian Hayden thinks that plants and animals were domesticated for one reason: politics.[23] Hayden starts from the same point as Flannery, that in order to understand domestication, we have to adopt a forager perspective. Hayden studies transegalitarian societies like the Akha people of Southeast Asia (Thailand, Laos, Myanmar, and southern China). In these societies, competition for status is an important social dynamic, but differences in status or wealth are not particularly pronounced. Hayden thinks that these dynamics of competition are fundamental to human societies, since there are always individuals who are more aggressive and acquisitive than their peers.[24] These individuals are compulsive status seekers and are often extremely innovative in finding forms of competition that fit their existing social structure. One way that families in transegalitarian societies compete is by hosting feasts, creating an opportunity to show off their wealth and to make others in the community indebted to them.

Among the Akha and the other Southeast Asian societies Hayden studies, feasts provide opportunities to eat meat, usually pig, and drink fermented rice wine. Meat is not a part of the daily diet, and so the opportunity to eat large quantities of meat only comes during special, celebratory occasions. Figure 4.3 shows that early domesticates in different parts of the world often included grains, the basis for fermented beverages; meat animals, which provide fat and protein; and foods that add flavor, like chili peppers.

Hayden suggests that a desire for reliable luxury foods to serve at feasts drove the first cultivation rather than a need to supplement the diet with daily staples. In some parts of the world, stands of wild grains were dense and easy to exploit, but in other regions wild ancestors of grains were not particularly productive and required a good deal of labor to collect and process. Hayden cannot imagine that foragers would even bother cultivating them unless they offered a special benefit, in this case concentrated starch that could be converted to beer. Why would foragers put in the time to raise pigs if they could easily hunt wild ones, unless a surplus of meat was needed for a party? To Hayden, this extra effort only makes sense in the context of competitive feasts. Only later would the resulting domesticates have become productive enough to support the community as staples.

Each of these models articulates a different scenario for how human societies might have begun the process of domestication and ended up as farmers. Some emphasize the role of innovation, as a response to difficult conditions or for political gain, while others emphasize the goal of risk minimization. In some, societies moved relatively quickly from domestication to agriculture, while in others the process was slower, with cultivated plants incorporated into a foraging diet for a long period of time before the shift to agriculture occurred. Some focus on the benefits of agriculture pulling people toward this lifestyle, while others suggest that people were pushed toward agriculture by pressure from a growing population or a changing climate.

The only way to evaluate these ideas is to move past generalized scenarios to look at the archaeological evidence from different parts of the world. Of course, the process might have played out differently in each of the early centers of domestication. There is probably not one right answer, and thus it is more useful to ask about the circumstances under which different scenarios might have played out. Domestication occurred early in both the Near East and Mexico, but the trajectories each region took toward agriculture look very different. In both cases, agriculture spread from these centers to adjacent but very different regions. Farming spread north and west from the Near East into Europe, and north and east from Mexico to the southeastern United States. The next section addresses each of these cases in turn, before returning to these scenarios to evaluate which do a better job in helping us understand this key shift.

The Birth of Agriculture in the Near East and Europe

Megafauna like mammoths did not survive the end of the last Ice Age, and so postglacial foragers in the Near East and Mediterranean could not sustain a highly mobile, big-game focused Paleolithic way of life. Their diet had to diversify, in the Broad Spectrum Revolution discussed at the end of chapter 3. The warmer, wetter climate after the Ice Age allowed Natufian foragers to flourish, and populations grew in the Near East.[25] A sudden cooler, drier trend between 12,800 and 11,500 years ago caused grasslands to spread and forced the Natufians to adopt new strategies to find food. Archaeologist Ofer Bar-Yosef believes that some Natufians returned to an extremely mobile lifestyle at this point, but that others began to settle down and focus on smaller animals, grass seeds, and other resources that were more labor-intensive but also more reliable.

By the end of this cool, dry period, relatively permanent villages were scattered across the region, from the eastern shores of the Mediterranean, through Turkey, and south into Iraq and Iran.[26] At Abu Hureyra, near the juncture of several rich ecosystems along the Euphrates River in modern-day Syria, around two hundred foragers settled into a small village of round pit houses.[27] They gathered wild wheat, rye, lentils, and other seeds from abundant grasslands and hunted gazelles and wild goats in the nearby hillsides, finding enough food that they did not need to move often. They developed specialized tools to harvest and process seeds, and archaeologists find small, polished blades of flint that would have been embedded into sickle handles, grinding dishes, and storage bins at the center of their villages.

Over the course of Abu Hureyra's 4,000 years of occupation, plant and animal remains reveal a slow transition from wild to domesticated varieties. The first morphologically domesticated rye—that is, rye shaped by selection for larger size and a shatter-resistant rachis—at Abu Hureyra dates to about 11,000 years ago. It can be hard to tell whether animal remains come from wild or domesticated varieties. However, several lines of evidence, including the proportions of different species, the representation of different ages and sexes among the animals consumed, and some features such as changes in the size of horns, suggest that sheep and goats were domesticated slightly later at Abu Hureyra, by 9,500 years ago.

The ages and sexes of the animals people ate also reveal animal domestication. Archaeozoologist Melinda Zeder explains that hunters and herders make different choices about which animals to kill.[28] Hunters might go after particular kinds of animals, like the largest or the slowest, or like the Neandertals discussed in chapter 3 they might try to ambush and kill a whole herd. The animal bones in hunters' trash heaps reflect these demographic patterns. In the first case, large males or older slower animals would be overrepresented. In the second, the trash heap would resemble the population of a living herd. Herders have different goals than hunters, however. They need as many females as possible to raise the babies that grow the herd, but they do not need excess males. They tend to kill and eat all but a few males when they reach adult growth, but eat females only when they are older and are no longer fertile. The trash heap of a herder should contain a lot of older females and male yearlings, and that is exactly what Zeder saw at the 10,000-year-old Iranian village of Ganj Dareh.[29]

By about 9,000 years ago, Abu Hureyra was a village of rectangular homes where as many as 5,000 farmers grew wheat, lentils, and rye and herded sheep and goats. People there continued to hunt gazelles even after becoming farmers, and they probably became devoted herders only after plant cultivation was well-established. Their bones show they did hard work, with women probably spending several hours a day grinding grains. Men, women, and children were buried with funeral offerings. Neither the burials nor the houses show much differentiation, which indicates that everyone was probably similar in terms of status and wealth. When Abu Hureyra was abandoned around 7,000 years ago, the region was dotted with similar farming communities.

Slowly, as domesticated plants and animals were adopted by people in neighboring regions, farming spread. The expansion of agriculture from the Near East into Europe provides us with an opportunity to look at a different kind of process: not the initial emergence of agriculture, but the spread of new, fundamentally different foodways.

One of the questions at the heart of archaeological investigations of agriculture in Europe is a fairly basic one: "Who were the first farmers in Europe?" One possibility is that Near Eastern farmers migrated into Europe, traveling over land and across the Mediterranean Sea. Farming supported larger populations, as we saw at Abu Hureyra, and expansion into less densely populated Europe could have provided an outlet to release some population pressure. Farmers could have been drawn by contact with foraging communities into existing networks of exchange and communication that spanned the Mediterranean region.[30] Archaeologists call this process, in which people carry ideas and technology as they migrate, *demic diffusion*. Another possibility is that the idea of farming, along with domesticated plants and animals, spread from community to community. European foragers would have learned about this innovation from their neighbors and adopted it for themselves. This process is termed *cultural diffusion*.

We know that pigs, cattle, wheat, and barley were not originally domesticated in Europe, but we need to look at the evidence to decide whether farming spread through demic or cultural diffusion. If agriculture was carried along with migrating farmers who colonized parts of Europe, then we should see discontinuities in local culture that go beyond just a shift from a foraging to farming lifestyle. Local crafts and artistic styles, burial patterns and other evidence of local culture would be replaced by new ones. We should also see genetic evidence of replacement, in the form of new, Near Eastern genes flowing into local gene pools. This genetic evidence could be ancient, in the DNA of people from Mesolithic and Neolithic burials, but it could also be embedded in the genetic codes of contemporary Europeans. If, instead, agriculture was a great new idea that got passed along and copied from one society to its neighbors, we should find more continuity in local culture and genetics that knits together foragers and farmers in the same region.

Many archaeologists have argued that farmers migrated into central and southern Europe between 5,000 and 8,000 years ago.[31] Geneticists see evidence for the arrival of Near Eastern genes into this area, discontinuities with earlier forager populations, and some intriguing hints that foreign males may have integrated themselves into European communities and partnered with local women. Archaeological studies in the western Mediterranean suggest that farmers filled in the landscape around existing forager communities and despite evidence for contact, maintained distinct identities.[32] In the British Isles, too, there seems to have been a relatively quick population replacement rather than local continuity, based on evidence that diet changed abruptly.[33]

Evidence from northern and northeastern Europe tells a different story, one that emphasizes local continuity. As farmers moved through Europe, it seems that some foragers remained on the margins, especially in climates where agriculture was initially much more difficult. Eventually, foragers in these areas fit farming into their existing cultural traditions. For instance, in ancient Denmark, farmers used ceramics not only to process dairy, a common culinary practice in the northern European Neolithic, but also for fish, a holdover from prefarming practices.[34] In southern and central Europe, personal jewelry styles shifted abruptly with the advent of farming and presumably the displacement of earlier peoples; however, in northern Europe, bead styles remained similar across the Neolithic transition, suggesting that foraging societies adopted agriculture while preserving other elements of their culture.[35]

In Europe and a few other regions of the world, dairy became an essential part of a farming diet.[36] Milk fats have been detected in the chemical residues left on the insides of early colanders and pots from across Europe.[37] Dairy was especially important in northern Europe, where short summers and long winters required a very different approach to farming than in sunny Turkey. Farmers had to rely on grains like oats, which can cope with a colder, shorter growing season, and on cows who could convert grass into fat- and protein-laden milk.

The first farmers faced a huge obstacle to incorporating dairy into their diets: they could not digest it. Most adult mammals do not produce lactase, the enzyme that breaks down lactose, or milk sugar, because they no longer need to digest milk. Many humans also stop producing this enzyme as adults; we generally refer to this as lactose intolerance, when actually the persistence of lactase production into adulthood is the exception in humans.[38] In a few parts of the world, such as northern Europe and central Africa, where herding cattle and eating dairy products were extremely economically important in the past, genetic mutations allowed some people to continue producing lactase later in life. These individuals could extract more nutrition from a diet featuring dairy products, and so the beneficial mutation slowly spread through these populations.[39] This is one way in which humans have genetically adapted to an agricultural diet in the last 10,000 years.[40]

Another way humans have adapted to dairy is by using the flexible tools of cuisine and culture. By fermenting milk, which allows microbial cultures to consume part of the lactose, cooks can produce more easily digested dairy products. These products include cheese, yogurt, kefir, and cultured butter, and are eaten by people around the world, even in populations where lactose intolerance is common. The first part of this book focused largely on genetic adaptation over the course of human evolution, but here the role of culture is clear. Cuisine is one way that humans adapt culturally, thus shaping the conditions under which future cultural and genetic adaptation takes place.[41]

The Near East is one of the oldest and best-known cases of the emergence of agriculture, but is it unique? How does the transition experienced by the community of Abu Hureyra compare to what happened at other communities in other parts of the world? In the next section, I explore how the origins of farming in the Americas compare to what we saw in the Near East.

THE FIRST FARMERS IN MEXICO AND THE US SOUTHEAST

Humans have been living in the Near East for at least 60,000 years. Migration to Mexico and the rest of the Americas came much later in human history. After 15,000 years ago, people began to trickle across the Bering Strait from Siberia, slowly spreading south along the coast or between glaciers.[42] Foragers who reached central Mexico found rolling plains full of yucca and prickly pear cactus that gave way to rocky highlands cut by arid canyons. They moved through this landscape eating seasonal resources such as jackrabbits, antelope, and, as the climate got warmer and wetter after the end of the Ice Age, dry scrub forest foods like deer and mesquite.[43] Happily for archaeologists, these foragers occasionally camped in dry rock-shelters that preserved the remains of the plants and animals they ate. Eventually, these remains started to include early domesticates like corn.

Cob fragments from one of these caves, Guilá Naquitz, have some key physical characteristics of corn, showing that people had already begun the domestication process by 6,200 to 5,400 years ago.[44] Cultivation of other plants began even earlier. Archaeologist Bruce Smith has identified 10,000-year-old squash seeds from Guilá Naquitz cave as domesticates because they are larger and a different color than seeds from wild gourds.[45] Dry caves like this probably were not the first sites of domestication, just places where remains were best preserved. New evidence, including microscopic samples of maize pollen, starch, and petrified cell structures, has shown that domesticated maize was present 8,000 years ago in the lowland Balsas Valley, the homeland of wild teosinte in southern Mexico.[46]

Despite planting the seeds of agriculture by beginning to cultivate or at least manipulate key plants like corn, people in this region did not abandon their mobile foraging lifestyle until much later. The earliest Formative (Neolithic) villages in Mexico date to about 3,500 years ago, more than six thousand years after the earliest plants were cultivated. Archaeologists Joyce Marcus and Kent Flannery believe that only at this point did corn become productive enough to support permanent communities.[47]

San José Mogote, in Oaxaca, Mexico, is a good example of one of these early villages. Key features of life in San José Mogote included cultivated plants like corn and avocados, pottery (initially made to imitate gourd bowls), permanent wattle-and-daub structures with thatched roofs, and a village population that was seven times larger than earlier hunting camps. As this way of life spread, San José Mogote households received trade goods from distant valleys across the region. For the first time, it was possible for some people to achieve higher status, as indicated by the special burials of two middle-aged men at San José Mogote. Villagers also practiced household rituals involving human figurines (mostly representing women), and built ritual structures with lime-filled pits at their centers (possibly to activate ritual plants like wild tobacco or jimson weed in initiated men's ceremonies).

Why was the delay between cultivation and sedentary agricultural life so much longer in Mexico than in the Near East? While humans came much more recently to the Americas than the Near East, cultivation and domestication were underway nearly as early. However, the structure of available resources in central Mexico was not as favorable to a settled life as in the Near East, where foragers could live in relatively sedentary communities by exploiting dense stands of wild grains. Making a living as a forager in central Mexico required moving around a lot more. Teosinte, the wild ancestor of corn, was also not as productive as wild wheat or rye and required a much longer process of intentional selection than did Near Eastern cereals (or rice and millet in East Asia, for that matter, where the process looked much more like the Near East example than the New World one).

In the Near East, archaeologists have documented the interplay between domesticated plants and animals, and between farmers and herders. With the exception of llama and alpaca herders of the high Andes, communities in the Americas tended to emphasize domesticated plants. There were some important domesticated animals in the Americas. Dogs traveled with hunters across the Bering Strait from Asia. In North and Central America, people domesticated turkeys, and in South America they kept Muscovy ducks and guinea pigs for meat along with llamas and alpacas for meat, wool, and as pack animals. However, hunting and fishing continued to be central strategies for obtaining meat even as agriculture intensified.

Domesticated corn spread quickly through the Americas. In Ecuador, distinctive microscopic cell structures from corn have been dated to almost 8,000 years ago, and maize residue was found on some of the region's oldest pottery that dates back to 4,200 years ago.[48] While the earliest maize was part of a diverse foraging diet, corn eventually became the staple grain from the southern Andes to the eastern United States. In many of these places, people had already experimented with cultivation and domestication of other plants on their own. The southeastern part of the United States is one place where the transition to a farming economy happened in two waves: first, people domesticated local plants, and only later did corn arrive from elsewhere and become central to a local farming lifestyle.

At the end of the last Ice Age, the middle Mississippi and southeastern United States were sparsely inhabited by highly mobile bands of hunters. As Ice Age megafauna became rare and eventually extinct, these Archaic period foragers turned their attention to smaller game (deer, birds, and small mammals), acorns and hickory nuts, seeds, mussels, and fish.[49] They moved seasonally from winter settlements to summer base camps with smaller transient camps in spring and fall. In Kentucky and Ohio, Late Archaic foragers buried their dead (and their dogs) with belongings reflecting their age and an overall equality among community members. People were generally healthy, though they suffered from occasional lack of food and wear and tear on joints and teeth.

As in the Near East, a diversified, broad-spectrum diet eventually led to independent experiments with cultivation and domestication. By 3,000 years ago, Late Archaic foragers in Kentucky were cultivating squash, plants with starchy seeds like goosefoot, knotweed, and maygrass, and plants with oily seeds like sunflower and sumpweed in mixed upland gardens.[50] The oldest morphologically domesticated knotweed identified to date comes from a mound in Kentucky and dates to about one thousand years after cultivation of knotweed probably began.[51]

Other than squash and sunflower, these plants are probably unfamiliar to the average American. Goosefoot, also called lambsquarters, belongs to the same family as better-known quinoa (native to the Andes). Both are pseudocereals from the genus *Chenopodium* with small, flat, round seeds that are high in protein and nutrients. These plants, along with undomesticated hickory nuts, fish, and game, formed a solid basis for a semisedentary horticultural economy in Woodland-period Kentucky. But corn had already begun its slow march north to revolutionize farming in North America.

Native Americans famously called corn, beans, and squash the "three sisters" because they are so amazingly complementary (figure 4.5). Corn requires a lot of nitrogen for adequate nutrition, and bacteria that live on the roots of beans transform nitrogen gas from the atmosphere into a biologically useful form. Corn provides a stalk for beans to climb, while squash's broad leaves and prickly vines provide ground cover and protection. Corn and beans together provide a complete protein, and all three are delicious together especially if you add some hot peppers.

At some point, cooks in central Mexico realized that if they soaked corn in an alkaline solution containing lime (calcium hydroxide), the skins would soften and the texture would change. This process, called nixtamalization, produced dough for the tortillas and tamales that have remained at the heart of Mexican cuisine.[52] Though cooks may not have realized it, nixtamalization has nutritional benefits as well,[53] allowing corn to form the base for cuisines of Mexico, Central America, and the US Southwest.

Unlike in Europe, there is no genetic or archaeological evidence that migrating groups carried corn and beans out of Mexico as they replaced existing populations—no evidence of demic diffusion. Instead, it seems these products spread through contact with neighbors and curious cultivators interested in trying something new. Corn reached the Ohio and Mississippi Valleys by AD 900–1000, and quickly became an important staple among

FIGURE 4.5. Maize, beans, and squash have complementary needs and are often grown together. (Robyn Cutright)

people living in small hamlets and homesteads, growing plants and hunting, and occasionally coming together as larger groups to bury their dead, worship, and construct mounds and earthworks.[54]

Corn fit into the horticultural lifestyle based on the Eastern Agricultural Complex I already described, but it could provide more calories than existing crops. Mississippian societies, which constructed enormous earthen pyramids at chiefly centers such as Cahokia (near Saint Louis), Moundville (Alabama), and Etowah (Georgia) grew corn intensively alongside starchy seed crops.[55] Farming came to support cities of more than 10,000 people, with surrounding farmsteads stitched together into regional populations of 100,000 in places like Cahokia. In Kentucky and the surrounding area, farming societies emerged in a long, two-step process that began with the small-scale cultivation of local plants as part of a mixed foraging strategy and ended with intensive agriculture of corn alongside older local crops.

WHICH MODEL IS RIGHT?

So what do these two completely independent examples of how farming emerged and spread say about all those models for the origins of agriculture? First, it is clear that the two cases look very different. In the Near East, sedentary foragers domesticated grasses like wheat and a whole range of animals. Once established, farming was carried in a Neolithic wave that spread across Europe from southeast to northwest, pushing foragers to the margins. Eventually, the remaining foragers made the shift to agriculture on their own terms. As agriculture pushed northward, it adapted, and the population adapted to it genetically and culturally.

In Mexico and elsewhere in the Americas, mobile foragers conducted the earliest experiments with domestication and remained residentially mobile for thousands of years after domesticates were present. Plants like corn spread through cultural transmission, and when they reached the United States they stood alongside local plants to become the agricultural base for large, complex communities.

In both scenarios, the process began when foragers took a broad-spectrum approach to minimize risk, as Flannery and others have argued. From the perspective of these foragers, domestication of some of the plants and animals in their environments was, at least at first, an unintended consequence of foraging calculus. The changing climate at the end of the last Ice Age and a growing population probably helped push foragers toward this broad-spectrum approach. Archaeologists debate the extent of population pressure before domestication,[56] but growing populations began to fill in landscapes in the millennia after farming villages first appeared, and probably pushed neighboring foragers toward adopting farming themselves.

Not all foragers adopted farming, though. Foragers lived alongside farmers for long periods of time in northwestern Europe, where it seems that farming was picked up, abandoned for a time, and then eventually added in to local foodways. Foragers lived alongside farmers in the ancient US Southwest and adapted cultivation to fit their needs in the Amazon, where societies like the historic Warí (chapter 7) grew corn while still relying heavily on hunting and fishing. Throughout this book, I discuss foraging societies from the present or recent past, like the Hadza (chapter 2), the Nunamiut (chapter 3), the maritime societies of the Pacific Northwest (chapter 5), the Nukak (chapter 7), and the !Kung (chapter 8). Farming was not the obvious choice for all societies, despite the pushes I described earlier. In fact, I will discuss some of the ways in which early farming lifestyles were more labor intensive and less healthy than foraging ones.

Agriculture did have some attractive features that may also have pulled communities toward farming. Farmers could store surplus food against the risk of future bad years, or intensify production to support a new kind of specialized, diversified, large community, like Cahokia or Caral. In both cases, cooking techniques that made new agricultural foods like corn and milk more nutritious helped transform them into dietary staples. And across the board, the social implications of the transition to agriculture were sweeping.

FARMING'S REPERCUSSIONS

Agriculture reshaped human cuisine and society in every region it reached. While the role of domesticated animals varied greatly among different regions, most early farming diets centered on just a few starchy staples and legumes: rice or millet and soy in East Asia; wheat, barley, chickpeas, and lentils in the Near East; corn (plus potatoes, quinoa, or amaranth) and beans in the Americas; millet, rice, and sorghum in Africa. Tropical farming, in places like Papua New Guinea and the Amazon, emphasized starchy root and tree crops like plantains, yams, and manioc. Reduced dietary diversity, alongside other aspects of farming economies, affected human health, biology, social organization, gender roles, religious practice, and relationship with the environment in fundamental ways.

It might seem that farming would improve human health by making it possible to produce more food. It is true that farming generates more calories on the same land compared to foraging. While many early domesticates were only barely more productive than their wild ancestors, cultural selection and improvements in farming technology eventually meant that one farming family could feed not only itself but others as well. This surplus production, in turn, could support a more diverse economy, where some people could become specialists like tool makers, religious practitioners, or long-distance traders. But did this ability to produce a surplus lead to better health?

The archaeological evidence tends to suggest that agriculture had a complex and variable, but often broadly negative, effect on the health of early farming populations compared to their forager ancestors, in a pattern that archaeologists George Armelagos and Mark Nathan Cohen have called "irregular patterns of ups and downs (mostly downs)."[57] In many parts of the world, early farmers were shorter, with worse teeth and more signs of poor health and malnutrition than foragers. Forager teeth tended to be worn from use, but farmer teeth tended to have more cavities. This is probably because farmers ate a lot of starchy grains, often boiled into porridge or soup, which left a lot of sugar coating the teeth. Foragers, in contrast, ate a more varied and fibrous diet.

The teeth and bones of early farmers often show ridges of interrupted growth, called enamel hypoplasias (on teeth) and Harris lines (on bones). As children, these early farmers were so malnourished or sick at times that their teeth and bones stopped growing. Archaeologists use the incidence of these episodes of interrupted growth to gauge the health status of different populations. In many parts of the ancient world, farming populations had more affected individuals, and individuals survived on average more incidents of starvation, than foragers. Farmers often also had more incidences of spongy porous bone caused by anemia and generalized bone disease than foragers.

Skeletal evidence of malnutrition suggests that early farmers regularly struggled with nonlethal but serious food shortfalls and poor health. Farming villages were larger, denser, and more permanent than forager communities, and this shift rather than agriculture itself might be responsible for the health impacts visible in the archaeological record. People in sedentary farming communities had to solve problems that mobile foragers never worried about, like what to do with the human waste and garbage generated by many people living closely together. With limited technology for waste disposal, early farming villages were fertile ground for pathogens and parasites.

Living closely with domesticated animals, as farmers did in the Old World, did not help either, since diseases can jump from animals like pigs and birds to humans. The health decline associated with early farming was likely due to these interrelated social, ecological, and epidemiological factors.

In many ways, life was harder for early farmers than for foragers. Ethnographic research showed that in the 1960s, !Kung foragers in the Kalahari Desert of southern Africa worked less than twenty hours a week to meet their needs.[58] The rest was time for socialization, leisure, and naps. In contrast, preindustrial farmers work up to sixty or more hours a week during key times in the agricultural cycle, because the work of clearing, tilling, planting, weeding, harvesting, and processing is intensive and demanding. Processing crops, especially grinding grains into flour, can take hours each day.[59] Farmers did not necessarily have much leisure, even though not everyone in the society was directly producing food.

As populations grew, farmers began to live in larger communities. This shift required new ways to promote shared identity, make decisions, and diffuse tensions. Foragers, who today generally live in small bands, tend to make decisions through consensus and protect individual autonomy. Those who disagree can just walk away. Foragers also tend to emphasize egalitarianism and maintain social mechanisms (such as reverse dominance, in which the group makes fun of anyone trying to assert themselves) to keep anyone from gaining too much power or influence.[60]

The socioeconomic calculus was different for early farmers. In most environments, farmers were able to amass more surplus than neighboring foragers.[61] Surplus food meant that not everyone needed to be involved in obtaining food all the time, but it also allowed for the possibility that some families could produce more than others. Farmers also had to manage tensions without just walking away from land their family had invested in for generations.

Archaeologist Ian Kuijt has studied the burials of Neolithic communities in the Near East in order to understand some of the social pressures the earliest farmers faced.[62] Sedentary foragers during the Early Natufian phase buried their dead with ornaments and personal belongings, but during the Late Natufian and early Neolithic (termed PPNA, or Pre-Pottery Neolithic A) period, all adults were buried basically the same way. They were laid out under house floors, on their backs, with no ornaments or belongings. Sometime after death, after their bodies had decayed, their skulls were removed. Groups of skulls were reburied together in caches, suggesting that they were used for some sort of communal ritual. Occasionally, skulls were plastered and cowrie shells placed in the eye sockets to reproduce facial features.

Kuijt finds this burial pattern interesting for a few reasons. We might expect the transition from foraging to farming to be accompanied by a big social shift, for the reasons I have already discussed, but burial practices did not change during this transition. Burial practices of Late Natufian foragers and PPNA farmers both emphasized community integration (caches of skulls were buried together) and deemphasized difference (everyone was buried in the same way) even as it was becoming possible to produce a surplus and become wealthier than your neighbors, and as storage shifted from communal space at the center of town to inside individual homes. As the Neolithic went on, the fact that some skulls were plastered and most were not probably indicates emerging social differences within communities. All this evidence adds up, for Kuijt, to hint that social tensions began to bubble up in early farming villages, but social and ritual institutions attempted to quell them.

Farther north, in Turkey, archaeologist Ian Hodder and a multidisciplinary team have studied the long-lived Neolithic community of Çatalhöyük.[63] Residents lived in tightly packed houses accessed through their conjoined roofs, with little change in village plan or social organization for over a thousand years. Hodder and his team have argued that daily household practices such as sweeping the floors and replastering walls, shrines, and the burial places of ancestors within houses helped to teach and reinforce shared values and maintain continuity.[64] Kuijt and Hodder both emphasize continuities in the household and ritual practices of Neolithic households that may have helped promote community cohesion and egalitarian ethos in the face of the social tensions brought on by a changing way of life.

Although agriculture has been understood as simply another example of how humans modify their landscapes through the process of cultural niche construction,[65] dramatic modifications often corresponded with widespread adoption of farming. Sedentism reduced the scale of the landscape through which humans moved on a yearly basis, but agriculture increased the carrying capacity, or the population that could be supported by a given territory, and the landscape continued to fill up. Foragers actively manipulate the landscape, but farmers make a much bigger impact by clearing and cultivating fields, irrigating or draining land, and raising grazing animals. Long-term pollen records at the bottom of lakes often reveal a regional shift from forests to grasslands as agriculture intensified.[66] Ancient farmers were increasingly dependent on the right mix of rainfall, sun, temperature, and other weather necessary for a successful crop to make ends meet, but the landscape also grew increasingly domesticated and crops increasingly dependent on human intervention. Ecological relationships shifted, and human impact reshaped farmed landscapes in new ways.[67]

The forager way of life did not end with the dawn of farming. Yet much of the blueprint of contemporary society, from our dependence on agriculture, to exchange relationships that are now global in scale, to our increasing impact on the environment and the huge growth of cities, can be traced back to the early farming communities I describe in this chapter. The people who grew cotton and traded for anchovies at Caral, built huge earthen mounds and grew corn outside the palisades at Cahokia, and replastered household shrines over the centuries at Çatalhöyük were pioneering a new way of life that would shape lives and cuisine for millennia.

5

"DRINKING BEER IN A BLISSFUL MOOD"

Feasts and Fancy Meals in the Past

Sometime around AD 1000, Wari lords gathered on top of a mesa in the southern Andes called Cerro Baúl.[1] The embassy was shutting down after centuries of representing Wari imperial power in the coastal Moquegua Valley. The temple, palace, storerooms, and other buildings had been abandoned in a planned, orderly fashion. Everyday tools and goods were packed away down the mountain, ritual offerings were buried, and thatched roofs were burned over the remains of celebratory feasts. In the meantime, the brewery kept producing corn beer, or *chicha*, flavored with spicy *molle* fruit to be served at these closing ceremonies.

Finally, only the brewery was left. After the final batch of *chicha* had finished fermenting, twenty-eight lords gathered in the courtyard of the temple. *Chicha* was poured from serving jars into twenty-eight tall, wide, decorated cups called *keros*. After drinking, the lords smashed their *keros* on the floor of the brewery, where they were covered by the burning structure. Having properly celebrated the abandonment of the community through conspicuous consumption and destruction, the Wari lords left Cerro Baúl's mesa top with the evidence of this last feast intact until archaeologists discovered it in the 1990s.

Remains of these ceremonial closing meals from Cerro Baúl and the surrounding Wari settlement suggest that beer drinking was accompanied by sumptuous meals of llama, guinea pig, fish, corn, and fruit, ritually important plants like coca and tobacco, and exotic animals from the Amazon basin and the high Andes. Meals like this, in which a group of people shares special foods for a special purpose or celebration, are known to archaeologists as feasts.

Feasts turn out to be fairly common across societies around the world. This chapter's title comes from a hymn celebrating beer brewing and drinking in

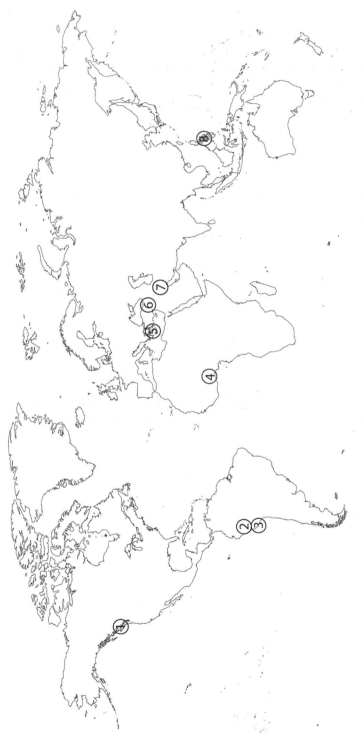

FIGURE 5.1. Map showing locations of key sites from chapter 5. 1 = Pacific Northwest region; 2 = Inca heartland; 3 = Cerro Baúl, Peru; 4 = Dahomey, Benin; 5 = Minoan Crete; 6 = Göbekli Tepe, Turkey; 7 = Sumerian Mesopotamia; 8 = Philippine chiefdoms. (Robyn Cutright)

ancient Mesopotamia, on the opposite side of the world from Cerro Baúl.[2] In this chapter, I focus on feasts, special celebratory meals that archaeologists have understood as a nexus of social, political, and economic negotiations for both hosts and guests in ancient societies. I discuss how archaeologists have analyzed the diverse motives and characteristics of feasts in the past, and I show how alcoholic beverages were central to feasting across the ancient world.

DEFINING THE FEAST

Feasts are expensive for hosts, so from an economic perspective we might say that feasts use hospitality to transform the host's surplus into social capital. Food and drink become a medium through which social messages are expressed, or political negotiations are carried out. Guests and hosts might not have the same goals or experience of feasts, but for both the occasion is slightly risky and the possibility of failure is real.[3]

Archaeologist Brian Hayden believes that feasts are ultimately about competition, which for him is a fundamental driver of human evolution and social change.[4] Self-interested hosts use feasts as one tool to win prestige and status and ultimately gain reproductive and economic success. Another archaeologist and feasting expert, Michael Dietler, thinks that such a view downplays the fact that feasts occur within particular historical and cultural contexts.[5] To Dietler, political and social dynamics at feasts cannot be generalized as simply adaptive behavior that promotes material gain. While feasts may be products of self-interest, people's ideas about what is in their best interest are defined by their cultural contexts and the social locations. Feasts are one way that people build prestige and status that gives them access to power and moral authority in their own society's terms. These opposing viewpoints reflect a central debate in anthropology about whether we should understand cultural practices as primarily adaptive in an evolutionary or materialist sense or whether culture itself is what constitutes the meaning that is performed through practice.[6]

Archaeologists from a variety of theoretical perspectives have been drawn to feasts in part because they have some clear material markers (figure 5.2). At feasts, larger-than-usual quantities of special food are prepared using large pots, served in large dishes, and consumed by many people using lots of plates and bowls. Hosts and guests use special serving wares, and hosts often focus on aesthetics and presentation in the food and surroundings. More alcohol is served at feasts than at daily meals. Archaeologists use these material markers to look for feasts in the archaeological record and have found them across the world, at many different times, from small-scale foraging societies to far-flung empires. However, not all feasts across this wide range of societies play host to the same social dynamics.

DIFFERENT KINDS OF FEASTS

Feasts are special purpose meals that create and maintain important social relationships, not just fill bellies. Within this broad definition, archaeologists have categorized feasts in different ways based on their purpose, participants, and politics.[7] Some feasts bring together the whole community, while others like the final toast at Cerro Baúl were restricted only to a certain group. Passover meals happen every year, while wedding feasts may be intended to happen only once in a lifetime. Different kinds of feasts might include different symbolic foods or actions and might impose different social expectations on their participants. For instance, the Wari lords who

FIGURE 5.2. Preparing *pib*, corn dough pies filled with meat and cooked in an earth oven, at a Maya family feast for the Day of the Dead in the Yucatán. Several characteristics of feasts are visible, including the communal preparation of larger-than-usual quantities of food, the use of large vessels and unusual modes of preparation (here, the earth oven), the participation of men as well as women in cooking, and the creation of special elaborate dishes. (Robyn Cutright)

gathered in the brewery were expected to smash their *keros* on the floor at the end of this feast, though they may not have done so at all feasts.

Because he focuses on feasts as a tool for self-interested competition, Brian Hayden categorizes feasts based on the goals of their hosts.[8] Alliance and cooperation feasts celebrate solidarity within or between groups and help generate political support. Economic feasts foster material gain through competition or acquisition of political positions, reward workers, or collect tribute. Diacritical feasts are exclusive to members of the elite and display wealth and status. The different goals of these feasts mean that they are held in different settings, with different kinds of participants consuming different kinds of food and drink. For example, the Wari feast described above best fits into the diacritical category, because a relatively small group of elite guests smashed their twenty-eight different decorated drinking cups in what was likely an exclusive event.

Michael Dietler's interest in the social and political content of feasts leads him to identify three different categories, or "modes of commensal politics."[9] Hosts of empowering or entrepreneurial feasts use hospitality to acquire power, prestige, and/or economic capital. Patron-role feasts subtly emphasize differences in power and wealth between the host, usually of higher status, and the guests, often workers, subordinates, or supporters. Finally, diacritical feasts, as for Hayden, celebrate and display elite status and wealth.

Neither of these systems captures every nuance of every feast, of course. The goal is not to perfectly categorize every feast by checking off the pertinent boxes, but to think through and sort out important differences in the politics, goals, and motivations that give feasts their different shapes. By looking at a few examples of feasts in each category from around the world, the differences (and overlap) between different kinds of feasts become clearer.

Empowering Feasts

Some people host feasts with the ultimate motive of garnering power, prestige, or wealth. Though I take the name of this section from Dietler's typology, this type of feast might also encompass some of Hayden's alliance and cooperation feasts, specifically those aimed at attracting political supporters or building ties with neighboring groups, and some of his economic feasts. Many celebrations in the contemporary United States, such as weddings, quinceañeras, and bar or bat mitzvahs, might combine rites of passage with lavish parties that hosts use in part to demonstrate their social and economic power and compete with rivals.

The classic ethnographic film *Ongka's Big Moka*[10] traces the trials and trib-
ulations of Ongka, a Big Man of the Kawelka tribe in Papua New Guinea. As
a Big Man, Ongka is a community leader who has not been elected to an official role or inherited power. Instead, Ongka uses his substantial charisma,
oratorical skill, and political savvy to coordinate the efforts of his community to host a feast. Some years previously, a Big Man from a neighboring group had invited Ongka's group to a ceremonial gift exchange called
a *moka*, where Ongka and company had been gifted pigs and other goods.
By accepting the gift and attending the feast, Ongka's group incurred the
obligation to repay the gift—with interest. In the film, based on the work
of anthropologist Andrew Strathern with Ongka and the Kawelka people,
Ongka conspires with, convinces, debates with, and berates his community
to contribute to a gift of six hundred pigs, cows, cassowaries, a motorcycle,
a truck, and over £5,000 in cash. If they can pull off the *moka*, Ongka and
his community will be temporarily short on pigs but will have garnered
great prestige.

Anthropologists have been able to find empowering feasts in many different societies. Some of these feasts have achieved legendary status among
anthropologists, such as the potlatch described by the father of American
anthropology, Franz Boas, in the late nineteenth century.[11] Feasts and potlatches were woven tightly into the social fabric of many distinct Northwest
Coast indigenous societies when Europeans arrived, and continued even as
the United States eventually tried to outlaw them and they took on the trap-
pings of Christian festivals.[12] Societies in this region foraged and fished the
rich Pacific Coast and developed complicated systems of status and class.
Boas believed that potlatches were investments of wealth in social relationships and prestige. Wealthy chiefs hosted feasts to celebrate milestones in
their children's lives, like naming and marriage; by hosting generously and
by giving overwhelming gifts of blankets, food, and money, families gained
prestige and favorable alliances.

Archaeologists have linked empowering feasts to fundamental processes
of social change. For instance, in many societies around the world, incipi-
ent elites have been able to establish themselves as politically and economically dominant, and power has been consolidated in the hands of only a few
political leaders such as chiefs and kings. Some archaeologists have invoked
feasting as a central dynamic in this process.

Before the Spanish arrived in the Philippines in the sixteenth century,
chiefs traded for exotic luxury goods with China and hosted highly osten-
tatious ritual feasts. Archaeologist Laura Junker has studied these feasts to

understand political and economic dynamics in Philippine society.[13] Her goal is to understand more generally how political leaders emerged in societies in which authority was hereditary but had to be built and maintained through personal alliances and loyalty rather than bureaucratic administrative hierarchies. Anthropologists often call such societies *chiefdoms*, and Junker is interested in how feasting helped chiefs in the Philippines compete for power.

Junker's work at two chiefly centers shows that wealth differences grew more exaggerated over time. By looking at ceramic fragments, animal bones, and plant remains in the deposits of trash left behind by inhabitants, Junker can tell that people were eating domestic species (water buffalo, chicken, and pig) as well as a broad range of wild forest animals and seafood. Wealthy families lived in larger houses, had fancier goods, and ate more domesticated animals, which were preferred feasting foods according to Spanish accounts. It is possible that rice was also eaten primarily by wealthy families and at ritual feasts, compared to root crops like yams and taro, which were available to all. Fancy Chinese porcelain, and especially porcelain plates and bowls perfect for serving food at feasts, became more common over time in chiefly communities. Lower-quality porcelain and decorated earthenware even began to appear in the refuse of lower-status households, indicating that nonelites eventually began to host their own feasts, albeit less flashy ones.

This evidence leads Junker to believe that the desire to host larger, showier feasts increased the demand for exotic pottery and allowed chiefs who maintained long-distance trade ties with distant China to obtain porcelain and host fancy feasts to compete for prestige. Status competition escalated over time, and even nonelites were drawn into feasts celebrating alliances and showing off the power of competing chiefs. In turn, this political dynamic drove the expansion of foreign trade across the region, linking competing chiefdoms more tightly even as they tried to show off their superiority. The central motor of this competition, according to Junker's work, was an empowering feast of roast pork and rice on a delicate porcelain dish.

Patron-Role Feasts

The Inca Empire ran on corn beer. Corn was a prized crop in the Andes, especially since it could not be grown at the highest altitude communities in this mountainous region. While people ate corn in stews and other dishes, one of the most important ways to prepare corn was to ferment it into *chicha*, or corn beer (figure 5.3). Archaeologists who study the Inca and the many ancient Andean societies that came before them know that *chicha* was commonly made and drunk in houses, palaces, and temples. They find the large urns used to store and ferment it, the cups and bowls used to drink it, and even sometimes the dregs discarded after straining.[14]

But what does it mean to say that the Inca Empire ran on corn beer? To answer that question, we first need to examine some of the challenges the Inca faced. In the span of about one hundred years, the empire expanded to control a vast swath of mountainous terrain from Ecuador to Chile. Administrators used knotted strings called *khipus* rather than a written language for accounting purposes, but they did not count money because the empire had no form of currency. Instead, taxes were paid in labor or in products.[15] Wheeled transportation was impractical in desert, mountain, and jungle landscapes; llama caravans carried goods long distances and herders walked alongside. The Inca countered limits on the speed of movement by building an impressive road system with a chain of outposts along which runners could quickly relay messages through the empire. However, they also had to figure out how to fund state activities like road construction, government activities, and wars of conquest in the absence of currency, across a rugged and diverse imperial landscape.

Many scholars believe that the Inca used existing Andean traditions of hospitality and labor sharing, manipulating these traditions to support their

FIGURE 5.3. Dried corn, sprouted corn, and two kinds of *chicha* in the Sacred Valley of the Incas. (Robyn Cutright)

own ends.[16] In Andean communities today, and we believe in the past as well, members practice a system of reciprocal labor obligations called *ayni*.[17] Farmers gather to help friends and extended family with labor-intensive planting or harvesting. The host whose fields are being worked provides food and drink and sends his helpers home with some of the harvest. The labor party is festive: participants joke and talk (and drink) as they work. The host also incurs the obligation of helping those who helped him with their fields; this is what we mean by reciprocal labor obligations. There is no formal accounting, but participants keep track and know if someone regularly shirks their responsibility to work.

This kind of labor sharing is central to the way that Andean communities constitute themselves, and is deeply embedded in social relationships between individuals and families across the generations.[18] Labor reciprocity exists in other cultural contexts as well. In graduate school, my friends and I moved often as we conducted doctoral research abroad and moved back and forth through student apartments. It was common for one of us to convene the rest to help move, and we always compensated our helpers by providing beer and pizza. By receiving help, we also incurred informal social obligations to help out with future moves. Even if we did not reciprocate with exactly the same people, we paid into the social system and, when we moved, got paid back with help in a way that is roughly similar to the *ayni* system. This analogy gives some sense of how reciprocity works but does not illustrate how fundamental *ayni* reciprocity is to Andean people's worldviews and sense of themselves as embedded in networks of reciprocal relationships.

Ayni relationships exist between social equals. In Andean communities, relationships involving labor and obligation can also be hierarchical. The mayor or the town priest can convene members of the community to work on projects for the common good, such as cleaning canals or re-roofing the church. In these cases too, community men turn out to complete the task and enjoy a festive work party. They are served a meal, often communally prepared by the women of the community, and have plenty to drink. However, in this case providing food and alcohol is enough to discharge the obligation. In pre-Hispanic communities, local elites rather than mayors or priests probably organized something similar. Many archaeologists believe that the Inca could have taken advantage of this system by inserting themselves at the top of the hierarchy, claiming that everyone in the empire owed them labor repaid by hospitality, which included corn beer.

By drawing on existing traditions, the Inca developed a labor tax or *mit'a* system in which every family owed labor to the state. This labor could take the form of farmwork, road construction, mining, or fighting in the army. The Inca engineered impressive agricultural terraces to expand the amount of lower-altitude land available to produce corn. They could feed workers with corn in stews, but to be truly festive, a work party needs beer too. To produce the corn beer known as *chicha*, the Inca turned to specialists who could be supported by the state. Some of these specialists were women who lived together in facilities called *aqllawasi*, where they learned how to brew *chicha* and weave intricate cloth. This labor was essential in symbolizing state hospitality and reciprocity.[19]

By providing the beer and food to support festive work parties, the Inca could convert staple products like corn into labor to build and run their empire. By feeding specialists like the women of the *aqllawasis* as well as other craftspeople, the Inca converted these staples into highly valued but easy to transport goods like cloth and metal objects that had deep symbolic significance and radiated wealth. These items then clothed Inca lords, played central roles in Inca rituals, and could be given as gifts to local lords and allies.[20]

In this system *chicha* cut across social boundaries and types of feasts. Made from sacred corn, *chicha* was an essential component of rituals and celebrations. When anthropologist Catherine Allen spoke to Andean villagers in the 1980s, they told her that when they drank too much *chicha*, their ancestors also drank from their excess.[21] *Chicha* helped the state fulfill its role as host to festive work parties, but it was also the symbol of Inca hospitality toward local lords and allies. Archaeologist Tamara Bray has argued that the most distinctive Inca pottery exported to the provinces took the form of plates for serving meat and jugs for serving *chicha*.[22] By inviting local lords to feasts where special food and drink were served, the Inca played the magnanimous host, but they also reinforced the status differences between themselves and locals and incurred obligations that locals could never quite return.

This asymmetry is the essence of the patron-role feast. On the surface, feasts might seem to build solidarity between hosts and guests. In systems like the *ayni*, as farmers take turns hosting and participating, ties of hospitality link extended families and communities through the metaphor of shared food, drink, and labor. But when there is a hierarchical difference between hosts and guests, the dynamics of hospitality shift. Hosts offer hospitality that guests cannot hope to reciprocate because they do not have access to the same surplus wealth or ritually charged goods and spaces. All guests can offer in return is their loyalty and allegiance to their host.

The Inca took advantage of this unevenness when they hosted feasts in the provinces. They gave away coveted goods in the state style, which archaeologists tend to find concentrated in the households of local elites.[23] For instance, under Inca rule, local elites in the Upper Mantaro Valley held onto their power in their own communities and used their access to Inca goods to emphasize their important role in the new hierarchy to their followers.[24] But the Inca Empire was still on top; Inca governors could still bring to bear extensive institutional power and resources as they hosted feasts for elites and for commoners. Local elites could not hope to compete on this playing field; they were hopelessly outclassed even as they probably enjoyed a nice time at state feasts.

Diacritical Feasts

Diacritical, or "distinguishing," feasts put power and wealth on display not by including commoners, workers, or employees in an uneven exchange, but by excluding them altogether. These feasts usually include luxury foods and emphasize food quality and style over sheer abundance of regular food like beer or pork.[25] Also present are symbols of wealth and rank and the finest serving wares. Diacritical feasts tend to take place in smaller, more restricted spaces within palaces, temples, or elite dwellings, so that guests can dine in private.

In the past, diacritical feasts occurred in highly stratified societies, where the differences between elites and commoners were strongly marked. One of the earliest parts of the world to see dramatic differences between royalty and commoners was the Near East. As I discuss in chapter 4, Natufian and PPNA communities faced the potential for increased social tensions as storage became private and status differences started to emerge. By the Early Dynastic period, between 4,900 and 4,350 years ago, some people in Mesopotamia had begun living in cities ruled by royalty and temple authorities. In the early twentieth century, Sir Charles Leonard Woolley discovered and excavated royal tombs in the city of Ur, in contemporary Iraq.[26] These tombs contained royal burials, but also evidence of sumptuous diacritical feasting.

Banquet scenes on Mesopotamian seals and other objects generally show small groups of seated participants being attended by servers and enjoying music, singing, and dancing (figure 5.4). Guests drink alcohol through straws from large pots or conical cups, and while the images do not depict large stacks of food, they do show animals being brought either to be consumed at the feast or sacrificed. Since Mesopotamia produced some of the earliest written documents, we can read about the feasts that took place in the Late Uruk and Early Dynastic periods in Ur. The word "banquet" in Sumerian literally meant "the place for beer and wine."[27]

In the Royal Tombs of Ur, archaeologists found conical cups made of silver like those pictured in images of banquet scenes, along with drinking bowls, serving vessels, and drinking tubes, made of gold, copper, silver, and polished stone. Texts refer to a ritual of graveside feasting, a practice I discuss in chapter 7. Archaeologist Louise Steel emphasizes the luxury experienced by guests at these feasts. Everything—the music, the food and drink, the cups and dishes made of highly decorated, precious materials, the jewelry and other adornments of lapis lazuli and other lustrous jewels, even the space itself—contributed to a highly charged experience that would overwhelm the senses of the participants. This aspect is key to a diacritical feast, where abundance is important, but class and style are paramount. The elite status of the guests was indicated by their ability to attend, since only other elites were allowed to participate, and reinforced by the luxurious surroundings and the sensory experience.

Archaeologists have evidence of other kinds of feasts and communal food consumption in Mesopotamia, occurring alongside diacritical feasts in very different social contexts. Archaeologist Susan Pollock documents how in Uruk and Early Dynastic times, rations were distributed to laborers in standardized, mass-produced, undecorated bowls.[28] The bowls could have contained grain (likely barley), bread, or perhaps beer. Workers might also

0 cm   5cm

FIGURE 5.4. Lapis lazuli cylinder seal showing a banquet presided over by Queen Pu-abi. (Cylinder seal of Pu-abi, Ur, Early Dynastic III [2600 BC], item 121544, courtesy of the British Museum, London)

have been fed meals during the workday, in addition to receiving monthly rations of unprocessed grain. Over time, Pollock points out, these bowls got smaller, which might indicate that they were more likely to be used for beverages or small food portions. This is another example of the kind of patron-sponsored work party feasts thrown by the Inca.

Elite feasts like the ones at Ur legitimize or naturalize hierarchy. Those who can gain access to such exclusive spaces are understood to be worthy and deserving of luxurious treatment. The emphasis on class and style at these feasts means that only those with social capital, the knowledge of the correct ways to act in such circumstances, can participate fully. For those on the outside, participants are simply a distinct kind of person, with a complex set of knowledge that they seemingly inherited, but actually learned as children from their elite parents.

The same logic of social capital is at work at fancy and expensive restaurants in the United States, which expect patrons to demonstrate a certain amount of knowledge (which fork to use, what an *amuse-bouche* is, how to eat a snail, which wine goes with fish) to navigate the experience. Those without this capital might feel out of place and be discouraged from trespassing into the world of the upper class. Diacritical feasts use exclusivity and highly charged, restricted access surroundings to emphasize difference, in contrast to patron-role feasts that emphasize solidarity and obscure difference, and to empowering feasts that seek to competitively create difference.

Why Categorize?

The preceding sections discussed feasts that exemplified each category, as defined by theorists of feasting Brian Hayden and Michael Dietler. Not all feasts fall neatly within the boundaries of these categories. In West Africa during the era of transatlantic contact and trade, royal leaders in the kingdom of Dahomey hosted private feasts to build political influence. Archaeologists J. Cameron Monroe and Anneke Janzen believe that in Dahomey, royal palace architecture highlighted three arenas of power.[29] Palaces had an exterior area where public ceremonies were staged, a series of courtyards and structures within the walls where state politics took place, and a private zone deep inside the palace where royal domestic life and internal politics intertwined.

Feasts and ceremonies that took place in exterior spaces had a patron-role flavor. Kings distributed wealth and hospitality so that they could incur obligations from subordinates, who would be able to repay the favor only with allegiance and tribute. Feast sponsors, royal or not, gained prestige by building a reputation for providing lavishly for followers, and so there was an aspect of empowering or competitive feasting as well. In the early eighteenth century, Dahomey kings gave away vast stocks of wealth goods such as cloth and cowrie shells to followers during celebrations of royal ancestors. In doing so, Monroe and Janzen believe, kings were essentially showing off the immense wealth differences between themselves and their followers, and in doing so further entrenching social inequality through a combination of empowering and diacritical elements.

What is most interesting about Dahomey feasting dynamics is the role of women in the private, internal palace zone. Hundreds of women, including craftswomen, officials, warriors, and servants, lived sequestered lives deep within palaces and conducted their own negotiations for power and influence at private feasts. Monroe and Janzen's interpretation of the ceramic and animal bone remains from these feasts suggests that individual hosts provided nice meals within private palace spaces to garner prestige in what was undoubtedly a context of political intrigue and negotiation.

As this example shows, different kinds of feasts can coexist in the same society, and even at the same meal. A single feast might have both competitive and solidarity-building aspects. Still, categories are useful because they help us consider how motivations, goals, and contexts of feasts can differ, and how these different kinds of feasts would show up in the archaeological record. Andean work-party feasts, for instance, would supply large quantities of *chicha*, brewed and served in many large jars, but would not necessarily require a lot of highly decorated ceramics in official state styles. Simply the fact that the state was offering abundant hospitality might be enough to meet the goals of the hosts. Diacritical feasts, on the other hand, would feature highly elaborate serving wares and exclusive spaces, just like we saw at the closing feast at Cerro Baúl. Many extended families within one community might use empowering feasts to compete for prestige, and so an archaeologist would expect to find some large serving vessels in each large household, while diacritical feasts might only occur in special rooms deep within palaces.

The examples in this chapter show that foragers, farmers, and people living in postindustrial economies all take hospitality seriously and build social bonds by sharing special meals together. Feasts turn out to be malleable social tools that can be used to build solidarity and also to compete, to host lower-class workers and also to emphasize the social and economic gulf between commoners and elites, to celebrate highly charged rituals and also to one-up the neighbors. Besides the common thread of hospitality and the warm feelings generated by breaking bread together, feasts also tend to share a certain ingredient: alcohol.

THE ROLE OF ALCOHOL

Alcohol is one reason that feasts are especially malleable, meaning-rich social contexts. Alcohol is a special kind of food that needs additional consideration here because of its potential to transform social interactions and relationships by altering our perceptions and lending a heightened sense of emotion or significance to an event. Humans are not the only animals to consume alcohol; wild chimpanzees use leaf sponges to drink naturally fermented palm sap, for instance.[30] The ability to break down ethanol, the alcohol in beer, wine, and distilled spirits, evolved in a common ancestor of humans, chimpanzees, and gorillas about ten million years ago.[31] Primates may be adapted to associate ethanol with the high nutritional value of ripe fruit and thus be primed to seek it out; in other words, a preference for mind-altering food and drink may be hardwired into the human brain.[32] Alcohol runs deep in our evolutionary history.

Alcohol is produced when yeast ferments the sugars in fruits, grains, or tubers into alcohol. As the full aisles of your local liquor store attest, there are endless variations on this basic process. Archaeologist Justin Jennings and his students have thought through the process of making different kinds of alcohol by looking at the main alcoholic beverages produced by several ancient societies.[33] They distinguish wine, made of high-sugar ingredients like fruit or honey that can be directly fermented, and beer, made of grains or tubers which need to have some starch converted to sugar (a process called saccharification) before fermentation can occur. The distillation process is a further step, which concentrates the alcohol in beer by heating it and condensing it into hard liquor like vodka or rum. Beer and wine were much more common in ancient societies than distilled spirits.

The *chicha* that helped lubricate the economy of the Inca Empire is a good example of a beer.[34] There were, and still are, many different recipes for *chicha*, but the basic process is the same. First, the corn must be saccharified. Andean brewers use two main methods for converting starch to sugar. One way is to get the corn damp and allow it to germinate, and then dry and grind it. The germination process begins to break down some of the stored energy in the starch into sugars to grow the new sprout. Another, more colorful way is to grind the corn and then chew mouthfuls and spit them out.

The amylase enzyme in saliva starts to break down starch into sugar, as you notice if you hold a soda cracker in your mouth until it starts to taste sweet.

Whether the corn is sprouted and ground, or ground and chewed, the next step is to boil it in water to continue to break down the starch. Several rounds of boiling, cooling, and straining help to extract the sugars and separate out the chunky grounds from the sweetened liquid. When I helped my good Peruvian friend Señor Andrés Bazán make *chicha*, he also added beans during cooking to add flavor and "make the *chicha* more nutritious" (figure 5.5). After the final straining, grounds might be fed to livestock and the liquid is cooled and poured into a large urn or jug to ferment.

In US breweries and distilleries, chemistry labs monitor and propagate proprietary strains of yeast. In Andean home breweries, the fermentation jars are not washed between batches, so their rough pottery interiors already

FIGURE 5.5. Making *chicha* in the Jequetepeque Valley, Peru, with Andrés Bazán. (Robyn Cutright)

contain the yeast culture that will go to work on the new beer. As the yeast consumes sugar and excretes alcohol, the mixture starts to bubble vigorously. Several days later, the *chicha* is lightly alcoholic and ready to serve. It goes bad after about a week, so *chicha* must be made a few days in advance of the party or a feast where it is to be consumed. Hosts would thus face large labor demands to produce enough for large feasts.[35] The same general process, with adjustments for each grain and desired end product, was used in Mesopotamia and Egypt to make wheat or barley beer, in Asia to make rice beer, and so on.

Wine made from fruit, honey, agave syrup, and other sugary substances can skip the saccharification step and go straight to fermentation.[36] For instance, makers of grape wine start by harvesting and pressing the grapes to extract the juice. Natural yeasts from the grape skins and yeast hanging around in jars from the previous batch start the fermentation process quickly, and after it slows wine can be sealed into smaller bottles or jars. In antiquity, wine would have been consumed within a year of production, because bottles could not be perfectly sealed and eventually the wine would turn into vinegar through further microbial action.

Archaeologist Alexander Joffe believes that alcohol played a central part in the politics of the Near East and Mediterranean.[37] Throughout the Near East and Egypt, alcohol and drunkenness were recognized and celebrated. One Sumerian poem, "Hymn to Ninkasi," was dedicated to the goddess of brewing. It celebrates beer brewing by poetically walking the listener through each step of the process.[38] Beer drinking was also celebrated in art. An Egyptian image of a party shows a maid handing a cup to a lady, telling her to get drunk. The lady replies, "I shall love to be drunk."[39] This chapter takes its name from another Sumerian song celebrating the opening of a tavern, which Jennings and colleagues also used to title their article on the production sequences of various ancient alcohols. Part of the song goes, "Drinking beer, in a blissful mood / Drinking liquor, feeling exhilarated / With joy in the heart and a happy liver."[40]

In the United States, the government generally frowns on public drunkenness outside of specific, regulated contexts (such as bars or outdoor events with permits). Joffe thinks that in contrast, the state played a key role in sponsoring drinking in the Near East and Egypt, but that wine and beer played different social and political roles. In ancient Egypt, according to Joffe, beer and bread production were interconnected, and local elites as well as state institutions worked to secure control over combined bakery/ brewery production facilities. Being able to produce such essential foods, which filled bellies and altered moods, allowed elites and the state to support followers and act as providers, strengthening the loyalty of workers.

Wine, in contrast, was an imported product. Some wine was produced in Egypt, but it was also imported from the Levant on the eastern shore of the Mediterranean. During the Early Bronze Age, 3500 to 2350 BC, the economy of the Levant was focused on producing oil, dates, and wine for export to the growing Egyptian state, first as part of an Egyptian colonial occupation during Egypt's First Dynasty, and later as local communities began to urbanize and orient themselves toward long-distance trade. In Egypt, elites used their access to imported goods like wine and oil as one way to display their status (similar to how US elites might serve French wines or single-batch artisanal mezcal), and containers in the Levant style eventually made their way into elite tombs in Egypt as symbols of wealth and access for foreign trade networks.

Joffe's examples of Egypt and the Near East link alcohol, the types of feasts discussed above, and political processes like urbanization and the growth of the ancient states. New archaeological evidence from a very old and very exciting archaeological site called Göbekli Tepe in Turkey also links alcohol to very early ritual celebrations and feasts among mobile foragers at the end of the last Ice Age.[41]

When German archaeologist Klaus Schmidt arrived at the Turkish site of Göbekli Tepe, or "potbelly hill," in 1994, no one had realized how much the low, lumpy hill had been built up over time by human activity. As Schmidt dug down into the layers of human occupation, he realized he had found something unprecedented—a series of at least eight, but probably closer to twenty, large circular enclosures had been built, used, and covered over by people living in the region around 11,500 to 10,000 years ago. The enclosures contained five-meter-tall T-shaped stone pillars carved with scary beasts—boars, scorpions, snakes, foxes, vultures—along with other animals like aurochs and gazelle. While the monumentality of these enclosures was impressive to archaeologists, what really made this discovery exciting was who built them: foragers.

Historically, archaeologists have tended to doubt that foragers built big architectural monuments. The reasoning went that foragers were thinly spread across the landscape and would have lacked the human resources, motivation, and leadership to coordinate the construction of large structures. We now know that view is not accurate. For instance, foragers living at the site of Poverty Point in Louisiana 3,400 years ago built enormous C-shaped earthen mounds.[42] And, though Göbekli Tepe is contemporaneous with the very beginnings of agriculture farther south in Mesopotamia, Schmidt and the rest of his team have not found remains of domesticated plants or animals at Göbekli Tepe. It is clear that even though foragers did not build huge monumental architecture to the scale that settled city dwellers did, they did build monuments on the landscape. In fact, it is possible that rather than being a product of settled communities, monumental architecture and the ceremonies that took place around it were the catalyst that brought people together.

Feasts and ceremonies definitely took place at Göbekli Tepe.[43] The archaeological team found large limestone basins that have been associated at other sites in the region with brewing beer. In the rubble used to fill in abandoned enclosures, the team found large amounts of smashed gazelle, ass, and aurochs bones, which probably represent feasting detritus. They found no evidence that anyone lived permanently at Göbekli Tepe, meaning that people came together from the surrounding landscape to build the enclosures and to eat, drink, and dance there. Archaeologists actually have images of dancing from this period, including one bowl with an image of two people dancing with a figure that looks like a turtle. This image might hint that altered or heightened perceptions were an important part of these feasts.

The picture that emerges from Göbekli Tepe is fascinating. It supports Hayden's view that feasting could have generated economic demands for grain from which beer could be brewed, meat, and other surplus food.[44] Increased focus on domesticating and cultivating grains might have been a response to the desire to host these perception-altering events. Evidence from the site of Göbekli Tepe also suggests that rituals that drew foragers together from across the region could have provided the impetus for greater regional cooperation to build the circles and to provide beer and meat, which may have led the move toward a more settled, agricultural life.[45]

It is no accident that the team highlights how sensory perception may have been altered by consuming alcohol (or other substances) at Göbekli Tepe feasts. One of the enduring characteristics of feasts is a heightened sense of social connection and meaningfulness, often helped along by that oldest of social lubricants, beer. Archaeologist Yannis Hamilakis argues that consumption is important not just from an economic perspective, but also from the perspective of the body.[46] Food and drink provide nutrition, but are also consumed by the body and experienced through the senses.

For many of us, food is not simply a package of the calories and vitamins we need to survive. We respond to the way food looks. Smell and taste trigger memories; we link the sizzle of bacon with the taste of coffee and the luxury of a lazy weekend morning. Food shapes, and is shaped by, memory and bodily experience. Hamilakis says that we need to pay attention to the embodied meaning of food and drink in the past in order for our reconstructions to do justice to ancient people and societies.

This approach is especially important when it comes to feasting and alcohol because of their heightened social and sensory significance. Hamilakis's work focuses on how wine and oil were used on ancient Crete. Olive trees and grapevines are well-suited to the Mediterranean environment, but Hamilakis suggests that we need to consider the foods produced from these plants as having a very different relationship to humans than that of grains and pulses like lentils. Wine is consumed for its enjoyable psychosocial properties (in other words, it makes you feel good), and oil provides fatty unctuousness and a base for ointments and perfumes. Both took time and infrastructure to produce and were probably available primarily to elites rather than consumed by everyone as daily staples.

Elaborate palaces with space for storage, elite residences, and rituals appeared on Crete beginning around 2000 BC, and continuing through what are called the Protopalatial and Neopalatial periods. Wine was already being produced by this time, and olive oil may have been as well, though it only becomes clearly visible in the archaeological record a bit later. Drinking vessels, cups, open courts and public spaces, and pig bones are all abundant in archaeological excavations of palaces, which suggests what Hamilakis has called an "explosion of drinking and feasting ceremonies" in Minoan Crete's palaces.[47] Feasts were recorded in the pits dug to contain their remains and likely inscribed in social memory as well. Palace feasts would have woken the senses, with wine, heady perfumed oils, spices, and pork smells combining with the sounds of music, the movement of dancing, intoxication, and the spectacle of wealthy elites and elaborately built spaces to create a memorable experience for participants.

Hamilakis argues that we cannot understand the political role of feasts without understanding how the body's experience of feasting and drinking creates meaning and memories. Feasts rely on alcohol, food, and spectacle to become highly charged rituals of consumption. Their highly charged nature allows them to be mobilized in many different social and political contexts, across so many different societies.

In fact, from the work reviewed in this chapter, it seems as though feasting has been implicated in every important dynamic human societies have been involved with over the past 10,000 years. From building solidarity in the earliest farming communities, to serving as a medium for status competition among self-aggrandizing individuals and communities in 1970s Papua New Guinea or chiefs in the fourteenth-century Philippines, to making pronounced wealth and power differences in third millennium BC Ur seem natural, and even to mobilizing neighbors to harvest some corn, feasts seem to be able to accomplish anything their hosts desire.

This range provides quite a buffet for archaeologists to choose from as we theorize about past societies. With such a broad range, we run the risk of losing track of the details, and making feasting too much of an all-purpose, homogenized social institution that can explain everything. Instead of just identifying feasting, we need to focus on what makes feasts work in different kinds of political contexts and how feasting can help us understand how power was wielded in past societies. In this, Dietler is correct to remind us that feasts are culturally constituted and draw their power to generate prestige and status from their particular social and historical contexts. Feasts may be spectacular moments where hospitality and hierarchy meet, but we will see in the next three chapters that they are not the only politically, religiously, and socially important meals.

6

THE TASTE OF POWER

Cuisine, Class, and Conquest

B y all accounts, the Aztec king Moctezuma enjoyed opulent, over-the-top royal meals. Bernal Díaz, a Spanish soldier who helped Hernán Cortés conquer the Aztecs in 1519, later described one of these meals as including an incredible variety of three hundred dishes in over thirty styles, including fowl, fish, meat (Díaz heard one of these meats might be human flesh, but he could not verify it), fruit, and tortillas.[1] Moctezuma and his guests also consumed large quantities of frothy chocolate and a strange plant called tobacco. They ate from fine red and black pottery and cups of gold. The king washed his hands with special basins and towels before eating and was shielded from the view of other banqueters with a wooden and golden screen. As he ate, he was entertained with jokes, stories, and songs.

The Spanish writer and friar Bernardino de Sahagún detailed the vast variety of foods served to Aztec lords: white and hot tortillas, large tortillas, thick tortillas, long buns, layered dainty tortillas, tortillas of sifted corn so delicate they were almost translucent, tortillas of tender corn, or maize tassels, or amaranth seeds; tamales of various shapes, colors, flavors, and fillings; fowl in stews, or roasted, or wrapped in dough, or one fowl stuffed inside another, casseroles made of fowl or frog or fish or locust or shrimp with sauces of ground squash seeds, tomatoes, chilies, or fruit. In Sahagún's account, Aztec nobility ate meals clearly befitting their high status.

For the Aztecs, and for many other societies with class structures, food was one means by which wealth, status, and class identity could be communicated. In this chapter, I discuss some of the ways that archaeologists and others have defined elite cuisine and identified it in the archaeological record. Class differences between elites and commoners are only one form of inequality that existed in past societies. Later in the chapter, I use case studies of slavery in the United States, European colonial expansion, and

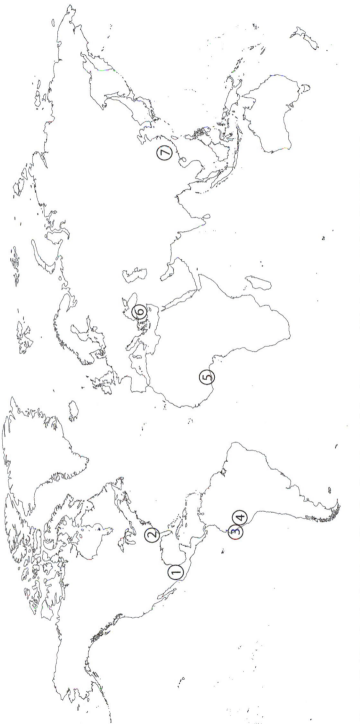

FIGURE 6.1. Map showing locations of key sites from chapter 6. 1 = Aztec central Mexico; 2 = southern United States; 3 = Jequetepeque and Zaña Valleys, Peru; 4 = Upper Mantaro Valley, Peru; 5 = western Africa; 6 = Gordion, Turkey; 7= Changsha, Han Dynasty China. (Robyn Cutright)

imperial conquest in the Andes to show how archaeologists have used food to shed light on systems of inequality and experiences of oppression and resistance in the past. First, however, I return to the Aztec Empire to explore what archaeological evidence and historical records can (and cannot) tell us about the relationship between class and cuisine in the ancient world.

CUISINE AND CLASS IN THE ANCIENT WORLD

The Aztec Empire coalesced when three powerful central Mexican city-states formed an alliance in the fourteenth century. Aztec elites benefited from a tradition of urbanism and political hierarchy that stretched back over a millennium but reached new levels of codifying and symbolizing status through food. Texts written and illustrated by native scribes and Spanish observers in the days after the Spanish Conquest reveal how the Aztec connected food with social identity and status; the Codex Mendoza, written during the early days of the Spanish Conquest, shows a girl learning to grind corn with her kitchen supplies arrayed around her. Being a proper woman meant learning to prepare tortillas and other foods at the heart of Aztec cuisine.

The Aztec capital, Tenochtitlán, sat at the heart of an agricultural landscape that produced corn, beans, chili peppers, squash, and turkeys. The Aztecs also traded across a wide range of tropical, highland, lake, and coastal zones, which filled Tenochtitlán's central markets with a riot of diverse and colorful foodstuffs. Sahagún included the following products in his description of Aztec markets: tamales made with fish, hot peppers, tadpoles, rabbit, beans, red fruit, turkey eggs, or honey; tortillas of all sorts including bean, amaranth, and prickly pear cactus; and sauces of tomatoes, chilies, beans, mushrooms, squash, avocado, and fruit. Though corn lay at the heart of many of these dishes, the Aztecs clearly prized variety in market food. Markets also made finely decorated dishes available to commoners who could purchase them, according to archaeologist Michael Smith's excavations in rural and urban households outside the capital.[2]

The broad outlines of Aztec cuisine were drawn by the plants and animals present in central Mexico and the economic systems in place to produce and distribute them. But in a society stratified by class, cuisine also played a role in signaling and reinforcing class differences. Everyday meals for Aztec commoners were based on corn tortillas flavored with sauces of herbs, seeds, and peppers. Adding beans, insects, and small animals provided protein, and squash, tomatoes, and other vegetables variety and nutrients.[3] According to written accounts, Aztec elites elaborated on this base with more meat, more variety, more exotic ingredients, and more complex recipes. Texts also indicate that the Aztecs also had sumptuary rules determining who could eat, drink, and wear what. For example, only men and elderly women were officially allowed to drink pulque, a thick drink fermented from agave nectar. Pulque was for commoners, while lords, kings, and warriors were supposed to enjoy more prestigious chocolate instead. At least according to written sources, Aztec cuisine was one way in which elites differentiated themselves from commoners.

British scholar Sir Jack Goody set out to identify common themes that differentiated elite and commoner cuisines across a diverse set of societies in Africa, Europe, and Asia.[4] While Goody's ultimate aim was to figure out why a high cuisine developed in some societies but not others, his description of elite high cuisine provides a useful set of criteria to apply to archaeological examples. In the next section, I describe the characteristics that Goody believed are shared broadly by elite cuisines across cultures. I then apply these characteristics to archaeological discoveries from three societies, including the Aztecs, to evaluate how well they fit.

Haute Cuisine and Luxury Foods

In Goody's account, high cuisine usually features exotic, expensive, or rare ingredients and spices. Foods might be costly because they are imported, labor-intensive to grow or process, or rare. In many civilizations, elite cuisine is heavy on meat, particularly high-quality cuts, or exotic animals. Recipes are complicated, with ingredients highly transformed from their natural state. Because preparation is complicated, cooking is done by specialists (chefs), who tend to be men even in societies where daily cooking is done by women.

Artistry and aesthetics are emphasized by elaborate high cuisine presentations (figure 6.2). Medieval European menus provide a good example of the kind of artistry and transformations Goody highlights. Medieval feasts required a lot of cooks, servers, guests, spices, and species of animal (some stuffed inside each other). Goody cites the Archbishop of York, who held a feast in the mid-1400s at which fifty-seven cooks and even more servers and cleaners served two hundred guests. This probably means that the food being prepared was extremely elaborate and time-consuming, and the cooks were likely highly trained. Feasts took place in halls warmly decorated with tapestries, and the lord's family and distinguished guests were physically separated from the rest of the participants at a raised table where they could be visible to all. In Díaz's account, discussed earlier in the chapter, the Aztec king Moctezuma was separated by remaining hidden from view. Feasts in Medieval Europe and Aztec Mexico were accompanied by music and other performances to increase the pageantry of the occasion.

Like Aztec royalty, medieval European nobility ate multiple courses of highly transformed ingredients.[5] Dishes included wine thickened with egg yolks, meat pies, chickens stuffed with grapes and herbs, game birds in almond milk, and pears poached in a sauce of cinnamon, red wine, sugar, ginger, saffron, and vinegar. In these recipes, ingredients were heavily manipulated rather than being served in naturalistic forms. Recipes were also highly spiced, featuring pepper, salt, cloves, mace, cinnamon, saffron, ginger, citrus, and honey. Since many of these spices were imported, using them added to the expense and exoticism of the feast.

FIGURE 6.2. Haute cuisine features highly transformed and rare or expensive ingredients and a focus on artistry and presentation, as seen in this octopus dish from the restaurant Maras in Lima, Peru. (Robyn Cutright)

High cuisine also emphasizes complicated dining etiquette, such as know-ing which fork or glass to choose from a complex place setting. In elite con-texts, a formal meal is an elaborate, time-consuming pageant that takes place in a space physically removed from where the food is prepared. Because all these elements require ample resources as well as specialized knowledge on the part of cooks, servers, and diners, they create an exclusionary at-mosphere that separates elite cuisine from the cuisine accessible to other members of society. In this way, high cuisine becomes a performance that separates elites from commoners, displays this separation in an exclusion-ary way, and sets up barriers to social mobility. It also creates a set of aspira-tional goals for those who wish to enter the elite class.

More recent discussions of elite cuisine have focused on the concept of luxury foods.[6] Luxuries are refinements of basic necessities that many peo-ple in a society desire, but only a few can obtain. The social context here is essential: both desire and supply are socially constructed. Consuming lux-ury foods is a way to symbolize status and exclusivity. Some luxuries be-come democratized as supply increases or technology to mass produce them becomes available. When this happens, these foods are no longer lux-uries. The concept of luxury foods highlights important missing pieces from Goody's model: that social context is essential, and that high and low cui-sines change over time.

Archaeological Signatures of Elite Cuisine

The written accounts I cited earlier emphasize how Aztec elite cuisine was distinguished from everyday commoner cuisine by special elaborate prepa-rations and sumptuary rules. However, early Spanish writings were often motivated by a desire to emphasize the sophistication of the indigenous states that had just been conquered, often through comparison to what the author was familiar with in Europe. Archaeological evidence from Aztec communities actually suggests that commoners had access to many of the same foods and dishes as elites through the empire's network of markets.

Archaeologist Michael Smith argues that there was no distinct state or elite pottery style that marked elite feasts, and elites and commoners all par-ticipated in feasts within their households and communities.[7] Using deco-rated vessels reflected wealth, in that elites had more and used them at feasts associated with the highest rituals, but these fancy vessels were not exclu-sively associated with elite identities. Though he suggests that elites may have had restricted access to some perishable luxury items that could have included some specific foods, Smith believes that texts overemphasize the strictness of rules regarding consumption.[8]

Archaeologist Elizabeth Brumfiel has found evidence for household consumption rituals, or ritual feasts, across elite and commoner households during the Aztec period.[9] However, her work in the community of Huexotla suggests that after the Aztec state became more dominant, elite household feasts began to use less complex serving wares. To Brumfiel, this means that local political autonomy waned under Aztec rule, and elite household consumption rituals became less powerful. This evidence suggests that highly decorated serving wares were not exclusively linked to elite identity, but were part of complex political, social, and economic choices made by all Aztec people according to their social locations and political goals. Taken together, the work of Brumfiel and Smith calls into question whether we can easily identify luxury foods or the hallmarks of elite cuisine in the archaeological record.

It may be easier to see elite cuisine at a singular special-purpose meal, as opposed to in an archaeological record accumulated across decades of daily meals and feasts. For this reason, I turn now to two elite banquets that were preserved in the burials of nobles from Turkey and China. At the site of Gordion in central Turkey, the tomb of a Phrygian king who died in 700 BC contained the remains of a royal feast.[10] The king's coffin was covered in richly dyed textiles and was accompanied by what appear to be banquet tables and a 150-vessel drinking set that included large vats, buckets, jugs, and drinking bowls. Organic residues in these vessels suggest that guests were drinking a mixture of grape wine, barley beer, and honey mead, contrary to generations of party advice to avoid mixing one's spirits.[11] Mycenaean and Minoan vessels from the Mediterranean have also been found to contain the same mix, which may have stretched rarer grape wine by adding more readily available ingredients. Alongside the fermented punch, revelers ate a stew of barbequed sheep or goat meat, lentils, and honey, wine, and olive oil.

Not all of Goody's characteristics are visible here. However, the emphasis on meat, the data suggesting multi-ingredient combinations, and the presence of fancy serving ware hints at the outlines of an early Turkish haute cuisine. One feast alone does not provide enough social context to concretely identify luxury goods, but it is likely that the wine present in these vessels would have represented luxury to guests at this feast.[12]

Around 170 BC, the Marchioness of Dai was buried in China. Her body was wrapped in layers of silk, charcoal, clay, and four coffins, which sealed off oxygen to such an extent that her body was almost perfectly preserved, including her type A blood, her double chin, and her clogged arteries. Lady Dai clearly lived a life of luxury, inactivity, and rich food. Included in the tomb are remains of her last feast, consisting of a full range of lacquer vessels including vases, cups, and jugs still containing dregs of wine and over one hundred baskets, containers, and sacks of food.[13]

As with Aztec high cuisine, abundance and variety were both emphasized at Lady Dai's last feast. Meat included deer, pigs, cattle, boar, pheasants, quails, ducks, and sparrows, and fruit comprised persimmons, peaches, pears, and plums. Echoing broader Chinese culinary trends, grains like wheat, millet, and rice formed the cornerstone of the meal, with meat, fruit, and pickled condiments as flavorings.[14] The range of bowls and plates in the tomb hints that the feast featured a variety of dishes. As in Turkey, we can identify some of the cornerstones of Goody's elite cuisine: abundance, variety, complex preparations and sequences of dishes, and a focus on esthetics in both food and serving wares. One meal does not, however, provide enough social context to identify foods that would have symbolized exclusivity and luxury.

These descriptions of elite meals suggest that social, political, and economic hierarchies are symbolized by a deep gulf between elite cuisine and everyday commoner foodways. In complex, hierarchical societies, wealth determines access to food (in terms of its quality, quantity, or even particular kind of food); at the same time, food becomes a powerful register for communication about social, political, and wealth differences. When food is invoked as a way to communicate power and wealth, cuisine can be exclusionary. It can come to symbolize access to power and social capital. It can also be a tool of resistance against hegemonic power wielded through conquest and oppression, as illustrated by the archaeological evidence from plantations in the United States South and conquered Andean communities I discuss in the next sections of this chapter.

CUISINES OF THE ENSLAVED AND THE FREE IN THE ANTEBELLUM SOUTH

Slavery was the most oppressive institution in US history. The legacy of the enslavement of millions of Africans and African Americans continues to shape the United States in profound ways. Long-term racial wealth disparities, for instance, can be traced back to slavery and were reinforced by structural racism long after slavery ended.[15] In my town of Lexington, Kentucky, thousands of enslaved individuals were sold at Cheapside Market. Today this space hosts a farmers' market and popular bars and restaurants;

only a historical marker hints at its painful past. Raising people for the slave market was a lucrative strategy for some white farmers in central Kentucky during the early nineteenth century, some of whom vaulted into the upper class over the course of a single generation.[16] A few of these families are still locally prominent, while families of those who were sold as slaves have had to struggle with legal and social constraints against class mobility and wealth inheritance. Wealth and class status gained through trade in human lives continues to shape our local and national social landscape today.

On pre–Civil War plantations in the US South, drastic cultural and economic differences separated families living in close proximity. Plantations were enclosed hierarchical ecosystems, where the food prepared in kitchens in the main house, the homes of white overseers, and the cabins of enslaved people came from the same markets and fields but reflected the status of those who consumed it. Remains of this food provide archaeologists and descendant communities with important insights into the daily lived experiences of enslaved people, wealthy elites, and others in between, revealing the deep connections between food, status, and identity in the United States' past.

Reconstructing Plantation Diets

Relying on historical records to investigate food and hierarchy on plantations is tricky, because the records were written almost exclusively by plantation owners and overseers.[17] We know, for instance, that planters generally supplied food to their enslaved workers, either cooked food or a weekly quantity of meat, often salt pork; grain, either flour, cornmeal, or rice; and sometimes additional items such as molasses. Owners could dock this ration as punishment or increase it at holidays or labor-intensive periods in the agricultural calendar. The account books and diaries of plantation managers suggest that owners controlled slave diets by providing a limited set of provisions.

Financial records from plantations indicate that in many parts of the South and the Caribbean, enslaved populations were also permitted or encouraged to supplement their rations with food they grew or foraged.[18] In South Carolina, it was customary to allow families substantial land for gardens and time to work that land after daily work quotas were reached. Financial records from the Caribbean mention that plantation owners bought food and game from enslaved individuals. This strategy was designed by plantation owners not to improve the lives of their enslaved workers but to reduce the cost of supporting them by making them provide for themselves. However, it did provide some enslaved individuals with a narrow space for independent entrepreneurship within the constraints of the system.

Enslaved workers in southern cities had little opportunity to grow or cook food outside the main house kitchen, although they did exercise other small forms of control over their lives and surroundings. One urban slave quarters in Savannah still preserves a blue-painted ceiling, which its residents believed would ward off spirits and ghosts.[19] Archaeological research shows that the individuals who lived there had access to more diverse foods, dishes, and personal items than was common at more rural plantations. The experience of slavery was not homogenous but varied by location and region.[20]

While historical records help us understand some of the economic, social, and culinary realities of plantations, they tend to record these realities from the perspective of the owners. No written records describe what the people who lived in those Savannah slave quarters ate. Frustratingly, diaries and account books often skip over aspects of daily life that the writers took for granted, even though these parts of everyday life may be extremely interesting and unexpected to us today.

Archaeology thus provides an important counterweight to historical records of plantation life. In the antebellum South, literacy and the resources to write and preserve documents were limited to only a small segment of the population, but everyone ate, lived in structures, and produced trash. This means that unlike the written record, the archaeological record preserves the experiences of enslaved Africans, poor whites, and plantation owners. Archaeological projects at plantations across the southern United States, from Virginia to Tennessee and from Kentucky to Louisiana, have shown how hierarchy shaped plantation diets, called into question some assumptions about the diets of enslaved people and planters alike, and emphasized the diverse experiences of enslaved Africans and African Americans.

For instance, planters' records indicate that they supplied enslaved people with rations of pork, but many excavations have turned up a wide variety of animals in slave quarter kitchens.[21] Domesticated animals such as pigs, and to a lesser extent cows and sheep or goats, provided the most meat to slave quarter kitchens at the Hermitage Plantation in Tennessee, Thomas Jefferson's Monticello in Virginia, and other plantations. However, animal bones recovered from household trash indicate that enslaved cooks prepared catfish and other local fish, local shellfish like mussels, domestic birds like chickens and wild birds like quail, and small game such as squirrels, possums, and woodchuck. These foraged foods were not recorded on official records but supplemented and diversified the rations owners provided.

The use of wild animals also reflected class and identity among white landowners. Zooarchaeologist Elizabeth Scott's work at Nina Plantation in Louisiana shows that after the Civil War, the Anglo-American family who moved there from Philadelphia ate less wild meat and fish than the French Creole family who had owned the plantation before the war.[22] At the same time, the gap between the meats cooked in the main house and the workers' quarters narrowed after the war, as free workers' diets matched more closely the diet of their Anglo-American employer. In this example, regional and ethnic food traditions interacted with class hierarchies and race to shape cuisine across the plantation.

Even off the plantation, archaeology lends nuance to historical records of diet and cuisine. People in the Upland South region, enslaved and free, supposedly ate mostly pork in the nineteenth century. Archaeologist Tanya Peres argues that few people actually ate this classic cuisine, though, and those who did were the wealthiest planters.[23] Kentucky was not able to import or produce enough food in the mid-nineteenth century to feed everyone a diet of pork, and not everyone could have afforded it anyway. Those with fewer resources and less access to the market, such as poor white farmers and enslaved Black workers, hunted a variety of wild game to supplement what they could produce or buy. The wealthier you were in nineteenth-century Kentucky, the less diversity was on your table (at least in terms of meat).

At wealthy plantations, enslaved households might even have eaten more pork than rural white landowners in Kentucky.[24] At Monticello, the Virginia plantation of the US president Thomas Jefferson, bones from domestic meat animals such as cows and pigs were very common even in trash deposits associated with slave dwellings. Written records indicate that enslaved workers were given perceived inferior cuts of meat such as feet and necks, but the archaeological remains at Monticello question this. Patterns of cutmarks on bones show that at least some cuts of meat were roasted and carved, rather than being cooked in the more stereotypical one-pot stews that can make good use of even the lowest quality parts of the animal. There was variation among the different enslaved households; some kitchens had greater access to higher quality cuts and even full carcasses.

As archaeologist Diana Crader writes in her discussion of diet at Monticello, it can be hard to extrapolate from faunal assemblages to the actual diet. One of the most common forms of pork in rations was salt pork, which is boneless and therefore largely invisible in the archaeological record. Archaeologists are not able to gauge how much salt pork, bacon, or similar products were consumed across plantations. Those who worked in the plantation house kitchen may have brought home scraps or leftovers, which could account for the high-quality cuts of meat found in some households. In this case, high-quality cuts would not indicate generous provisioning of enslaved workers in general. It is even possible that trash from elsewhere on the plantation was occasionally dumped in old slave cabins or discarded near occupied ones, mixing together food remains from slave and planter diets. Still, Crader argues that plantation hierarchies were more complicated than just a "master-slave" binary, and that historical records fail to provide the full picture of these complicated dynamics.

At the Hermitage Plantation, Andrew Jackson's estate near Nashville, archaeologist Brian Thomas reports that not all houses in the slave quarter had the same access to pottery and building materials.[25] Houses closer to the plantation house were more solidly built and had nicer ceramics. This probably indicated the control of the planters in imposing status differences based on favoritism or different roles on the plantation. But Thomas found that other differences among the households of the enslaved did not follow the same lines. In fact, the households closest to the plantation house had the lowest quality cuts of meat, and all houses had access to the same range of species. The situation was more complicated, and to Thomas more contested and negotiated among planters and enslaved workers, than we might think from just looking at what the planters wrote.

If enslaved plantation workers were supplied with rations of cornmeal and salt pork to be supplemented by their own gardening, hunting, and fishing, leftovers from the plantation house, and/or stolen goods, rather than receiving meals already prepared and dished out, then we need to regard plantation workers as playing an active, albeit severely constrained, role in creating their own foodways. Archaeologist Larry McGee argues that the meals prepared in the cabins of enslaved people were determined to some extent by what owners provided and the seasonal, regional, and economic availability of ingredients.[26] Importantly, however, they were also shaped by individual family members' preferences and their ability to procure wild foods or garden vegetables. While it is hard to see elements of cuisine like flavorings, recipes, and deliciousness in the archaeological record, McGee thinks it is important to envision the ambiguities and clashes that must have surrounded cooking and eating activities that were not fully dependent on the owners' dictates. In McGee's account, food could even provide a limited means for resistance and defense of identity and self for those enmeshed in the violent and exploitative institution of slavery. In this process, a new American cuisine was born.

Forging an American Cuisine

Looking at plantation diets in the antebellum South gives us an opportunity to see how power and hierarchy interact with culture, cuisine, and tradition. The colonial period in the Americas was a time of culture contact and change, and on plantations this meant the brutal incorporation of African and Native American people and technology into an ostensibly European hierarchy. Yet a new cuisine arose in the spaces left by European overseers, created through overt or subtle resistance to European norms on the part of enslaved Africans, enriched by Native American traditions and ingredients.

West African and African American ingredients and cuisine have made a clear contribution to southern foodways, even though that contribution has sometimes been overlooked or appropriated by white chefs.[27] The slave trade brought people to the US South from many parts of Africa with distinct cuisines, languages, religions, and traditions. There was no one historical African cuisine, just as there is no one contemporary North American cuisine. Yet enslaved Africans incorporated ingredients and dishes familiar to them into colonial and pre–Civil War American cuisine. African plants such as rice, okra, and black-eyed peas became agricultural and culinary staples in the South. Enslaved cooks already had experience with New World ingredients like corn, peanuts, and chili peppers, which had been brought by the Portuguese to the West African coast.[28] When possible, they continued to cook these foods in familiar ways in the United States, and these ingredients made their way into savory southern stews, corncakes, and grits.

Historical archaeologist Leland Ferguson has studied the pottery produced in rural and enslaved households in South Carolina as a way to understand the experience of enslaved people and the possibility for resistance.[29] The low country along the Atlantic coast of South Carolina and Georgia was not well-suited for growing wheat, tobacco, or sugar, but eventually colonial planters realized that they could use the expertise of skilled farmers from rice-growing regions of West Africa to make rice a central agricultural commodity. They imported West African rice varieties and enslaved rice farmers from places like Sierra Leone and Angola.[30]

On Carolina rice plantations, enslaved workers were generally allowed to fish and garden after finishing the day's quota.[31] Enslaved African Americans also hunted game and herded cattle, another commodity that linked South Carolina and West African colonial economies. In doing so, they developed deep knowledge of the South Carolina wilderness. These conditions gave enslaved families some autonomy in shaping daily meals, and Ferguson suggests that they also provided space to subtly resist the European ideology that justified slavery. In this space, enslaved Africans could create a subculture that emphasized different symbols, values, and ideas.

As Ferguson reconstructs the story, plantation owners and other members of European American elite society tried to structure their world in a rational, hierarchical way.[32] They built plantation houses in Georgian style and used imported dishes to show off their appreciation for quality manufacturing and their access to expensive commodity markets. These goods and buildings symbolized the wealth and status considered to be natural to those at the top of the hierarchy. But in rural households and slave quarters, everyday pottery was made by hand in a style archaeologists call Colono ware.[33] In many parts of West Africa, women were traditionally the primary potters, and they could have carried on this role in South Carolina. Kitchens were also stocked with gourds and European pots, reflecting the mixed culinary traditions at work.

Colono ware pottery usually included many small bowls and jars as well as a few bigger ones. Ferguson points out that these forms fit within broad West African culinary traditions, which often place a starchy staple like rice, ground corn, or mashed cassava root at the heart of the plate and season it with smaller amounts of vegetable and meat relish or stew. This means that enslaved cooks might have been using these dishes to cook meals in a West African tradition. So, Ferguson concludes, even as plantation owners used one symbolic system to place themselves at the top of the hierarchy, enslaved African Americans maintained their own subculture that might have helped emphasize solidarity, tradition, and a separate identity from the European American planters. This subculture would have been an effective site for resistance.

Overt resistance, the subtle rebellions Ferguson identifies, contact with European and Native American cuisines, and sharp but complicated status and class distinctions shaped the foodways of enslaved African Americans on plantations. Regional cuisines emerged throughout the South that brought together influences from Native American culture and varied regions in Africa and Europe in a process of creolization.[34] Sometimes African culinary and cultural traditions remained at the core of American practices. Aspects of West African language, folklore, and cuisine are still evident in Gullah and Geechee communities on the Atlantic Coast of the Carolinas and Georgia, communities that are home to descendants of the enslaved rice farmers I mentioned earlier.[35] Elsewhere, the dominant culture of a particular part of the United States, often European in origin, provided the vocabulary, and the grammars of other traditions survived in recontextualized or translated forms.[36] Thus Mary Randolph, the white author of a well-known cookbook from the early nineteenth century, could suggest to her European American readers that they should cook their okra and rice soup in an earthenware pot (perhaps reminiscent of handmade Colono ware) without overtly acknowledging the African origin of the ingredients, recipe, or tradition.[37]

Today, the African and Native American roots of southern cuisine are not always acknowledged. Food historian Michael Twitty is an expert on the culinary traditions of enslaved Africans and African Americans.[38] As a historical reenactor, he experiments with dishes that would have been made by enslaved cooks and writes about the powerful role of food in identity and cultural resistance. Twitty points out that barbecue is an American tradition forged from a fusion of Native American and African culinary practices of spicing, smoking, and slow roasting meat over open pits.[39] As barbecue became popular in the colonial and antebellum United States, enslaved men were often charged with preparing it. Though popular narratives do not always recognize the role of slavery and colonialism in shaping barbecue, Twitty argues, much of the innovation and variety in regional barbecue traditions today can be traced back to these cooks.

Grits provide another example of these complex dynamics. Grits are coarsely ground cornmeal or hominy that is cooked into porridge, seasoned with salt, butter, or cheese, and served in many parts of the United States today with breakfast or as a bed for savory stews. As I discussed in chapter 4, corn was domesticated in Mexico and moved north to become a staple for Native Americans across the present-day United States. When European colonists arrived, they learned from indigenous farmers how to grow corn, and they probably saw some sort of hominy mush.[40] Colonists would already have been accustomed to oatmeal and other grain mushes. West African cuisines also had a place for starchy porridges accompanied by a flavorful sauce or stew, and enslaved African cooks could easily transform cornmeal or hominy rations into mush or grits. Grits represent the culinary fusion that took place in the spaces in and between the violence of slavery and conquest in the United States.

But grits are also an example of the relationship between Goody's haute cuisine and everyday nonelite meals. At Husk, a famous Nashville restaurant dedicated to southern ingredients and foodways, an appetizer portion of shrimp and grits today costs $16.[41] A main course of catfish with zucchini, borage (an easy to grow garden herb), and Carolina gold rice grits sells for $30. Food historians and archaeologists find corn, rice, local seafood and fish, squash, and kitchen greens in records and excavations related to slave quarters and poor farmsteads dating to the same time period when plantation owners were modeling their meals on English high cuisine, serving beef pies and English peas. Two hundred years later, these same ingredients and preparations are part of American high cuisine, cooked by (white male) celebrity chefs, and eaten by those with ample social and financial capital.

This example highlights the role of context, class, and culture in shaping the symbolic meanings of foods. As we saw Mary Douglas argue in the introduction to this book, there is no universal structure to a meal; instead, cultural grammars and vocabularies give meaning to particular foods and dishes. The social restrictions created by the price point, the participation of a famous chef, and the elaborate preparation of specific, single-origin heirloom varieties take foods that have historically been associated with marginalized traditions and, in essence, gentrify them. By placing grits, catfish, and barbeque at an elite table, white chefs may seek to reclaim an overlooked past but run the risk of erasing a history of violence by appropriating the hard-won traditions of others.

COLONIAL DISHES

Specific foods and dishes are given meaning by their social and cultural contexts, and these meanings shift over time. This means that cuisine may be altered by powerful processes such as conquest, exploitation, and political change. At the same time, as in the example above, cuisine can be a site for everyday resistance and identity maintenance among the conquered.

The culinary creolization of the antebellum South is one facet of a larger process of exchange between New and Old Worlds sparked by Columbus's voyages at the end of the fifteenth century. This process, called the Columbian Exchange (figure 6.3), reshaped the ecology and cuisine of the world as American plants, animals, and diseases spread to Europe, Africa, and Asia, and vice versa.[42] Many of the products that we closely associate today with particular regions actually originated elsewhere. For instance, the Caribbean is known for producing rum from vast sugarcane plantations, but sugar was introduced to the New World as a plantation crop and economic commodity.

Anthropologist Sidney Mintz chronicled the rise of sugar as a colonial commodity and a central element of the British diet.[43] Along with other colonial products like tea (from Asia), coffee (originally from Ethiopia), and chocolate (cacao is from the tropical Americas, but became popular in Europe once sugar and milk were added), sugar "was transformed from a luxury of kings to the kingly luxury of commoners"[44] between 1750 and 1950.

Luxury trends often percolate downward through social strata (the opposite of what happened to grits).[45] At the beginning of this chapter, I defined luxury foods as refinements on necessities that are widely desired but not widely accessible. Sugar was no longer a luxury once it could be eaten cheaply and regularly by the working class. After cheap milk chocolate became widely available, chocolate makers in Europe capitalized on the quality and expense of their products to retain luxury status.[46] Today, European brands like Ferrero Rocher and Lindt are available in the grocery checkout line, and the truly expensive chocolate is single-origin rain forest certified organic. The signifiers of wealth and luxury might change over time, but, by definition, luxuries are desired by many and attainable only to a few.

Increased desire for and consumption of sugar—to sweeten tea and porridge and to make jam to be eaten with bread—by the British working classes drove colonial sugar production and subsidized a growing urban

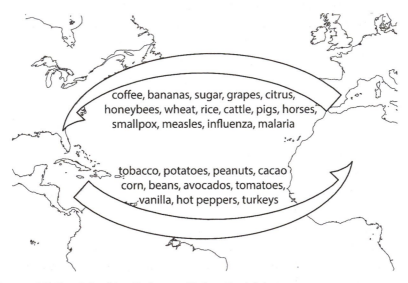

coffee, bananas, sugar, grapes, citrus, honeybees, wheat, rice, cattle, pigs, horses, smallpox, measles, influenza, malaria

tobacco, potatoes, peanuts, cacao corn, beans, avocados, tomatoes, vanilla, hot peppers, turkeys

FIGURE 6.3. The Columbian Exchange. (Robyn Cutright)

population's turn to wage labor. Mintz argues that working-class desire for sugar was not, in itself, enough to reshape British diet. Instead, this new diet was linked to an emerging capitalist global economy that enmeshed British consumers with Caribbean plantations and industrial mass production.

Mintz argues that the British working classes learned to eat sugar in the context of fundamental shifts in the way they lived and worked (in city factories rather than on rural farms) and that those in power profited from the deep social transformations reflected in, but also made possible by, this new diet. Sugar, combined with tea and mass-produced bread, made it possible for the working class to spend less time cooking and more time working for wages, which they would then spend buying sugar and tea. In other words, this shift facilitated the exploitation of the British working classes. The story of sugar, as told by Mintz, reveals how asymmetrical relations of power and class struggle shaped cuisine.

The story of wheat in the Americas is another example of how power and desire were intertwined with culinary change and the flow of plants and animals in the Columbian Exchange. In colonial Mexico, corn tortillas remained a staple because introduced European wheat did not grow well on local farms. This made European-style wheat bread a status symbol. Historian Jeffrey Pilcher has written that members of the aspiring elite in colonial Mexico would step outside after meals to ostentatiously brush crumbs off their clothes; corn tortillas do not produce crumbs, so what they were really showing off is having eaten wheat bread.[47]

When New World products were introduced to Europe, they were often initially viewed as luxuries (cocoa), novelties perhaps useful as aphrodisiacs but not much else (potatoes), beautiful but possibly poisonous (tomatoes), or unfit for human consumption (corn). Eventually, however, some of these products supported a huge population increase in Europe during the eighteenth and nineteenth centuries.[48] New World crops proved useful in rotation with Old World crops, since they made different demands on the soil and lacked local pests. Root crops, and especially potatoes, produce good yields with relatively little work, which made them essential in places like Ireland where poor tenant farmers struggled under an oppressive economic system. Of course, the story of the Irish potato famine would not have been possible without the Columbian Exchange.

Just as it is hard to imagine Caribbean economies and cuisines without pork, coffee, rice, bananas, or sugar, it is difficult to think of Italian cuisine without the tomato, or Thai cuisine without the chili pepper, or Eastern European and Russian without the potato. These foods were incorporated into the deep culinary grammar of these places in ways that made local sense but nevertheless exerted an intense transformative power on the flavor profiles and ingredients we associate with these cuisines. Today, we are all products of colonial Columbian Exchange in many ways. Simply celebrating the global flavors that were forged by this colonial transformation, however, risks downplaying its coercive and violent aspects.

CONQUEST KITCHENS

I discuss above how global systems of extraction and oppression brought disparate cultures and foods together in southern plantation kitchens, and the cuisine that emerged was something new, forged by inequality and contact. Culture contact, inequality, and coercion, and the culinary hybrids that emerge, are also associated with imperial conquest. My own research in Peru focuses on how local diet, cuisine, and household practices were affected when rural communities were conquered by the pre-Inca Chimú Empire.[49]

At the broadest level, I am interested in what we can tell about political control by looking at local food. When many historians and archaeologists write about conquest, they refer to something that happens only at the top level of government. It may not matter much to peasants where their taxes are going, just that they have to pay taxes. At the same time, I hesitate to think of rural households as stuck in timeless tradition with no part in larger politics. I am also wary of downplaying conquest's traumatic, transformative impact. These competing perspectives drive me to study this topic in greater depth.

I focus on the Jequetepeque Valley, on the Pacific coast of Peru. This valley was conquered around AD 1320 by the Chimú Empire as it expanded along a wide swath of the coast. The battle they fought for control of the Jequetepeque was so fierce and bloody that local residents mentioned it to Spanish chroniclers three hundred years later. After the Chimú won, they razed the walls of an important local community called Farfán, placed two sacrificed women on top of the wall, and built their own compound above it.[50] At Farfán, Chimú administrators oversaw the agriculturally rich lower valley, stored products, and hosted elite visitors and feasts. The Chimú built other administrative centers elsewhere in the Jequetepeque aimed at controlling the flow of water and people through the valley, invested in canals and other aspects of the farming infrastructure, and sent a member of the royal family to represent their interests at Farfán.

Given Chimú interest in reshaping the farming landscape of the Jequet-epeque and the local remembered trauma of the conquest, I was curious whether local families and communities experienced a dramatic transition under Chimú rule, or whether rural life continued relatively unaffected. I chose the farming community of Pedregal, located only a few miles from Farfán, as the focus of my investigation.

I assembled a team that included Peruvian archaeologists, a few under-graduate students from the United States, and local workers who had ex-perience from Farfán, and set to work. We spent four months digging into Pedregal houses to find broken pottery, fish and mammal bones, plant re-mains, broken tools, and discarded fragments of textiles and other house-hold goods. Because the Pacific coast is so dry, even corn cobs and cotton seeds were preserved. When we had collected our sample, we returned to the lab to analyze it and look for changes through time in what households were doing, and what people were eating.[51]

The results were surprising. Over the course of Chimú rule, people in Pe-dregal households processed more corn and cotton. This means that they were probably emphasizing these products more heavily in their fields, ramping up production. Corn and cotton were labor-intensive to grow and process, but the distribution of remains told me they were probably ex-ported to somewhere like Farfán. Even though they were probably spending more time producing these crops for Chimú administrators, Pedregal resi-dents continued doing the same range of activities and eating the same mix of fish, shellfish, and animals like guinea pig, dog, and llama (figure 6.4). They continued burying their dead and holding feasts around low platform mounds at the heart of their community, and they seem to have cooked their meals in the same kinds of pots in the same way. Household and com-munity organization and local culinary practice remained constant, even in the face of conquest and reorganization of the regional political and eco-nomic situation. Whatever impact the Chimú had on local identity or au-tonomy, I see it archaeologically more as an intensification of pressures that already existed rather than a dramatic upset.

Other archaeologists have looked at the bigger and better-known Inca Empire and have found that the Inca ruled at least in part through providing food and hospitality to conquered subjects.[52] Sometimes, Inca rule substan-tially altered local cuisine and social organization. One of the most compre-hensive studies of the impact of Inca conquest was carried out by archaeol-ogists Terence D'Altroy and Christine Hastorf, along with a team of other archaeologists and specialists, in the Upper Mantaro Valley in the highland

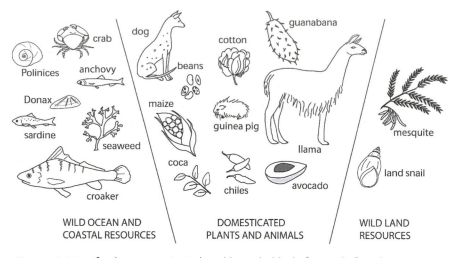

FIGURE 6.4. Key food resources in Pedregal households, before and after Chimú conquest. (Robyn Cutright)

Andes.[53] This project documented many aspects of Mantaro Valley life in the two periods preceding Inca conquest and during the Inca occupation, from the way that people settled on the landscape and located communities and fields, to the kinds of goods that they produced in their households, to what men and women ate. The overall picture from the Mantaro Valley is one of some continuity, but also of changes that stretched down into the microlevel of everyday life.

In the earliest period, scattered communities dotted the valley edges and farmers grew corn along the river and potatoes on the higher elevation slopes. Eventually, regional competition developed and people resettled in larger clusters in higher, more defensible locations. Perhaps as a result, the diet shifted away from corn to include more potatoes and high-altitude crops like quinoa. Christine Hastorf identified this change by taking soil samples from the floors of houses occupied during each period and counting up all the charred remnants of potatoes, corn, quinoa, and beans so that she could compare the crops that were being processed and consumed. Communities during this period contained both elites and commoners, and elites had more access to metal, fancy ceramics, and corn. Hastorf also tested the bone isotopes of men and women who died during this period. As you recall, different plants process energy through different metabolic pathways, and these characteristic signatures are visible in the bone chemistry of those who consume them. Luckily for archaeologists in the

New World, corn's metabolic pathway is distinct from that of other plants like potatoes. Though she was only able to test a few individuals, Hastorf found that during this period, men's and women's diets were fairly similar in terms of consumption of corn compared to other plants.[54]

Inca conquest brought many changes to Mantaro Valley life and cuisine. The Inca prized corn above other crops, in part because it could be brewed into corn beer, called *chicha*. This was an essential part of the Inca reciprocity-based economy and the empire's hospitality-based provincial polities. Because corn does not grow above a certain altitude, valleys with good agricultural land at a low enough altitude were extremely valuable to the Inca, and they reshaped the settlement and farming systems of the Mantaro Valley to focus on corn production. Communities moved away from their hilltop defensive settlements after the Inca subdued regional competition, and people moved to smaller communities near the valley floor. Charred corn fragments were more common in the samples Hastorf gathered from Inca-period household floors, echoing this renewed focus on corn. The Inca built a system of storehouses in the valley to centralize and store surplus corn.

The status differences that had existed in Mantaro Valley communities before the Inca persisted, but narrowed. Local elites maintained their prominence, according to the Inca system of allowing existing hierarchies to persist as long as they supported Inca rule, but the Inca now sat at the top of the heap. Many other household activities, in both elite and commoner households, continued as they had before Inca arrival. Local households were not dependent on the state for basic resources, though they were linked into a wider network than before. Interestingly, bone chemistry suggests that after conquest, men and women ate more differentiated diets when it came to corn. Men's bone isotopes showed a greater percentage of their diet was coming from corn than women. Hastorf believes that this could be due to the importance of drinking *chicha* at political or work party feasts hosted by the Inca. It may be that men were drawn more tightly into the imperial network than women, even though women played a key role in producing the corn beer that lubricated the network.

D'Altroy and Hastorf's Mantaro Valley project focuses a good deal on how Inca strategies reached into local households and kitchens. But sometimes, postconquest change is the result of local strategies to negotiate imperial impositions and cope with violent transitions. Archaeologist Parker VanValkenburgh has excavated an early Spanish colonial period community on the coast of Peru, one valley north of Pedregal; in comparing animal remains from colonial and pre-Hispanic garbage, he and zooarchaeologist Sarah Kennedy found a good deal of change in the local diet.[55]

Some of this change reflected a response to the pressures of the Spanish Conquest. The local population had collapsed due to disease, which disproportionately struck elders with knowledge of foraging and farming practices. Colonial authorities demanded more tribute in kind, rather than demanding labor as the Inca had before them. People would have had to scramble to meet these demands with a smaller, less healthy population.

In response, local residents spent less time fishing off shore and gathering shellfish and other wild coastal resources so that they could focus on meeting Spanish demands. They made up for this loss by adopting European animals like goats and chickens. It turned out that these animals were better adapted to local desert climates than indigenous animals like llamas, which evolved in the cooler and wetter high Andes. Adopting these new species was a strategic innovation, a way of using local ingenuity to take advantage of new opportunities in the broader context of the violence and trauma of conquest, demographic collapse, forced labor, and loss of language and belief systems.

Studying food allows researchers to peek into the inner workings of ancient homes and communities. Looking at what people were growing, cooking, and eating during a period of big regional changes provides a new perspective on what these changes actually meant from the point of view of an average person. The three Andean examples presented here suggest that conquest most readily affected how food was produced and distributed. This had some impact on daily diet, especially in the Mantaro Valley, but it did not necessarily change the overall cuisine or range of foods included in the diet. It was harder for empires to reorganize elements of daily life such as recipes, the way food was prepared, or how families were run. This could mean that conquest was not a big deal at a local level. It could also indicate that cuisine is resistant to imposed changes, either because it is inherently conservative or because people hold onto culinary traditions as a means of resistance.

Similar dynamics of culinary conservation and resistance are visible in the West African traditions maintained by Gullah and other African American communities over centuries of enslavement and struggle for autonomy and in the persistence and recovery of cultural foodways and food sovereignty by indigenous nations in North America.[56] In some cases, conquest opened up new opportunities by making new plants, animals, or technology available to be used to local ends. If Hastorf is right that Inca-period men ate more corn than did women, then conquest could also reach into the household to reshape daily meals and gender relations.

These daily dynamics are a long way from the royal Aztec meals with which this chapter began. The humble meals of Pedregal farmers, the dishes that emerged as echoes of resistance to the oppression faced by enslaved Americans, and the feasts of Lady Dai and Moctezuma all, however, illustrate how social hierarchy shapes, communicates, and is reinforced by cuisine. In chapter 8, I look more carefully at how daily meals provide insight into larger social and political processes by stepping even further inside the kitchen. The examples in this chapter demonstrate that power, wealth, and class shape the meals we eat. Some elite meals are so highly elaborated that they become ceremonial occasions. Chapter 7 explores what happens when food truly becomes ritual.

7

FOODS OF THE GODS AND SACRED MEALS

The ancient Moche people of Peru left archaeologists with many mysteries. Their pottery depicts finely drawn scenes of hunters, warriors, plants and animals, and fantastic figures that combine human and animal characteristics. One scene repeats across many different pots. On the top register, several figures dressed in elaborate regalia face a larger individual dressed in a crescent-shaped headdress and beautifully decorated tunic. One of the figures holds out a goblet. On the lower part of the scene, smaller figures cut the throats of naked, bound prisoners. Archaeologists call this the Presentation Theme, based on a guess at what this scene represents.[1] But, since Moche civilization collapsed more than a thousand years ago without leaving any written records, archaeologists have struggled to capture the full meaning of the scene.

Over the past few decades, archaeological discoveries have helped us better understand this scene.[2] At Moche pyramids across the north coast of Peru, including Sipán, Ucupe, and San José de Moro, archaeologists have found royal tombs with central figures dressed in versions of the elaborate regalia pictured on the pots. At one site, they have found many tombs of women representing the "Priestess" figure that holds the goblet in the Presentation Theme. Archaeologists have also found sacrificed warriors, whose bodies reflect a history of violence and who were killed and left exposed in ceremonial plazas. These discoveries hint that the scene describes a ceremony that was held at these Moche ceremonial centers by elites or priests who dressed as supernatural figures whose attributes combined human and animal features. Ceramic versions of the goblet have also been found in tombs, and when residue on the inside is tested, it turns out that they likely held human blood.[3] This may be the ultimate food of the gods.

Food does not simply nourish the body. It feeds the soul. So far, I have argued that for humans, food is not just a biological requirement, it is a

Figure 7.1. Map showing locations of key sites from chapter 7. 1 = Mesa Verde, Colorado, United States; 2 = Late Woodland Virginia, United States; 3 = Maya Belize; 4 = Moche region and Farfán, Peru; 5 = Warí territory, Brazil; 6 = Viking territory, northwestern Europe; 7 = Mycenean Greece; 8 = Neolithic, Xiajiadian, and Shang China. (Robyn Cutright)

cultural realm through which we make meaning in our lives. Regular foods can take on sacred meanings, and the act of eating and drinking (or fasting) together can heighten the experience of shared religious and social rites. Food rituals and prohibitions exist across contemporary world religions. Many Muslims and Jews avoid pork, Catholics skip meat on Fridays during Lent, and many devout Hindus and Buddhists avoid eating meat altogether. Sharing bread and wine in remembrance and celebration of Christ is one of the central moments of Christian services. Foods imbued with deep historical and symbolic referents lie at the heart of the Jewish Passover seder. Given the wealth of contemporary examples, it is logical to suggest that sacred foods and religiously charged meals also played a role in how people ate in the past.

Chapter 5 discussed the political and social significance of feasts, a specific type of special purpose meal, and chapter 6 explored how some foods held special significance for signaling wealth and status. Politically and socially significant feasts are not always sharply distinguished from sacred or religious meals and ceremonial foods. People in most past societies probably did not separate religious and political ceremonies as distinct occasions. Instead, the religious and political were intertwined; sacred and secular were blurred. In this chapter, though, I focus on the ritual use of food in the past, the kinds of foods that were considered sacred, and the contexts in which these were consumed.

SACRED FOODS

What foods might have been considered sacred to people in the past? Foods that are exotic and expensive, prepared in elaborate labor-intensive dishes, tend to characterize elite or haute cuisines around the world. Yet in the contemporary sacred meals I just mentioned, some of the most deeply meaningful foods are humble and commonly consumed on a daily basis: bread and wine, bitter herbs and eggs. In this case, the religious context and symbolic content set these foods apart as sacred. Another category of sacred foods includes "foods of the gods" set aside for divine consumption. Burnt offerings, animal sacrifices, ambrosia, and the shell of the thorny oyster are examples of this category. Finally, some sacred foods may be selected because of their transformative power: alcohol, hallucinogens, and other drugs fall into this category. In the sections that follow, I provide some examples of the first two kinds of sacred foods; food and drink that alter perception are described later in the chapter.

Sacred Context

According to the work of archaeologist Christine Hastorf, some foods are considered luxuries because of the role they play in rituals, special meals, and other highly charged social contexts.[4] Ceremonies and rituals can lend everyday staples new meanings, as in the case of Aztec rituals discussed by art historian Elizabeth Morán.[5] In the Aztec Empire, foodstuffs and ceremonial meals were central parts of both household and public rituals. Morán documents how ordinary foods such as corn, amaranth, and chili peppers were used in ceremonies ranging from weddings to large-scale celebrations of seasons and deities. During one yearly ritual, a priest would make a cornmeal cake and wait for a god's footprint to crumble it. The god's eventual arrival was celebrated with music and the distribution of balls of cornmeal dough to the people. The Aztec also used food for its aesthetic value, painting the faces of sacrifice victims with amaranth seed paste and forming images of gods from ground amaranth and maize mixed with maguey syrup, with beads for eyes and corn for teeth.

A second way that ordinary foods can become special, according to Hastorf's analysis, is by having special prized varieties. In the United States, we can buy apples year-round at the grocery store, and the same few varieties, such as Red Delicious and Granny Smith, are readily available. In the fall, though, we might see the store flooded with local apples in a wider variety only available during the harvest, and we might use these in special seasonal dishes. In a similar way, Hastorf suggests that special varieties of corn were selected for rituals in the Andes.[6] Later in the chapter, I discuss evidence that the pre-Inca Moche people prized larger varieties of corn for burial offerings, even though corn was also a daily staple.

A third way to set ordinary food apart is to serve it in large quantities. Abundance gives everyday food special meaning, just as a traditional US Thanksgiving spread elevates humble ingredients like potatoes, apples, green beans, and turkey to symbolize family and harvest. To illustrate this aspect, Hastorf uses the example of funeral ceremonies in the early highland Chiripa society in the Lake Titicaca region of the Andes. At these feasts, people ate the full spectrum of daily foods but in larger than usual quantities.[7] Similarly, ancient Egyptians celebrated a Festival of Intoxication. Tomb paintings picture elite banquet guests vomiting, presumably from overindulging. Irish stories describe feasts at which a whole year's food was served, including wine, boar, and wheat cakes cooked in honey. In these cases, the foods themselves were ordinary, but consuming them in abundance (or overabundance) signaled a special meal.[8]

Consuming sacred or special foods can symbolize and reaffirm social distinctions. In one example of how participation in ancient food-based rituals was shaped by gender and status, bioarchaeologist Christine White studied skeletal remains from seven Maya sites in Belize.[9] She found that according to bone isotope signatures, elite females consumed less maize and less meat than elite males. Nonelite females, on the other hand, consumed a diet very similar to that of nonelite males.

What social context was responsible for this difference between elite men and women? One possibility is that men ate more protein and more maize on a daily basis, perhaps because of variation in snacking opportunities or gender ideology that dictated a more carnivorous diet for men. Another possibility, which White favors, is that men participated more frequently in rituals where they ate meat, perhaps specifically the meat of dogs and deer that had been fed on maize to prepare them for ritual feasts (accounting for the high meat and corn signatures in male skeletons). While Maya women had access to authority and power through membership in elite families and on the basis of their key role in preparing and serving food that fueled religious and political ritual, bone chemistry suggests they may not have been the central participants in these particular rituals.

Sacred Sacrifice and Divine Consumption

Archaeologist Christine Hastorf's final example of a luxury food in the Andes is a food that draws its power not from rarity or abundance but from its life-giving properties: human blood.[10] Her example of this sacred food comes from the Moche scene at the beginning of this chapter. Archaeologists are convinced that a version of this scene was periodically played out at Moche ceremonial centers, and that the blood and human sacrifice pictured there were real. A mysterious fruit called the *ulluchu*, which is pictured in the scene, may have served as an anticoagulant that would allow the blood to remain liquid so that it could be extracted from the sacrificed victim, poured, and even drunk.[11] Because of its symbolic power of life and death, Hastorf suggests that human blood may be one of the most symbolically charged ritual foods. In Moche sacrifice ceremonies, it might have been consumed by humans dressed as deities, and perhaps by extension by deities themselves. Other examples of ancient human sacrifice, for example the large-scale ceremonies of the Aztec in Mexico, also emphasized the literal and figurative consumption of human flesh and organs to maintain order in the world.[12]

Some sacred foods were literally food for the gods. In the Andes, the shell of the thorny oyster *Spondylus* was crunched up and consumed by the gods in a Quechua myth. *Spondylus* was imported into the central Andes from the warm coastal waters off Ecuador and left as offerings, strewed before the king as he walked, and fashioned into elaborate jewelry and figurines. Archaeologist Mary Glowacki has suggested that *Spondylus* flesh was also consumed by humans, and that its seasonal toxicity would have given it hallucinogenic properties recognized by Andean shamans.[13] While I am not convinced that *Spondylus* flesh was regularly eaten hundreds of miles from where it was collected, *Spondylus* shells do have wide ceremonial use across the Andes. Other famous foods that confer immortality and feed the gods included the nectar and ambrosia of the Greek gods, amrita in Hinduism, mead in Norse Valhalla, and cacao in Mesoamerica.[14]

As this brief review shows, a food might be sacred for a number of different reasons, and not all sacred foods really were foods (for humans, anyway). The context of consumption was at least as important as the substance itself and often played a central role in converting everyday foods to sacred ones.

"FAST" FOOD

If abundance can signal a sacred or socially meaningful meal, going without can be a sacred act as well. Fasting, rather than feasting, is central to many religious celebrations. Fasting does not always entail foregoing food completely; it can mean not eating during particular times of the day or avoiding specific foods. Fasting and feasting are paired in some world religious traditions today, as the feast of Mardi Gras precedes the fast of Lent in many Catholic regions, or Eid celebrates the end of Ramadan for Muslims. In some Aztec rituals, the tension between fasting and feasting was emphasized visually and ritually. Elizabeth Morán recounts annual rituals dedicated to the deity Chicomecoatl, in which people first ate and drank at a festival, then began a fast.[15] A young girl was chosen to impersonate the deity and was ornately decorated with chilies, squash, vegetables, corn, and other seeds. The visual abundance of the food made an intentional contrast with the hunger fasting celebrants surely felt. Eventually, the deity impersonator received blood offerings from the audience, and then was decapitated and flayed in a bloody but deeply symbolic representation of the balance between life and death, hunger and abundance, and the mutual sacrifice of gods and humans central to Aztec cosmology.

Unlike feasting, fasting does not produce material evidence to be preserved in the archaeological record, and so it is basically archaeologically invisible.[16] To complicate matters, textual evidence shows that fasting was defined differently across past societies. For instance, the Spanish chronicler Father Bernabé Cobo describes participants in Andean religious festivals fasting for days.[17] In this context, fasting meant abstaining from salt, chili peppers, corn beer, and sex. In addition to fasts, major religions today also observe food taboos. The introduction reviewed how anthropologists have tried to understand religious food taboos from structural, ecological, and historical perspectives, none of which quite match up with the insiders' own explanations. Both food taboos and fasting can be difficult to see archaeologically, because it is hard to securely attribute the absence of a specific food to religious prohibitions.[18] Even when archaeologists know for sure that a particular food was supposedly taboo, it can be hard to conclusively identify a conspicuous absence as the specific product of religious avoidance.

Despite the difficulty, some anthropologists have attempted to think through the material signatures of food avoidance. For instance, archaeologists Gustavo Politis and Nicholas Saunders studied the Nukak, foragers who live in the northern Amazon.[19] The Nukak do not neatly separate the natural world from the supernatural or the human worlds. Instead, for the Nukak as for many other societies, the boundaries between these worlds are permeable and intertwined. The Nukak believe that at death, one of a person's spirits "puts on the clothes" of the animal ancestor of his clan and returns at night to the forest where it prowls in the form of a tapir, deer, or jaguar. They do not eat these animals and avoid other species as well in a complex system that takes into account sex, pregnancy, parenthood, and other circumstances.

To Politis and Saunders, the ecological or adaptive consequences of consuming the taboo species are not sufficient to explain the taboo.[20] While the Nukak avoid the tapir, for instance, neighboring groups in an identical environment eat it happily. Politis and Saunders argue this system shows that food preferences are culturally constructed. Culture tells us what is edible, and what is not, and so each society eats only a subset of possible foods from its environment. Thus, in this view mythology and ideology, not ecology and economy, give taboos their shape.

Politis and Saunders also document the archaeological patterns produced by this kind of food taboo system and highlight the potential for confusion and misinterpretation. The white-lipped peccary is eaten exclusively by men and is taboo for women. Peccary are butchered near the kill site, usually some distance from the camp, and then grilled at the edge of camp for men to eat. Future archaeologists would find peccary heads at the butchering site and long bones discarded around the grill. Other animal bones would have a different pattern of discard, as they are brought back to the camp whole for women to cut up and cook. It is possible that patterns of differential treatment of different species could alert archaeologists to the presence of food taboos, but there is a lot of "noise" in the signal, such as the fact that the Nukak scavenge leg bones from completely taboo deer that have been killed by jaguars to make bone flutes. In this way even animals that are most strictly avoided might still contribute their bones to a future archaeological site. These examples show how hard it is to use the archaeological record alone to identify the religious fasts or food taboos likely practiced by people in the past. They also reiterate how central social and cultural context is to making foods sacred. However, there is a class of food and drink that seems to be almost universally granted ritual significance: those that alter sense and perception.

DIVINE VISIONS

Humans seem primed to search out hallucinogens, inebriants, and other psychoactive substances. Ninety percent of societies in one cross-cultural sample had culturally patterned ways of creating altered states of consciousness.[21] In chapter 5, I showed how alcohol has played a central role in feasting, political competition, and the origins of agriculture. However, beer and wine are not the only ancient substances that forged transcendent social ties by creating a heightened sensory experience. Here, I more carefully examine how psychoactive plants were used in sacred contexts.

In prehistoric societies, use of psychoactive plants was generally embedded in ritual and ceremony. In a contemporary Western context, we tend to associate drugs with recreational use and addiction, but it would be misleading to think of most prehistoric drug and alcohol use this way. These substances allowed everyday consciousness to be transcended and facilitated communication with spirits, deities, and ancestors.

Cannabis and opium poppy, as well as plants such as the *Ephedra* shrub, the blue water lily (*Nymphaea* sp.), and mandrake root (*Mandragora officinarum*), saw very early use in Europe, Asia, and Egypt.[22] Remnants of opium poppies and instruments for consuming the drug have been found in archaeological contexts around the Mediterranean dating back to the earliest farming communities eight thousand years ago. The oldest seeds of the opium poppy found to date were in a religious cult room in a Neolithic village. The fact that seeds were here, rather than charred in a kitchen hearth or mixed with household trash, links even the earliest opium consumption to ritual contexts. In chapter 5, archaeologist Yannis Hamilakis drew our attention to the sensory experience of attending a feast in a Minoan palace.[23] It turns out that the wine and scented perfume oils may not have been the only heady experience at these feasts. In Minoan and Mycenaean palaces, images of poppy seed capsules were shaped in stone and precious metal, and small pipes were used to inhale opium smoke. All in all, the use of psychoactive substances like opium and cannabis is well documented in the ancient world and was consistently linked to spiritual or religious experience.

Andean societies have long employed their own set of hallucinogenic substances such as the San Pedro cactus (*Echinopsis/Trichocereus*) and ayahuasca (*Banisteriopsis caapi*) in shamanic practices. At the early religious

FIGURE 7.2. Anthropomorphic Chavín deity holding a hallucinogenic San Pedro cactus. (Redrawn and modified from Richard L. Burger, *Chavin and the Origins of Andean Civilization* [London: Thames and Hudson, 1995]: figure 125. Robyn Cutright)

pilgrimage center of Chavín de Huántar, stone carvings depicted a fanged deity holding the San Pedro cactus (figure 7.2). Images also show individuals with freely flowing mucus, perhaps related to consumption of another hallucinogen, *vilca* (*Anadenanthera colubrina*), using decorated snuff spoons.[24]

Anthropologist Bonnie Glass-Coffin has tracked images related to San Pedro and shamanic ritual through Andean prehistory.[25] She believes that San Pedro's use as a vehicle for shamanic transformation and rituals related to water, fertility, and ancestors has persisted for millennia. Today on the north coast of Peru, shamanic healers use the hallucinogen to divine the causes of illness and to travel between the worlds of the living and the dead. They are widely known for their power; even in the modern metropolis of Lima you can see small cardboard signs stuck to lampposts and utility poles advertising the services of northern healers. Hallucinogens alter the senses, providing ritual participants with transcendent, otherworldly experiences that nudge open the door between this world and the supernatural.

MORTUARY MEALS

As I discussed, everyday foods take on new meanings in contexts that are charged with emotional, spiritual, or social meaning. In past societies special ceremonial meals accompanied many different kinds of life-cycle rituals, from Aztec naming ceremonies to medieval European weddings. Funerals and other rituals surrounding death and burial may be some of the most emotionally charged contexts in which food plays a role. This is the case in the examples of the Phrygian king and the Marchioness of Dai from chapter 6 and at many US funerals followed by a wake at a funeral home, place of worship, or family member's house. Special funeral foods may be associated with these events, but often the meal itself includes food that would be just as likely to appear at a church potluck or weekend meal. Sociologists think about death as a rip in the fabric of society. If this is the case, then the act of eating and drinking together helps to reaffirm social bonds and begins to repair that fabric. This charged social context, rather than the specific dishes, is what makes the meals special.

By looking at the kinds of food and serving vessels placed in burials, archaeologists can infer something about which foods were considered appropriate for funeral contexts, and in this way, try to understand something of the symbolic importance of specific foods or recipes. We can also try to reconstruct the kinds of social gatherings that occurred at funerals and the roles that food and drink played in cementing social bonds. In this section, I provide a few examples of mortuary meals and their associated social dynamics.

As a graduate student, I helped excavate a cemetery belonging to the Lambayeque culture at the site of Farfán, in the Peruvian coastal desert.[26] One thousand years ago, Lambayeque dead were buried in a long, low mound, each accompanied by a few grave goods. Women were buried with weaving baskets, children with small figurines made of gourd or clay, and all people with at least a few utilitarian ceramic cooking pots, bowls, and jugs that often contained food remains (figure 7.3). Many of the cooking pots were covered in soot from having been used over open fires; these were not vessels specially made to place in burials but everyday cooking utensils that had been repurposed as grave goods. I wondered whether the food had also been repurposed from daily use to serve as a final meal or offering for the afterlife.

To find out, I counted up all the different kinds of plant and animal remains in each pot. After I excavated at a small nearby village, I was able to compare the assemblage of plants from the burials to the assemblage of plants in household trash. The comparison showed that corn was much more common in the burial offerings than it was in the trash of Lambayeque households, and other foods like fruit, avocados, and chili peppers were much less common. Corn, whether alone or mixed with beans or fish,

FIGURE 7.3. Funerary food from Lambayeque burials at Farfán. *Left*, a cooking pot containing two cobs of corn and a spoon. *Right*, an individual with cooking pot, bowl, plate, and gourd. The pot contained food remains protected by the inverted bowl. (Robyn Cutright)

seems to have been especially valued as a funeral offering. At the nearby site of Pacatnamú, archaeologist George Gumerman found that varieties of corn with larger ears and more kernels were preferred in burials but were less common in households.[27] In these cases, an everyday staple like corn took on special meaning when included in emotionally, symbolically charged burial rituals.

Some food in burials may be intended to accompany the dead along a journey to the next world. Famously, this was the case in ancient Egypt. Pharaohs and elites had their graves furnished with food, implements, and representations of the workers they would need to reestablish their luxurious lifestyle after the journey to the underworld to be judged by Osiris. Archaeologists have even found the remains of funerary boats, designed specifically to carry the dead king to his tomb along the Nile, and then buried alongside the tomb after use. For the ancient Egyptians, you could quite literally take it with you when you went.

The Vikings of northwestern Europe are also famous for their boat burials, in an interesting echo of these Egyptian practices. Dead warriors were placed on boats to make the journey to the afterlife, and then the whole boat was burned to sever the connection between living and dead. This practice makes it hard for archaeologists to see all the details of Viking burials, and we rely on accounts of travelers and missionaries to fill in the gaps. Not all evidence of Viking burials went up in smoke, however, and archaeological study shows that food played an important role in these rituals.[28]

By carefully examining the soil of cremation mounds, archaeologists have discovered that food accompanied the dead on their journey.[29] Common foods included cattle, pigs, cabbage, grain, fish, and fruits, but the menu may have varied based on the preferences of the deceased. Buckets placed at the feet of the dead contained food or drink, and some graves also contained ceramic containers left as gifts by mourners. It is especially interesting that some graves were physically modeled after cisterns or chests that mimicked the structures the Vikings used to store food. Economic wealth, and the ability to produce and store agricultural surplus, were symbolized in the way the dead were interred, linking class, food, and death visually and ideologically.[30]

The Viking case illustrates the multiple purposes of food in rituals, especially emotionally charged ones like funerals. Food simultaneously fed the individual dead person on his or her journey and helped to comfort survivors by gifting dead loved ones with something they enjoyed in life or by outfitting them properly for death. For pre-Christian Vikings, food offerings could also invoke the protection or attention of the gods. Food and drink shared at graveside feasts or wakes stitched together the social fabric with threads of commensality, but it also emphasized differences in wealth or status.[31]

In Viking burials, wealthier or more prominent individuals commanded more grave goods and animals and bigger feasts. In some cases, food served at the feast was collected as tribute, symbolizing the flow of goods from followers to ruler, who then shared them at the feast. Burials also symbolized gender hierarchies and identity. Food and the tools used to prepare it, including grinding stones and serving wares, were often placed in women's burials. In some cases, such as at the site of Oseburg in Norway, even queens were provided with the necessary tools to cook and serve large amounts of food and beer, including enormous barrels that could hold as much as five hundred liters.[32] This practice could indicate that elite women's power lay partially in their role in preparing and presiding over feasts in their husbands' halls.

In another case from early medieval England, a quernstone (a large stone used to grind grain) was placed over a woman who was buried face down, missing limbs, and in a contorted position. The stone seems to seal in someone who might have been dangerous even after death.[33] The presence of bodies in bogs all over northern Europe and the British Isles suggests that some individuals were regarded as deviant, criminal, or dangerous and needed to be buried in ways that might protect the community. In these two examples from Scandinavia and the British Isles, food preparation and serving tools were used to send two very different social messages about women. In one case, they revealed the power derived from hosting; in the other, a desire to socially constrain deviance or malevolence even in death.

In China, funerary feasts helped convert family members into ancestors. They linked the living and dead more closely and reinforced or reshaped social bonds in the community. Remnants of these feasts were interred alongside newly created ancestors, and archaeologist Christopher Fung has found evidence that the meaning of food in these burials changed through time.[34] Fung studied burial rituals between 5000 and 2500 BC in northern coastal China, a time when social inequality was just beginning to appear. By analyzing the location of ceramic pots and other artifacts in relation to the bodies of tomb occupants, he was able to see that funeral customs shifted from drinking alcohol to presenting food and were later intensified by communal drinking at the graveside. Increasingly, rituals emphasized mourners and their consumption of food and drink, as opposed to providing drink to the dead. Community social relationships became the focus, even as relationships of unequal power and wealth arose within communities.

Later in Chinese history, during the Lower Xiajiadian and Shang periods, archaeologist Sarah Nelson believes that graveside feasting created connections with the dead, converting a recently deceased member of the community into an honored ancestor.[35] Cooked meat offerings left for the dead, as evidenced by the presence of animal bones in excavated burials, decreased in popularity through time. Serving dishes for meat and alcohol became more elaborate and varied by the Late Shang period. Based on this evidence, Nelson argues that the living feasted at the graveside, consuming increasingly elaborate meals in order to create alliances and connections to the dead.

EATING THE DEAD

In a few rare cases, the dead themselves constitute mortuary meals for the living. Cannibalism can be a difficult topic to think about from a scientific perspective because it is so emotionally charged. Many have heard about the Donner Party, the soccer team who survived a plane crash in the Andes, or shipwrecked sailors resorting to cannibalism to survive. These horrific stories emphasize the gory lengths to which survivors can go to stay alive. But survival cannibalism is only one context under which humans eat each other.

Archaeologists have identified evidence of what they call terroristic cannibalism under conditions of social breakdown or warfare in the US Southwest.[36] In the twelfth century, a prolonged drought destabilized communities that depended on farming corn in the already dry landscape of southern Colorado and northern New Mexico. As the drought wore on, a complex social, political, and economic network centered at Chaco Canyon, New Mexico, began to break down. For several centuries, Ancestral Puebloan people at Chaco had been trading exotic goods such as macaws and chocolate from Mexico, building a vast network of roads, and bringing trees over 50 miles through the desert to construct enormous Great Houses.[37] By the middle of the twelfth century, for reasons we don't fully understand (but were probably at the very least exacerbated by the drought), construction had stopped at Chaco, its inhabitants had migrated elsewhere, and the region was thrown into a twenty-five-year period of instability.

For people living in the Mesa Verde region of southern Colorado during this time, the threat of violent raids was intensified by fears of terroristic cannibalism. Archaeologist Brian Billman and his team documented one episode of violence in which a household was destroyed and its inhabitants slaughtered and consumed.[38] Skeletal remains were highly fragmented, reminiscent of the way animals were butchered in similar cultural contexts. Billman recovered preserved human feces from the hearth that contained traces of human myoglobin—a protein that could only be the result of the consumption and digestion of human flesh. Essentially, raiders killed the family, cooked and ate them in their own kitchen, and left the remains in the hearth the next morning before abandoning the house. This kind of violent raiding and cannibalism must have sent a powerful message to nearby households and communities. As Billman and colleagues point out, it is compelling to think about the kind of social and economic stress that would bring a society to this point, and equally amazing to realize that by AD 1175, the climate of terror had ended as quickly as it began. Social order was restored and the region became a bustling center of Puebloan population for the next century.

The social context of mortuary cannibalism is completely different from this kind of terroristic cannibalism. The Warí, a small tribe in the Amazon, described to anthropologist Beth Conklin how they used to eat their dead loved ones rather than consigning them to the cold, wet, lonely ground.[39] When someone died, family members would be called in to attend the funeral. The closest loved ones would lie on the body and hold it tight until it was time for slightly more distant kin (in-laws, or affines in anthropological terms) to consume as much of the flesh as possible. For the Warí, consuming the physical remains helped the living move on and forget the dead. It also initiated a cycle of reciprocity between the Warí and the water spirits. The dead joined the water spirits' society and came back to the forest as animals such as peccaries. When a peccary was killed by a Warí hunter, it was understood as an ancestor offering himself to feed the community. Thus consuming the dead, according to Conklin's analysis, symbolically began this relationship of reciprocity in which the living and the dead fed each other.

The example of Warí mortuary cannibalism highlights the importance of social context and belief. A food, even one as precious as human flesh, is given meaning by the social setting in which it is consumed and the set of beliefs in which it is embedded. The Warí and the Ancestral Puebloan raiders both consumed human flesh, and yet it meant something very different in each case.

OFFERINGS

Food and drink served as ritual offerings outside the cemetery as well. In Mycenaean Greece, as well as in later classical periods, burnt animal sacrifices were offered at sanctuaries and palaces. In one Peloponnesian sanctuary, archaeologists found a thick layer of burnt pig, sheep, and goat bones, along with drinking vessels, cooking pots, and animal figurines. By reconstructing the pattern of which bones were present, which were absent, and which were burned, archaeologists Yannis Hamilakis and Eleni Konsolaki were able to reconstruct what happened in the sanctuary.[40] Sheep or goats were butchered elsewhere and preferred cuts such as legs, shoulders, and rumps brought in as offerings. Very young pigs probably arrived whole. The meat was removed from some cuts before they were burned, and even parts of the animal with little meat such as hooves, jaws, and teeth were burned.

This pattern suggests that the meat from these sacrificed animals was eaten by humans, and then the remaining animal parts were given to deities to consume as burnt offerings. Hamilakis sees this kind of ritual as a rich sensory experience for participants who ate, drank, and witnessed the fire transform animals into offerings. In this sense, they shared an intense experience with ancestors or gods who consumed the sacrificed animals.

In other cases, ritual offerings are archaeologically visible because they are not consumed. Archaeologists Amber VanDerwarker and Bruce Idol analyzed the plant materials deposited at a Late Woodland period village in Virginia.[41] The Buzzard Rock II site, occupied AD 1200 to 1600, was a horticultural hamlet with a diet based on maize, beans, and squash as well as wild foods like hickory nuts and acorns. Most pits they excavated contained refuse created during processing plants, such as nut shells. Two contained an abundance of burnt corn fragments, mostly kernels. This is notable since the kernels would generally be eaten, leaving cob and husk fragments behind. The authors reason that these large caches of kernels, representing about 2.5 bushels of corn, must have been deliberately placed in the pits and burned. This could represent the disposal of spoiled corn at the end of the winter, but VanDerwarker and Idol suggest that it could also represent what they call "renewal ceremonialism," or the offering of valuable food in a ritual context such as mourning or purification.

In many New World societies, corn was a daily staple with deep symbolic meaning. The Popol Vuh, a sacred text of the Quiché Maya, recounts a myth in which humans were created from yellow and white ears of corn. Maize was a dietary cornerstone to be sure, but the Maya were also "people of corn" (*hombres de maiz*) in a more sacred sense as well. Aztec creation myths recount how the god Quetzalcoatl was charged with figuring out what humans would eat after the gods made them. He and an ant retrieved maize from Food Mountain and the gods distributed maize to the people (Quetzalcoatl and other gods and elements also eventually captured all of Food Mountain and obtained maize of many colors, amaranth, beans, and chia seeds).[42] Because of its symbolic power, corn was a common ritual offering in ancient North and South American societies.

In my work in pre-Hispanic Peru, I have found burnt offerings of maize in rural village kitchens. Just like at the Buzzard Rock II site, these small deposits of burnt maize cobs and kernels were probably offerings rather than cooking accidents because of their seemingly intentional placement and thorough burning. Figure 7.4 shows one of these offerings, which was deliberately placed in a food preparation area during a period of remodeling. Other corn offerings were placed to ritually close spaces before they were abandoned.[43] As with the example of mortuary meals, above, the context is what sets this corn apart from the other corn being processed, prepared, and eaten daily in these kitchens. Corn is a wonderful example of a food that carries multiple cultural meanings: it was at the heart of daily meals and at the same time (and perhaps because of its key role in daily cuisine) a particularly appropriate mortuary meal and a sacred household offering.

FIGURE 7.4. Burnt corn offering at Pedregal. (Robyn Cutright)

The case of corn reiterates again that there were often no clear distinctions between the kinds of foods used in sacred and secular contexts—except that the sacred context itself marked a distinction, a deepening of meaning, compared to quotidian meals. Much about the religious and spiritual lives of people in the past remains inaccessible to us in the present. Yet, because rituals are patterned, repetitive activities, they sometimes inscribe their traces in the archaeological record. As I have shown in this chapter, we can capture at least a hint of the deep links between food and the sacred in human prehistory.

8

DAILY BREAD

Everyday Meals, Gender, and Identity in the Past

About one thousand years ago, a small child died in the Lambayeque community of Farfán, on the Peruvian coast. The child was buried in a low mound at the foot of a rocky mountain at the edge of the community. Like other community members, the child's grave contained a cooking pot filled with food, covered by an inverted bowl. The child's burial was excavated by archaeologist Carol Mackey's team and the pots were brought to the lab for analysis; there I realized the plant remains inside looked strange.[1] The pot turned out to contain over nine hundred corn kernels that had been stripped of their tough outer skin, leaving only the soft starchy interior. This was a time-consuming way to prepare corn, and an unusual one. Other individuals had been buried with corn, but the kernels were whole, or left on the cob. A Peruvian colleague told me that today, rural mothers in the Andes might prepare corn in this way for children who are just beginning to eat solid food. Perhaps this was the last meal prepared by a mother for her toddler.

This find made me consider the ways in which food provides a window not just on sweeping processes of change but on the intimacies of daily life and the complicated workings of gender, family, and identity as they play out in households both past and present. Because as archaeologists we recover and analyze the material remains of the past in the present, we are privy to a physical connection to past lives. In this chapter, I show why it is so important to understand everyday life in the past and how archaeologists have used food as a window onto the intimate relationships and microscale dynamics of life in ancient houses and communities. I suggest that these relationships and dynamics are not only important in themselves but also in how they shed light on gender, power, and broader processes like conquest and ethnogenesis.

FIGURE 8.1. Map showing locations of key sites from chapter 8. 1 = San Francisco and Fort Ross, colonial northern California, United States; 2 = southwest United States; 3 = Maya Cerén, El Salvador; 4 = Spanish Caribbean; 5 = highland Ecuador; 6 = Late Intermediate Period Farfán and Ventanillas, Peru; 7 = New Kingdom Amarna, Egypt; 8 = Çatalhöyük and Hacinebi Tepe, Turkey. (Robyn Cutright)

EVERYDAY LIFE IN THE PAST

It is not always easy to see how regular individuals actually lived their lives in prehistory. Archaeologists deal with deep time, so we rarely view the past with the resolution of the human lifespan. For example, archaeologists divide the Archaic period in Kentucky into three subperiods, each several thousand years long.[2] Generations of individuals were born, lived full lives, and died during just the Middle Archaic period alone. So, while we know that the archaeological record was produced by humans living, throwing away trash, building houses and temples, and dying, it can be hard to know about any one individual's life.

For this reason, many archaeologists have focused instead on the big picture, the level of the society rather than the individual. Although this focus has shifted in recent decades, archaeologists have traditionally been interested in understanding the historical sequence of human occupation in a particular region, or the processes by which societies grow, change, or collapse—in other words, big questions about whole societies. Some would argue that one individual could have very little impact on these big processes, except maybe for important individuals like royals or elites whose decisions have the potential to determine the direction a society takes.

When archaeologists talk about specific individuals in the past, they often talk about kings and queens whose images and names were literally written in stone. A theoretical interest in elites as perceived decision makers and drivers of change has led to excavations of elite houses, which were often more durable and larger than those of the commoners. Until recently, archaeological conversations about the lives and meals of individuals in the past have been disproportionately influenced by the lives and meals of king and elites, even though they were always a minority in ancient societies.[3]

For similar reasons, discussions of food in the past often revolve around the meals of kings and wealthy elites (chapter 6), the role of food in rituals (chapter 7) and feasts (chapter 5), or the way food is caught up in broad processes of social change like the origins of agriculture (chapter 4). The social dynamics of daily meals in everyday households, and what they tell us about how gender, family, and identity are lived and negotiated, are much harder to see. However, this knowledge is essential to a full view of food in the past. This is a place where our own experience of life in the

FIGURE 8.2. Three kitchens: Pay Pay, Peru, in 2007 (*top*); Ventanillas, Peru, sometime between AD 1200 and 1400 (*center*); and Danville, Kentucky, United States, in 2019 (*bottom*). All these kitchens are sites of everyday life in their respective houses, despite their distance in space and time. The juxtaposition also highlights differences in the tools used, in the organization of space, in the dishes prepared, and the family units being cooked for. (Robyn Cutright)

kitchen most closely touches experiences of ancient people but also a site that informs us about what it meant to live in the foreign country of the past.[4] Figure 8.2 visually juxtaposes views of three kitchens, revealing connections and differences in lived experience.

Attention to nonelites, everyday life in households, and individual experience has become much more central to archaeological research since the 1980s. Archaeologist Cynthia Robin's book about ancient Maya farmers proclaims this perspective in its title: *Everyday Life Matters*.[5] Robin takes what she calls a "critical everyday life approach," which views everyday life as complex rather than mundane and mindless. It is the place where people shape and are shaped by their interactions with the world. Everyone, elites and commoners alike, people of all genders and ages, helps to shape everyday life in a community. While many archaeologists have focused on ancient houses to learn about everyday life, Robin believes that we should think about lived space more broadly as including all the spaces people make and use over their lifetimes. To accomplish this goal, her book describes excavations of outdoor spaces and fields as well as houses, as much of the everyday life of Maya farmers took place in these spaces.

Archaeologist Monica Smith's book, *A Prehistory of Ordinary People*, expresses a similar concern for the everyday decisions and experiences that shape the material record of the past.[6] She argues that we should look at how individuals in the past acted in deliberate ways and made choices. Change or lack of change in diet, technology, settlements, and social structure are the aggregate result of these choices. From this perspective, individual actions are actually what constitute society; society cannot be understood as separate from them.

After she introduces this perspective, Smith turns to food. She argues that food is a "particularly rich realm for understanding the relationship between creativity and habituation as activities that are interwoven through the process of multitasking."[7] This means that tradition and memory play an important role in cooking, but so does adaptation to the availability of ingredients and the specific circumstances of the family, the day, and the meal. Some of the big processes outlined in this book, such as broad spectrum shifts in foraging practices, the transition to farming, or conquest and cultural change, might be boiled down to a series of daily decisions made by cooks in hundreds of houses over thousands of years. Whether to brew beer or bake bread, hunt a wild goat or milk a tame one, make a tortilla or a tamal—these ordinary decisions and tasks are the basis of larger continuities or changes in a society.

FOOD TRADITIONS, FOOD REVOLUTIONS

Life in the town of Çatalhöyük was very stable. This early farming community in what is now Turkey was occupied between 7400 and 6200 BC. Houses were so tightly packed together at Çatalhöyük that you would have to walk across your neighbor's roof to get to your own home's rooftop door. It can be hard to get along with neighbors when everyone is so tightly packed together; conflict resolution can be even more difficult when there is no strong centralized authority to hand down rules and settle disputes, as seems to have been the case at Çatalhöyük. And the thousand years during which Çatalhöyük existed was a time of change. Farming was becoming more important even though most people still foraged widely through the landscape, and other technological innovations like pottery were spreading. How was Çatalhöyük able to maintain such a strong sense of continuity and stability in the face of such broad change and the potential for social tensions to disrupt community ties?

Members of the team that has excavated at Çatalhöyük since the early 1990s believe that everyday domestic activities such as cooking and cleaning played a role in this remarkable persistence.[8] The typical house at Çatalhöyük consisted of a central space where residents gathered around a hearth to cook, eat, and socialize, flanked by smaller rooms used as storage spaces. The central space also contained well-plastered platforms, under which family members were buried when they died, and religious altars and imagery. Houses lasted for a few generations and then were abandoned, reused, or rebuilt. Internal spaces were kept clean and well-maintained during the lifespan of the house, and the use of space within them was carefully patterned.

In general, domestic activities can reflect a sense of order and tradition, but they also help replicate and recreate that order through the generations. Cooking, of course, is a central domestic activity. Archaeologist Christine Hastorf believes that we can understand the cook's role in continuity and change in Catalhöyük households by looking at cooking and eating as foundational to the social life of the household.[9]

Hastorf's research shows that the diet of Çatalhöyük residents remained incredibly steady over the thousand-year life of the community. In contrast, diet in the United States has changed dramatically just over the past fifty years. Tortillas, sriracha, and organic apples are now available at any grocery store. Low-fat food was once popular, but now even bread can be low-carb. Americans ate 23 percent more calories a day in 2010 compared to 1970.[10] On the scale of centuries rather than decades, the American diet still looks fairly dynamic. In the early 1800s, the average adult man in the United States drank over seven gallons of pure alcohol a year (in 2010, the World Health Organization reported that the average American drank slightly less than 2.5 gallons)[11] and probably loved eel pie and turtle soup. From this perspective, the idea of a community maintaining a stable diet and cuisine for over a thousand years really is remarkable. More importantly, such continuity calls our attention to the social mechanisms that could have supported it and to the few changes that did occur.

At Çatalhöyük, remains of plants and animals, the organic residues left on pots and tools, and the bone isotopes of individuals buried under house floors tell us that people ate a healthy and varied diet.[12] Cavities and plaque on teeth tell us folks ate starchy food, and tooth wear tells us they ate nuts and grain that had not been finely ground into flour. People ate both wild foods (nuts, berries, tubers, hare, fish, and shellfish) and domesticated ones (wheat, barley, lentils, and goats). They stored food in their houses and processed it by drying, toasting, butchering, pounding, and fermenting it, inside the kitchen and up on the roof. In the early days of Çatalhöyük, people used clay to build ovens and made clay balls to drop into baskets or bags of liquids to boil them; only much later did they use this clay to make cooking pots. This shift, from clay balls to clay vessels, is probably one of the most profound changes in Çatalhöyük foodways.[13]

Çatalhöyük cooks, according to Hastorf and her team's many detailed individual research studies, used the central room of the house to bake bread, roast meat, toast grain, and boil porridge. Over time, cooks probably spent more time processing domesticated grains than before, and they adapted slowly to ceramic pots. To boil water without ceramic or metal vessels, cooks used flammable wooden bowls, leather bags, and baskets that cannot sit directly over the fire without burning. In order to boil liquids, cooks dropped hot objects into the liquid, which protected the perishable container from burning. Some cooks in the pre-Hispanic Americas used fracture-resistant rocks, while cooks at Çatalhöyük used clay balls. This process took time and constant tending, as clay balls had to be heated in the fire, dropped into the pot, and once they cooled fished out and replaced with hot ones.

The first ceramic pots appeared six hundred years into Çatalhöyük's occupation and were initially used to store grease. Toward the end of the community's life, people started putting pots over the fire, which archaeologists can discern from the pots' blackened exteriors. This shift perhaps allowed more multitasking on the part of the cook, as boiling food would not have required constant attention. This may have freed up labor or opened space for more elaborate meals with more different preparations. Also in these later chapters of life at Çatalhöyük, the oven moved out, away from the wall, toward the center of the main room, and pottery plates became more highly decorated. These changes would have drawn attention to the cook, the oven, and the presentation of food. The cook literally became more central to Çatalhöyük houses over time, presiding over the food as it cooked, in company with the ancestors and domestic ritual spaces.

Yet these changes are subtle. Hastorf thinks that food probably did not challenge the stability of the status quo. Instead, just like sweeping and re-plastering, it helped to habituate each new generation of Çatalhöyük residents to the set of cultural roles, rules, and expectations into which they had been born. Archaeologist Patricia Crown has argued that cuisine tends to be conservative and resist change, unless there are dramatic changes in the availability of resources such as ingredients, fuel, tools, or time.[14] As she tracked the cuisine of the ancient US Southwest from the earliest foragers to the period immediately before European contact, Crown only found a few moments where the cuisine fundamentally changed. First, the advent of farming brought in new plants and changed the way people made a living from the land. Once corn became the staple, the next culinary change derived from the need to balance labor, tools, and fuel. Over time, cooks were willing to put in more work grinding corn to save fuel. Women in the ancient US Southwest could easily spend over four hours a day grinding corn, but making cornmeal allowed them to toast tortillas quickly rather than boiling porridge or stew for hours. Crown interprets this shift as cooks making a trade-off, spending more time at the daily grind to reduce demands on other resources like fuel which they perceived as more limited.

Thinking about cuisine as shaped by economic trade-offs to conserve resources that cooks perceive as more limited, at the expense of other resources that seem more abundant, offers a lens through which to understand contemporary cooking in the United States. Over the past century, home cooks have seen dozens of innovations aimed at reducing labor and time in the kitchen. Obvious examples include microwaves, fast food, frozen dinners, meal delivery services, and little plastic containers of prechopped onions, peppers, and butternut squash in the grocery store produce section. These strategies, along with a shift in expectations regarding food preparation, have in fact saved time in the kitchen. According to food writer Michael Pollan, American cooks today spend an average of twenty-seven minutes a day preparing food, about half as long as in the mid-1960s.[15] This change responds to real shifts in US economic and social structure, such as the increasing need for dual incomes in middle-class households, increasing instability and a fraying social safety net for those living in poverty, and broader opportunities for women in professional careers as well as cultural shifts in expectations of leisure and entertainment.

If these cooks perceive time as the resource that needs to be conserved, what are they willing to trade off? The examples above suggest that they are willing to accept more packaging, more industrial processing, and longer-distance transportation in exchange for reducing prep time. Following Crown's analysis, it may be that cooks in the United States do not perceive these resources (fossil fuels, plastics, industrial production) as limited in the same way they perceive that their busy schedules affect the amount of time they have to prepare dinner, even though in fact these resources are nonrenewable and have a huge environmental impact. Such calculus has helped shift American cuisine, and Crown's analysis would suggest that it should not shift again unless cooks' perceptions of resource scarcity change.

WHO COOKS?

Christine Hastorf ultimately concludes that at Çatalhöyük, the cook played a central role in domestic activities, and thus in the life of the community. Based on evidence from the bodies of the individuals buried at Çatalhöyük, she thinks that older individuals spent a lot of time around the hearth, and that they may have been the ones in charge of preparing food.[16] Figuring out who cooked, and what the place of the cook was, is not an easy task for archaeologists. So how do we know who cooked in ancient kitchens?

One way to answer this question is to use analogies to societies that we can observe through anecdotes and specific case studies. Another way is to use cross-cultural research.[17] Cross-cultural databases such as the Human Resources Area Files gather together reports visiting anthropologists compile on societies around the world. By pulling together information on how different tasks were assigned by gender in these societies, cross-cultural researchers can try to find patterns. It turns out that cooking daily meals is almost always done by women, along with tasks like childcare and gathering water and fuel.[18] This means that in the absence of other evidence, the safest guess is that women were in charge of cooking daily meals in past societies, just as in the present ones in the sample.

Of course, tasks that are culturally associated with one gender might actually be carried out by an individual of another gender when circumstances demand. Among !Kung foragers of the Kalahari desert, hunting is gendered

male. Men make arrows and track and kill animals. However, a famous ethnographic description of the !Kung mentions that women and even young
girls kill small or vulnerable animals when they come across them.[19] Likewise, men cook on hunting trips even though women are the cooks at home.
Cultural ideals can be fairly fluid in practice, and gender categories are not
fixed, either. Though *man* and *woman* are the most common gender categories, many societies have three, four, or even five genders, all with different
roles and symbolic associations.

Still, an assumption that women tend to be the everyday cooks in most
societies is probably not a bad one. We can support this assumption with
additional evidence when it is available. For example, Hastorf looked at skeletal evidence to see which groups at Çatalhöyük spent more time around
the hearth. Researchers in the US Southwest find evidence of wear and tear
on women's backs, knees, and shoulders associated with corn processing.[20]
Kneeling at bins pushing heavy grinding stones back and forth for hours
a day took a distinctive toll on women's bodies; this wear helps us identify
women's labor in this society.

Images and texts can also help us identify how different tasks were gendered in the past. Aztec books depict girls being trained to grind corn and
make tortillas, surrounded by kitchen equipment.[21] A letter explaining Inca
society in words and images to the Spanish king shows women spinning
and weaving at key stages of the life cycle.[22] Ancient Egyptian texts mention
that women were active in conducting business and administering households.[23] All these lines of evidence tell us that, while women were probably
not the only cooks, they took primary responsibility for preparing the daily
bread (or tortillas) in many past societies.

If women did the bulk of the food preparation, what was the place of the
cook? How was this task embedded in gendered relationships within households, as well as in the broader society? We might think of cooking from
scratch, every day, using fuel and water you physically carry to the kitchen,
as degrading drudgery—but was it? Hastorf has already suggested that Çatalhöyük cooks wielded a sort of central authority or at least a central role.
Other observers have also highlighted the way that power and approval (or
disapproval) can be expressed through cooking.

Anthropologist Mary Weismantel studied the role of food in the ways rural Ecuadorians thought about themselves and the world in the 1980s.[24] In
the homes she studied, serving and preparing food was the duty of women
in a gender system in which men and women had complementary roles
and obligations. Meals often consisted of a stew with large chunks of meat,

potatoes, corn on the cob, or other ingredients. The senior woman in the house served the household and guests in order of status by selecting the appropriate pieces for them. This allowed her to signal status or approval by picking the best piece of meat or of course to signal the opposite.

Weismantel tells a story from her fieldwork that illustrates how women used their power as cooks to express themselves. A young wife was living with her husband in his parents' household. They went out to the village festival, but the husband abandoned her to get drunk with his friends. Getting drunk at festivals was within the scope of acceptable male behavior, and so even though she was furious, as a junior woman in her in-laws' house she did not feel free to express it. She would have been out of bounds to complain too loudly about something men just did from time to time.

He arrived home late and drunk. Early that morning, she got up to make him breakfast. Perfectly embodying the traditional role of woman and wife, she prepared him a large, rich, spicy soup and served him a heaping bowl, which he regarded with bleary hungover panic. Having been served by his dutiful wife, his complementary duty now was to eat what she served, and he could not. Now he had committed a foul, and she had every right to complain, and she did so loudly, channeling her frustration from the night before. His parents watched the scene unfold, amused at his predicament. The young wife had used her traditional role as cook to express her hurt feelings and shame her husband for his behavior the night before. The role of the cook gave her subtle and situationally limited, but real, social power.

Of course, this one story does not mean that things always ran smoothly in the kitchen, only that we should not assume that the role of the cook was always subservient. Cooking is often wrapped up in gender roles and relationships within families and communities. This means that when we look at the archaeological remains of food preparation and serving, we might be able to read something of these relationships.

Archaeologist Joan Gero has studied the role of women in different parts of the Andes, and her work provides a glimpse inside the kitchens of a site called Yutopian, in present-day Argentina.[25] Along with archaeologist Cristina Scattolin, Gero documents how Yutopian families organized their living space. Rather than making a strict distinction between the hearth where daily meals were prepared and the hearth where copper was heated to make tools, families allowed these tasks to overlap. Given that cooking is usually gendered female and metalworking is usually a male activity, this means that men's and women's spheres spatially overlapped in the households that made metal tools (which tended to be the wealthier households). At the same time, grinding stones clustered together. This means that women from different households might have gathered to grind corn together. Daily chores provided opportunities for people in the community to cooperate across genders and families.

This was also true in the ancient Maya community of Cerén, where women were visible to each other while working at their grinding stones, and in pueblos in the US Southwest, where women set up production lines of mealing bins to bring corn from a coarse grind to a fine meal. These examples show that domestic tasks probably provided an opportunity for ancient women to gather, socialize, gossip, and commiserate in a way that our own domestic labor in the United States often does not. Many cooks toil away in individual houses, out of sight of neighbors, and cooking and cleaning can become isolating drudgery. While grinding corn by hand was far from easy, the spatial organization of ancient kitchens tells us that women did not necessarily undertake it alone.

Kitchens were places where women made connections to other women in the community and to family members of all genders and ages. At the village of Cerén, which was quickly abandoned during a volcanic eruption and preserved intact like a Central American version of Pompeii, women worked together around five grinding stones, or metates, clustered together in one structure.[26] Archaeologist Tracy Sweely argues that this structure was used to prepare food for some sort of community social organization, since a single household probably would not need five identical grinding stones. Women from different generations and families may have sat together discussing family and community dynamics and sharing religious or practical knowledge as they prepared corn. However, women seated at the metates would not all have been able to see each other as they worked. Only one grinding stone was positioned where the user could see all the others—so was one woman directing or supervising the others? Grinding corn could have been an opportunity for solidarity and connection, but at the same time it was shaped by hierarchical power relations.

Cerén's quick abandonment and preservation gives archaeologists a chance to reconstruct what they call "taskscapes," the spaces created by the arrays of interlocking domestic tasks that took place in households.[27] Sophisticated spatial analysis shows archaeologists how grinding stones served as culinary stations, with tools and small jars arrayed within arm's length of the person working at the metate. (Figure 8.3 offers a contemporary example of a culinary station.) Next to one of these culinary stations, researchers found the remains of a duck that had been tied by one foot to the central post of the house. Whether it was a pet or waiting for the pot, the duck was well taken care of, provided with a bowl of corn and a water bowl within easy reach. These findings remind us that ancient kitchens were vibrant spaces at the center of household and community social landscapes.

In the community of Amarna, a workers' village in New Kingdom Egypt, families were supplied with rations of grain as payment for their labor.[28] Bread and beer were essential, intertwined foods in ancient Egypt. Everyone

FIGURE 8.3. Contemporary Maya example of a culinary station that includes a metate, or grinding stone, and a griddle that holds tortillas and tomatoes (*above*), and collaborative kitchen work (*below*) at a community display for the Day of the Dead near Mérida, Yucatán, Mexico, 2013. (Robyn Cutright)

ate bread, but we need to look more carefully inside Amarna houses to understand the social interactions that occurred as bread was prepared and consumed. Stone mortars had to be used to remove the husks from the emmer wheat grains as they were milled into flour with stone querns. Bread was made from this flour mixed with water and baked in cylindrical ovens. Archaeologists can identify where bread was produced by looking for the mortars, querns, and ovens used in the process.

Most households in Amarna had the tools to make flour. Fewer had a mortar to dehusk the grains first, but the ones that lacked a mortar had access to grinding facilities in nearby streets. It might be that some households could not afford grinding stones, or that some households were linked through family relationships to households with grinding facilities and chose to make this work communal. Only half the households had ovens, but it is likely that ovens were located on the roofs where they would be harder for archaeologists to identify. This would be a smart choice to avoid heating the whole house while cooking bread. Most families could probably bake their own bread, but the various steps in flour and bread preparation would have been somewhat communal for Amarna residents.

Daily kitchen work helped to define and reproduce relationships within the family, community relationships, and even the relationship between the family and the state. In some cases, kitchen life was even what defined the family. In the Ecuadorian communities Mary Weismantel studied, newly married couples might build a separate dwelling space adjacent to the home of the husband's parents, but this space probably would not contain a kitchen. Instead, the couple would eat in the kitchen of the husband's mother and his larger extended family. The new wife would need to wake up early and dart through the predawn darkness to get the fire going and start breakfast. Not until the new family was fully established, perhaps with children of its own, would it have enough significance to establish a kitchen of its own.

GENDER AND ETHNICITY IN THE KITCHEN

Some of my favorite examples of ancient kitchen dynamics come from studies focused on how ethnicity and identity were expressed through daily meals. Ethnicity has a powerful impact on what we eat. An ethnic group defines itself based on a shared history and origin story. Ethnicity is not always or only assigned by others; it is often a way in which people identify themselves with a shared history and tradition. It is not necessarily stable and fixed, but rather embodied through practice and material culture: language, holidays, clothing, and food.

The city of Milwaukee, Wisconsin, has a large festival ground on the shore of Lake Michigan. The different ethnic groups that played a role in building Milwaukee each host their own yearly festival. Irish Fest, German Fest, Festa Italiana; festivals for Native Americans, Mexican Americans, African Americans, and Polish Americans alternate through the summer. Each festival has traditional music, art, souvenirs, and most of all food, from fry bread tacos to bratwurst. Food is one of the ways ethnic groups present themselves to the broader community and celebrate their identity and heritage in contemporary Milwaukee. It is also a way in which identity is negotiated and debated—who decides which foods come to represent an authentic expression of ethnic identity? Some version of these public dynamics probably occurred in past societies as well. For instance, archaeologists have theorized that decorations on serving vessels helped to express identity and affiliation at past feasts.[29]

But the food we cook in our own kitchens also celebrates ethnic identity and heritage, albeit in less publicly visible ways. The food we eat, the pots and pans we use to cook, and the way we eat our meals reflect our multilayered identities in ways that are not necessarily consciously thought through and put on display. They reflect our view of comfort food cooked in a way that is appropriate and proper. What we consider to be appropriate or comfortable is shaped by our culture and our family history.

Pierre Bourdieu was an influential French sociologist who was interested in how we negotiate our daily lives through patterns and routines.[30] He argued that as people move through their houses and communities, they unconsciously learn what is proper and what is not. Part of this learning takes place through observation, and part takes place through physical, bodily movement through the environment. By following these learned patterns, members of a society reinforce them and replicate them for future generations. This means that aspects of daily life do not necessarily need to be consciously thought out to be perpetuated.

One example of this kind of patterned behavior is the classroom. When students walk into a classroom at the beginning of the semester, they automatically move toward the chairs or desks facing the board. The professor enters and automatically occupies the podium in the front of the room. Professors and students are so well socialized into the built landscape of the college that it never occurs to them to do otherwise. And yet, this behavior also encodes a specific hierarchical relationship between the students (seated in identical chairs, facing toward the board) and the professor (standing alone at the board, facing the students). Professors and students replicate and re-affirm this relationship by moving into their places unconsciously, without question.

The kind of embodied habits learned through socialization and repli-cated in daily practice without too much thought play a large part in struc-turing society, according to Bourdieu's theory. When archaeologists look at the past, we need to pay attention not just to what people display in public, but also to the different aspects of identity that shape how people cook daily meals for themselves, the patterns of habit they unconsciously repeat with-out question. This is exactly what archaeologist Gil Stein did to understand who was living in one particular neighborhood at Hacinebi Tepe.[31]

Hacinebi was part of the earliest colonial expansion in the world. Around 3700 BC, the Uruk civilization in southern Mesopotamia created a network that linked trading partners in modern-day Turkey, Iran, and Syria with cit-ies in what is today southern Iraq. Uruk presence is visible to archaeologists in the form of trading posts and enclaves throughout this region, and this presence is relatively easy to identify through characteristic artifacts, archi-tecture, and administrative technology such as seals that marked owner-ship. It is much harder to know whether Uruk expansion was supported through colonial imposition or through alliance. This was Stein's question regarding a specific Uruk enclave at the site of Hacinebi, in the Euphrates Valley of Turkey.

At Hacinebi, a small Uruk trading enclave was built within an existing lo-cal Anatolian settlement at the intersection of two important trading routes. The presence of a wide range of Uruk artifacts in one sector of the settle-ment indicates sustained Uruk habitation, rather than just local access to Uruk-style trade goods. But who were these Uruk inhabitants? Were they colonial administrators dominating the local community in order to con-trol the trade routes? Stein doubts it. Instead, he sees the long-lived enclave as evidence for peaceful economic interaction and fairly symmetrical polit-ical relations.

There is no evidence of systemic physical violence or fortifications that might signal a tense, defensive orientation. The Uruk community persisted and maintained a clear identity for several centuries, indicating that in-habitants continued to be in contact with faraway Uruk cities to the south. The enclave also managed to maintain a peaceful relationship with the lo-cal community, and Stein believes that multiethnic or intercultural house-holds helped to preserve Uruk identity and maintain peaceful local ties.

Specifically, he believes that Uruk men set up households with local women throughout the life of the enclave.

To identify intercultural households, Stein compares different aspects of food preparation and serving between the Uruk enclave and the local Anatolian community. Ceramics used for serving and storage tend to belong to the local style in the local Anatolian neighborhoods, but to Uruk styles in the Uruk enclave. This suggests that Uruk enclave households were displaying their affiliation with southern Mesopotamian cities when they served meals. Animals were also butchered differently in local and Uruk parts of the community. Animal bones found in the Uruk enclave display butchering patterns more similar to those of southern Mesopotamia. Since butchering animals was a male-dominated activity, Stein believes that this pattern is evidence for the presence of Uruk men in the neighborhood. However, local cooking pots predominated not only in the local parts of the community but also in the Uruk enclave. To Stein, this shows that local women were cooking in these households, using familiar vessels to prepare daily meals.

Both butchering and cooking are highly influenced by cultural understandings of what is considered normal, appropriate, and proper, and so they likely reflect identity and socialization. The mix of gendered patterns at Hacinebi seems to indicate intercultural households made up of Uruk men and local women. The use of Uruk-style pottery to serve meals indicates that these intercultural households probably wanted others to consider them to be Uruk. It seems that forging local alliances through marriage, while at the same time presenting a foreign Uruk identity, was a key strategy in the Uruk expansion. Stein's work at Hacinebi Tepe suggests that state expansion and the incorporation of provinces into colonial networks could be carried out within households, through intimate intercultural relationships between husbands and wives.

Colonial communities were often places where culinary and cultural systems came into contact, and intercultural households like those Stein identifies could serve as a tool of colonial expansion. Historical archaeologist Kathleen Deagan developed an influential model of these households based on her work in early Spanish colonies in the Americas.[32] While the earliest Spanish colonial communities in the Caribbean never adapted to local foodways, later colonists stopped producing European pottery styles and began to use locally made pots, native foods, and indigenous cooking techniques. Deagan attributes the persistence of local indigenous foodways to the agency of indigenous women present in colonial households as wives and servants.[33] In this model, intercultural, gendered interactions in multiethnic households and communities were central in forging a new, syncretic Spanish American culture.

Similarly, archaeologist Kent Lightfoot and his team identify a multiethnic community consisting of Russian colonists, Native Alaskan hunters, and local women at a fur trading outpost in northern California.[34] Like Stein, Lightfoot and colleagues use ethnic patterns and gendered tasks to look inside households. Animals were butchered using Alaskan techniques, but households were kept and food was prepared according to a local pattern by Native Californian women. In these three cases, intercultural households served as microscale stages for gendered dynamics of colonialism, ethnogenesis, and local women's agency.

Archaeologist Barbara Voss is critical of this household approach to colonialization.[35] By emphasizing colonial encounters that play out in intimate domestic settings, Voss believes, archaeologists underplay the brutality of colonialization. In fact, many encounters between locals and colonists were coerced and unequal in contexts other than marriage that limited the ways in which local people could act. By emphasizing intercultural households made up of local women and foreign men, Voss argues, traditional approaches often view the past through a heteronormative lens. Voss's work in colonial San Francisco shows that colonial policies were directed explicitly toward controlling and stigmatizing local expressions of sexuality and gender identity. While a focus on interethnic households might grant active agency to native women, Voss believes it does a disservice to them by limiting this agency to heterosexual household contexts in which relationships might be assumed to be consensual. In her words, this approach "domesticates" colonialism.

Voss thinks that a more useful approach to these colonial contexts emphasizes social diversity within both colonizers and colonized, rather than relying on a gendered colonizer/colonized dichotomy.[36] During her archaeological research at the earliest Spanish colonial community in San Francisco, Voss uncovered a midden of household trash accumulated during the first few decades of the settlement.[37] This trash, which included plant and animal remains and broken pottery, was relatively homogeneous. Everyone in the community, which records indicate included people of Spanish, African, indigenous, and mixed descent, ate a similar diet cooked in similar plain vessels. They preferred stews to the tortillas cooked on griddles historically assumed to be the cornerstone of Spanish colonial diet in North America. They also eschewed typically indigenous food preparation tools like grinding stones. In short, household culinary practice in the early days of the settlement minimized internal racial or cultural differences within the community but also avoided culinary practices associated with local Native Californian cooks. Voss argues that, in this case, domestic culinary practice helped to forge a shared Californian identity that both repudiated racialized hierarchies and marginalized local native people.[38]

It is hard to know how coercion, violence, practicality, and fondness might have played out in these ancient intercultural households and communities. It is clear, however, that colonial expansion brought into contact people with different understandings of how to cook, clean, and live in communities. In my research at Ventanillas, in the foothills of the Peruvian Andes, I am especially interested in how conquest and cultural identity played out through daily household life.[39]

Ventanillas became a prominent community about one thousand years ago, a time of transition for what is now coastal Peru. The complex Moche society, with its ceremonial centers of elaborately painted pyramids, royal burials dripping with gold, and human sacrifice ceremonies, had collapsed a century and a half before. The Lambayeque people who followed the Moche in the Jequetepeque Valley now looked north for influence, to an emerging regional power called Sicán. Archaeologists do not agree whether the Sicán state actually conquered the Jequetepeque Valley or whether they drew neighboring regions in through economic alliance or the power of a new religious cult that emerged at Sicán. People in the Jequetepeque put Sicán-style pots in their burials and built architecture that was inspired by, but did not exactly copy, Sicán architecture.[40]

People built Sicán-style architecture at Ventanillas as well. In fact, the three pyramids at Ventanillas look more like northern architecture than architecture elsewhere in the valley. Ventanillas occupies a key strategic location in the valley. The Andean coast is a narrow strip of desert punctuated by short rivers that flow down out of the mountains into the Pacific. Because it rarely rains on the coast outside of catastrophic, periodic El Niño events, farmers rely on irrigation canals to draw water from the river to their fields. Ventanillas is located near key canal intakes, which means it had strategic importance for those living farther down the valley.

Ventanillas lies in the middle valley foothills, where the coast transitions to the highlands, and the character of the landscape and the climate shift noticeably. Today and in the past, people make a distinction between coastal and highland populations. In the past, coastal and highland people spoke different languages, ate different food, made different pottery, did their hair differently, and were referred to differently by the Inca as they described their empire to the Spanish. These practices are all classic expressions of ethnic identity, which means that people on the coast probably understood themselves as ethnically and culturally different from those in the highlands. Where does that leave people in the middle valley, like the population of Ventanillas?

When I started to work at Ventanillas, the coastal-style pyramids made me think that Ventanillas must have been a coastal outpost on the frontier between coast and highlands. I wondered whether coastal presence was imposed, through conquest and control by coastal elites, or whether people at Ventanillas considered themselves to be coastal or perhaps reached out consciously to ally themselves with the powerful Sicán to the north and the coast in general. I also wondered what happened to Ventanillas when the Chimú conquered the valley in the early 1300s.

After testing living areas as well as public areas, I have found evidence that the Chimú were present at Ventanillas, but it does not look like they transformed it into one of their administrative centers. The pyramids are clearly inspired by northern Sicán or Lambayeque traditions, and people often changed and remodeled the configuration of the public architecture at the foot of the pyramids. But the interesting story really comes from the houses and the insights they offer into how people at Ventanillas understood themselves as middle valley residents in relation to coastal states like Lambayeque and Chimú. Were Ventanillas residents coastal folks living on the edge of a coastal state, in a border town that staked out control over canal intakes? Were they local middle valley people who had been forcibly, coercively, or enthusiastically incorporated into coastal states? Did coastal people take over, or establish an enclave of wealthy coastal elites who lorded it over local or highland populations? These questions boil down to questions of identity and ethnicity.

One potential answer lies in the same kinds of domestic culinary practices archaeologists have used to understand colonial San Francisco and Uruk Hacinebi. What kind of cooking pots did they use, what was in those pots, and what does this tell us about who they were?

Research shows that they used different kinds of pots. Based on my previous work on the coast, just a few kilometers from the Pacific at a site that dated to the same time period, I can identify the coastal versions of the standard Andean kitchen set. The set included round-bottomed cooking pots, or ollas; narrower-necked jars; open bowls and plates; and large, thick-walled urns to store water or ferment *chicha*. While I was digging at the coastal village of Pedregal, before I began my project at Ventanillas, my colleague

Howard Tsai was excavating the site just east of Ventanillas. This turned out to be a community with a very different set of jars, plates, bowls, and storage urns, one that looked much more middle valley and even highland in affiliation.[41] Thus I could compare what I found at Ventanillas to these two sites to determine which culinary set Ventanillas cooks chose to use.

I found a mix (figure 8.4). In most contexts where people discarded fragments of broken vessels, I found both coastal and middle valley cookware. Some cooking pots even looked very much like those that people all the way up in the highlands used. I found the same thing when it came to fancy serving ware: some coastal bottles, some middle valley red and white painted bowls. I saw no distinctive pattern—no shift through time from middle valley to coastal, no spatial distinction in which some neighborhoods used coastal cookware and others middle valley or highland. It looked like Ventanillas cooks were drawing from a mix of traditions.[42]

When I examined the food, I found that everyone was eating local products like corn and fruit as well as seafood from the coast (unfortunately, few foods that only came from the highlands). Some households placed more emphasis on seafood than others, though, so it looks like access to coastal foods came through family ties or individual connections rather than standardized provisioning of the whole community.

Currently, the view from the kitchen at Ventanillas does not support colonial imposition of a coastal enclave or colonial coastal overlords placed to control the middle valley. It does not look like middle valley and coastal

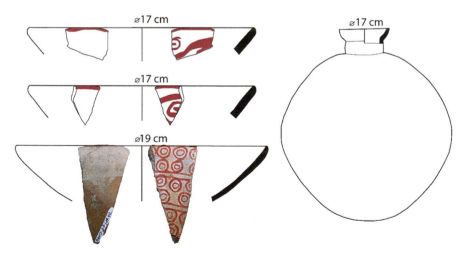

FIGURE 8.4. Middle valley painted bowls (*left*) and a coastal cooking pot (*right*) from Ventanillas. (Robyn Cutright)

elements were patterned by gender, though my colleague Carlos Osores and I are still looking at the animal bones for a pattern like that at Fort Ross and Hacinebi Tepe. Instead, it seems that Ventanillas families drew from both coastal and middle valley traditions, maybe eating something like an intercultural or hybrid cuisine. This could resonate with Voss's case, in which colonial households emphasized a newly forged shared identity. Yet Ventanillas residents built classically coastal pyramids, which may speak to an alliance with the powerful coastal state and probably cooperation in administering the canals. In this case, the process of coastal state expansion and governance was less one-sided, maybe less imposed, and certainly more multicultural and multiethnic than we might have thought.

This, in the end, is why I like to peer into the kitchen. It gives me a glimpse of how real people worked through regional alliances and conquests in the context of everyday decisions and interactions. I can get a little closer to how Ventanillas cooks thought of themselves and how that shaped their interaction with the state. I can imagine southern Mesopotamian diplomacy playing out at the tables of Uruk men and local Anatolian women. I can relate to women of the pre-Hispanic US Southwest making choices, sacrificing time to conserve fuel and feed their families.

As I imagine these scenes, though, I must remember that my choices and constraints, my experiences, and my worldview represent a starkly different way of living in and understanding the world compared to those of these past men and women. My own experiences can never tell me everything, or even very much at all, about these ancient lives. To imagine that I can, risks flattening the very real cultural differences that separate us. Yet, at the same time, I think this feeling of connectedness with the past is important. I believe that a powerful part of our shared identity as humans resides here, in the everyday, microscale domesticity I have described in this chapter.

CONCLUSION

We Are What We Ate

The goal of this book has been to show some of the ways that food has shaped us as humans and how what we eat has been shaped by culture and social structure through our long history as a species. Anthropologists study how biology and culture intertwine to make us human; as this book has shown, food connects us to and helps us understand both our biological and our cultural heritage. Food is "good to think,"[1] especially for anthropologists.

This book's survey of the role of food over the last four million or so years of human prehistory has revealed several themes. The first is that humans are the product of our specific evolutionary trajectory, molded by particular nutritional requirements, dietary constraints, and environmental conditions. Evolutionarily speaking, humans are omnivores and generalists. Like our primate relatives and our hominin ancestors, our teeth give us a varied, Swiss Army knife–style tool kit that can tear meat, grind grain, or crunch potato chips. Over millions of years, our shrinking guts and growing brains required (and were made possible by) low-bulk, high-quality foods such as meat and cooked tubers. We evolved a taste for the concentrated fats and sugars that were rare in ancient hominin habitats. A flexible generalist human diet proved a successful adaptation to fluctuating Pleistocene climates and a range that eventually expanded to encompass six continents. The legacy of natural selection for a flexible diet can be seen in the wide range of human diets today around the world. As long as basic needs are met, humans can thrive on everything from a vegan diet to one high in animal protein and fat.

Our generalist, omnivore legacy means that we must learn what is good to eat. Like other omnivores, we devote brainpower to learning what to eat and to keeping track of positive or negative consequences associated with particular foods. We are curious about but also suspicious of new foods. Much more than other omnivores, humans rely on culture to determine what is food and how to eat. This brings us to the second key theme of the book: humans are cultural eaters.

Culture transforms *diet* to *cuisine*. It embeds food within a web of social meaning. It also dictates technologies and practices that transform plants and animals into edible and nutritious food. From the perspective of some anthropologists, culture helps societies adapt to their environments. As in the case of the Tsembaga of Papua New Guinea, culinary rules about what to eat and when to eat it might help regulate a society's relationship with the natural environment. Food traditions such as fermentation can make otherwise hard-to-digest foods edible. Culture and cuisine have helped humans adapt to a broad range of ecosystems and subsistence systems, as we have seen in the case studies throughout this book. Cultural systems such as gender provide frameworks for the division of labor, which allows different members of the group to develop expertise in complementary skills. Human societies are, from this perspective, efficient networks of diverse specialists.

I argue, however, that cuisine is more than an adaptive mechanism. Cuisine is intensely social and imbued with meanings beyond the need to fill our bellies. Unlike strict cultural ecologists, I do not believe that these meanings serve only to ensure adaptive behavior. In this book, we have seen examples of ritual meals, political meals, and everyday meals at which dynamics such as gender, ethnicity, and identity are negotiated. Cuisine is shaped by class, by conquest and oppression, by imperial expansion, and by political strategies, so we need to bring these dynamics to the table too, in our analysis of food and culture. Culture transforms food into cuisine, but cuisine provides a window onto how we transform ourselves.

This is the third theme of this book—the story of how archaeologists and those in related disciplines have used food to understand the human past and what it means to be human at all. Archaeology, like any academic discipline, is a product of the society that performs it. We have seen how archaeological questions shifted as society changed. For instance, early models placed meat, men's hunting, and human dominance over the ecosystem at the heart of human evolution. More recently, archaeologists have reexamined assumptions about gender roles that lie at the heart of these models and emphasized the role of grandmothers, tubers, and human response to climate change in the same evolutionary story. Just as the stories archaeologists tell about the past reflect our own social organization, they also reflect the rapid pace of technological change. Much of the evidence reviewed in this book, such as ancient DNA, stable bone isotopes, phytoliths, and radiocarbon dates, has only been available for the last few decades. New advances are constantly increasing the resolution and confidence of our reconstructions of the past, and raising new questions.

So far, I have emphasized what we share as humans, and how we are similar to our hominin ancestors. But clearly what we eat today, and how we eat it, differs in significant ways from what most humans ate ten thousand years ago. Most people today eat a diet that is highly processed, rich in calories (though not necessarily nutrients), and global in scope compared to what people ate in the past. In many ways, though, we can understand our current food system as an intensification of trends that trace back to the origins of agriculture, or even further back in some cases.

Ten thousand years ago, some foragers in different parts of the world were "messing around" with plants and animals in ways that, intentionally or not, set them on the path toward agriculture. They began to modify some plant and animal species by selecting for desired characteristics, and this began a process of coevolution and codependence between humans, plants, and animals that has increasingly structured our world. Far from its humble roots as teosinte, corn has become a dominant global plant; in 2016–17, the world produced forty billion bushels of corn.[2] Even more striking are the calculations of one researcher that wild terrestrial animals now make up less than 3 percent of all terrestrial animal biomass. The rest is humans and domesticated animals, mostly cattle.[3] The species *Zea mays* (corn) and *Bos taurus* (cows) have become extremely successful because of their relationship with humans. In doing so, they have also become dependent on humans. Most corn grown today belongs to hybrid varieties that would not survive without human propagation. And humans, in turn, are dependent on these species and a few other domesticated staples. It would be impossible to support the current global population without highly productive crops. Returning to a Paleo diet is possible for only a few people, mostly those rich enough to afford a diet of unprocessed meat, produce, and nuts.

Alongside this codependence with a few domesticated plants and animals goes the ever-increasing modification of the landscape. Humans engage in niche construction, which means that we adapt in part by modifying our environment to better meet our needs; this modified environment then becomes the context for future natural selection. Culture is an extremely powerful force in modifying the conditions under which selection takes place. We humans have been modifying our environments for at least as long as we have been cultural beings.[4] Ancient civilizations such as the Inca invested the labor of thousands of people and used sophisticated knowledge of engineering to terrace, irrigate, and enrich their limited farmland (figure

C.1) in an empire-wide intensive modification of the landscape. Irrigation systems, fertilizer, pesticides, huge fields planted in just one crop, and genetic manipulation through both breeding and biochemistry have reshaped our global landscape along with the plants and animals we eat. Today, almost every meal reaches into multiple ecosystems across the world, a trend that began as foragers in many parts of the world focused on a broader spectrum of plants and animals after the last Ice Age.[5]

As dependence on a few staples increased, diet in many early farming societies narrowed. While agriculture had the potential to produce a surplus, it also left communities vulnerable to failed crops, shortfalls, and diseases related to sedentism and crowding. Hunger is still a global concern, though today it stems mostly from failures in food distribution rather than food production. The opposite problem, too much food, is also causing health problems in much of the developed world. While it might seem that we eat a wide variety of foods here in the United States, much of the processed food we eat is made from a few staples like corn and soy, fed to animals and processed into many unrecognizable forms.[6]

Domesticated plants and animals are subject to intensification. That is, humans can either select for more productive varieties, or develop technology

FIGURE C.1. Inca agricultural landscape near Pisac, Peru. (Robyn Cutright)

such as fertilizer, mechanized plows, and feedlot systems to cultivate plants and raise animals more efficiently at higher yields. Intensification itself has driven a few trends that continue to shape our lives today. First, intensive agriculture can support much larger populations on the same land compared to foraging. Global populations have grown dramatically, from perhaps fewer than twenty million people five thousand years ago to somewhere around seven billion people today (figure C.2). Agricultural production has, at least so far, kept pace with this growth through selection and genetic modification for productivity and disease resistance, technology, and increased inputs of fertilizer and pesticide. Another factor in human modification of the landscape is population; cities along with fields and farms have reshaped the earth's surface. Cities were first made possible by agricultural surpluses, and now for the first time in earth's history more people live in cities than in the countryside.

Agricultural intensification also allows some people to produce enough food to feed everyone. In foraging societies and the first farming communities, everyone had to be involved in gathering or producing food. As the potential for surplus increased along with the productivity of crops and innovations in agricultural technology, some people could specialize in

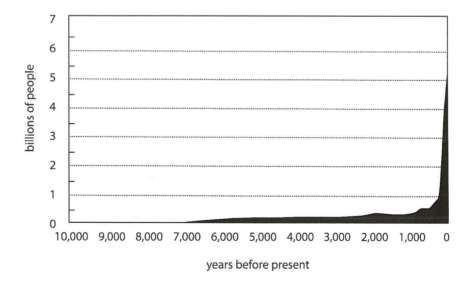

FIGURE C.2. World population from 10,000 years ago until present. (Redrawn and modified from "Key Theme 1: Patterns of Population," World History for Us All, accessed July 10, 2017, http://worldhistoryforusall.ss.ucla.edu/themes/keytheme1.htm, Robyn Cutright)

other occupations; not everyone had to be a farmer. The US economy has taken that trend to an extreme: in 2016, 1.6 percent of employed Americans worked in agriculture.[7] Most Americans today work in occupations that have little direct connection to producing food. Along with a diverse, specialized economy comes socioeconomic and political inequality, which can also be traced back to the early days of agriculture.

Even though our global, technologically sophisticated, large-scale food system might seem unprecedented, its roots can be found in the earliest farming societies ten thousand years ago, and even before. One way to better understand our present society is to look at the forces and trends that have shaped it over time and to ask how it is different from, and yet related to, past societies. This is one of the reasons that I study food in the past—to better understand my own experience and our present global system.

Another reason that I study food is to connect with the past, not just intellectually but in a real gut sense. When I teach the Paleokitchen course that inspired this book, I bring food to class. Students try roasted tubers during the unit on *Homo erectus*, test their knowledge of ancient grains during the section on domestication, eat ferments like yogurt, miso, and kimchi, and experiment with the Paleo diet. While the past is, indeed, a foreign country,[8] food can provide a bridge to the past just as it helps us experience and connect with different cultures today.

Many of the case studies in this book are a product of this growing archaeological attention to food, which has begun to move beyond fancy feasts and elite cuisine to look at the way that food reflects and engages with the everyday experiences of men, women, and children in the past. Ultimately, this research emphasizes the diverse experiences of being human, across cultures and through time. It also helps us understand in greater detail what we share and what it means to be human.

NOTES

Introduction

1. Amanda G. Henry, Alison S. Brooks, and Dolores R. Piperno, "Microfossils in Calculus Demonstrate Consumption of Plants and Cooked Foods in Neandertal Diets (Shanidar III, Iraq; Spy I and II, Belgium)," *Proceedings of the National Academy of Sciences* 108, no. 2 (January 2011): 486–91, doi.org/10.1073/pnas.1016868108. I have taken some liberty in describing this meal. Henry and her colleagues mention only that these plants were present in the teeth, and that the barley was likely cooked with water rather than dried or parched. Wild goat bones were found in the cave.

2. Amaia Arranz-Otaegui et al., "Archaeobotanical Evidence Reveals the Origins of Bread 14,400 Years Ago in Northeastern Jordan," *Proceedings of the National Academy of Sciences* 115, no. 31 (July 2018): 7925–30, doi.org/10.1073/pnas.1801071115.

3. Delwyn Samuel, "Bread Making and Social Interactions at the Amarna Workmen's Village, Egypt," *World Archaeology* 31, no. 1 (1999): 121–44, doi.org/10.1080/00438243.1999.9980435.

4. Mark S. Warner, *Eating in the Side Room: Food, Archaeology, and African American Identity* (Gainesville: University Press of Florida, 2015).

5. Paul A. Delcourt et al., "Prehistoric Human Use of Fire, the Eastern Agricultural Complex, and Appalachian Oak-Chestnut Forests: Paleoecology of Cliff Palace Pond, Kentucky," *American Antiquity* 63, no. 2 (April 1998): 263–78, doi.org/10.2307/2694697, among many other studies.

6. Michael Pollan, *The Omnivore's Dilemma: A Natural History of Four Meals* (New York: Penguin, 2006).

7. Nicolás M. Hamienkowski and Pastor Arenas, "'Bitter' Manioc (*Manihot esculenta*): Its Consumption and the Grater Used by the Indigenous Peoples of the Gran Chaco in its Preparation," *Journal de la Société des Américanistes* 103, no. 2 (2017): 205–28, doi.org/10.4000/jsa.15230.

8. I discuss this issue further in chapter 4.

9. Paul Rozin, "Psychobiological Perspectives on Food Preferences and Avoidances," in *Food and Culture: Toward a Theory of Human Habits*, ed. Marvin Harris and Eric Ross (Philadelphia: Temple University Press, 1987), 181–201.

10. William R. Leonard, "The Global Diversity of Eating Patterns: Human Nutritional Health in Comparative Perspective," *Physiology and Behaviour* 134 (July 2014): 5–14, dx.doi.org/10.1016/j.physbeh.2014.02.050.

11. "Staple Foods: What Do People Eat?" Food and Agriculture Organization of the United Nations, accessed August 3, 2018, www.fao.org.

12. Claude Lévi-Strauss, *Totemism* [*Le Totémisme aujourd'hui*], trans. Rodney Needham (Boston: Beacon Press, 1963), 89.

13. Claude Lévi-Strauss, "The Culinary Triangle," in *Food and Culture: A Reader*, ed. Carole Counihan and Penny van Estrik (New York: Routledge, 2008), 28–35.

14. Lévi-Strauss, "Culinary Triangle."

15. Mary Douglas, "Deciphering a Meal," in *Food and Culture: A Reader*, ed. Carole Counihan and Penny van Esterik (New York: Routledge, 2008), 36–54.

16. Mary Douglas, *Purity and Danger: An Analysis of Concepts of Pollution and Taboo* (New York: Routledge, 1966).

17. Mary Weismantel, *Food, Gender, and Poverty in the Ecuadorian Andes* (Long Grove, IL: Waveland Press, 1988).

18. Marvin Harris, "The Abominable Pig," in *Food and Culture: A Reader*, ed. Carole Counihan and Penny van Esterik (New York: Routledge, 1988), 67–79.

19. Roy Rappaport, *Pigs for the Ancestors: Ritual in the Ecology of a New Guinea People* (New Haven, CT: Yale University Press, 1968).

20. Steven Falconer, "Rural Responses to Early Urbanism: Bronze Age Household and Village Economy at Tell el-Hayyat, Jordan," *Journal of Field Archaeology* 22, no. 4 (1995): 399–419, doi.org/10.1179/009346995791974107.

21. Monica Smith, "The Archaeology of Food Preference," *American Anthropologist* 108, no. 3 (September 2006): 480–93, doi.org/10.1525/aa.2006.108.3.480.

22. Pollan, *Omnivore's Dilemma*.

23. Cynthia Robin, *Everyday Life Matters: Maya Farmers at Chan* (Gainesville: University Press of Florida, 2013), 2.

Chapter 1

1. "Caveman" is not a technical anthropological term, yet it has been used by diet promoters, advertisers, and cartoon artists to capture the public's attention. The term "caveman" evokes brutish primitives from some generic point in human prehistory. I hope to show a different perspective on the human past in this book, yet I use the term to be consistent with the oversimplified—and male gendered—popular usage I discuss here.

2. Loren Cordain, *The Paleo Diet: Lose Weight and Get Healthy by Eating the Food You Were Designed to Eat* (Hoboken, NJ: John Wiley and Sons, 2002). The term "Paleo Diet" is trademarked by Cordain.

3. Peter Menzel and Faith D'Aluisio have photographically documented some of this variation in *Hungry Planet: What the World Eats* (New York: Material World, 2007).

4. Chris Duvall, "Chimpanzee Diet in the Bafing Area, Mali," *African Journal of Ecology* 46 (2008): 679–83, doi.org/10.1111/j.1365-2028.2007.00883.x.

5. Andrew Whiten et al., "Charting Cultural Variation in Chimpanzees," *Behaviour* 138, no. 11 (January 2001): 1481–516, www.jstor.org.

6. Cristina M. Gomes, Christophe Boesch, and Colin Allen, "Wild Chimpanzees

Exchange Meat for Sex on a Long-Term Basis," *PLoS One* 4, no. 4 (April 2009): e5116, doi.org/10.1371/journal.pone.0005116.

7. Lucas Goldstone et al., "Food Begging and Sharing in Wild Bonobos (*Pan paniscus*): Assessing Relationship Quality," *Primates* 57, no 3 (July 2016): 367–76, doi.org/10.1007/s10329-016-0522-6.

8. Captive bonobos, in contrast, have been shown to share food with strangers. Even in the wild, bonobo females especially will initiate social and sexual behavior with females from other groups, unlike more xenophobic chimpanzees. Jingzhi Tan and Brian Hare, "Bonobos Share with Strangers," *PLoS One* 8, no. 1 (January 2013): doi.org/10.1371/journal.pone.0051922.

9. Richard Wrangham, *Catching Fire: How Cooking Made Us Human* (London: Profile Books, 2009), 15–36.

10. Wrangham (*Catching Fire*) sums up a number of studies on the differences between human and chimpanzee physiology and nutrition.

11. This description of the Grants' research is drawn from Jonathan Weiner's excellent book, *Beak of the Finch: A Story of Evolution in Our Time* (New York: Penguin Random House, 1995).

12. Scientific research on human evolution is constantly being published and evaluated. Some dates and conclusions are subjects of fierce debates, accepted facts can be called into question by new finds from the field, and our knowledge increases daily. Some of the information in this section, which is no means intended to summarize everything we know about hominins between two and four million years ago, differs from other textbooks and articles. It could even be outdated by the time this book is published. Unless otherwise noted, I have drawn dates and details on fossils and sites from *Reconstructing Human Origins*, 3rd ed., by Glenn C. Conroy and Herman Pontzer (New York: W. W. Norton, 2012).

13. Donald C. Johanson, "Lucy, Thirty Years Later: An Expanded View of Australopithecus afarensis," *Journal of Anthropological Research* 60, no. 4 (Winter 2004): 465–86, doi.org/10.1086/jar.60.4.3631138.

14. Raymond Dart, "Australopithecus africanus: The Man-Ape of South Africa," *Nature* 115, no. 2884 (February 1925): 195–99, doi.org/10.1038%2F115195a0.

15. Paleoanthropologists have offered a number of different interpretations of *afarensis* locomotion on the basis of these footprints. One fairly recent summary and discussion can be found in David Raichlen, Herman Pontzer, and Michael D. Sockol, "The Laetoli Footprints and Early Hominin Locomotor Kinematics," *Journal of Human Evolution* 54, no. 1 (January 2008): 112–17, doi.org/10.1016/j.jhevol.2007.07.005.

16. Herman Pontzer ("Economy and Endurance in Human Evolution," *Current Biology* 27, no. 12 [June 2017]: R613–21, doi.org/10.1016/j.cub.2017.05.031) provides a recent review of models emphasizing the efficiency of bipedalism. Also, see William E. H. Harcourt-Smith's summary "The Origins of Bipedal Locomotion," in *Handbook of Paleoanthropology*, ed. W. Henke and Ian Tattersall (Berlin: Springer, 2014), 1–36.

17. Manuel Hernández Fernández and Elisabeth S. Vrba, "Plio-Pleistocene Climatic

Change in the Turkana Basin (East Africa): Evidence from Large Mammal Faunas," *Journal of Human Evolution* 50, no. 6 (June 2006): 595–626, doi.org/10.1016/j.jhev01 .2005.11.004.

18. Peter S. Ungar and Matt Sponheimer, "The Diets of Early Hominins," *Science* 334, no. 6053 (October 2011): 190–93, doi.org/10.1126/science.1207701.

19. Based on their different metabolic pathways, grasses and sedges are referred to as C_4 plants, and fruits, roots, and nuts as C_3 plants. Dietary emphasis on these different categories can be reconstructed by looking at ratios of two different isotopes of carbon in preserved bones and teeth.

20. Ungar and Sponheimer, "Diets of Early Hominins."

21. Jonathan Wynn et al., "Diet of *Australopithecus afarensis* from the Pliocene Hadar Formation, Ethiopia," *Proceedings of the National Academy of Sciences* 110, no. 26 (2013): 10495–500, doi.org/10.1073/pnas.1222559110.

22. Ungar and Sponheimer, "Diets of Early Hominins"; Matt Sponheimer et al., "Isotopic Evidence for Dietary Variability in the Early Hominin *Paranthropus robustus*," *Science* 314, no. 5801 (November 2006): 980–82, doi.org/10.1126/science.1133827.

23. Thomas W. Plummer and Emma M. Finestone, "Archaeological Sites from 2.6–2.0 Ma: Toward a Deeper Understanding of the Early Oldowan," in *Rethinking Human Evolution*, ed. Jeffrey Schwartz (Cambridge, MA: MIT Press, 2017), 267–96; Briana Pobiner et al., "New Evidence for Hominin Carcass Processing Strategies at 1.5 Ma., Koobi Fora, Kenya," *Journal of Human Evolution* 55, no. 1 (July 2008): 103–30, doi.org/10.1016/j .jhev01.2008.02.001.

24. Richard Potts, "Environmental and Behavioral Evidence Pertaining to the Evolution of Early *Homo*," *Current Anthropology* 53, no. S6 (December 2012): S299–S317, doi .org/10.1086/667704; Ungar and Sponheimer, "Diets of Early Hominins."

25. The volume *Meat-Eating and Human Evolution*, edited by Craig B. Stanford and Henry T. Bunn (New York: Oxford University Press, 2001), sums up many different lines of research on this question.

26. The term "man the hunter" refers to early models that stressed the importance of hunting in human evolution. Scientists writing in the 1950s and '60s generally used the term "man" to refer to humans; for example, Jane Goodall's book on chimpanzees was called *In the Shadow of Man* (New York: Houghton Mifflin, 1971). I resist translating "man" to the contemporary usage of "human" to emphasize how these early models tended to focus a good deal of attention on what they assumed were male activities like hunting, stone tool making, and defense. Female activities received less attention, and assumptions about how (or even whether) different activities were divided by sex were generally not questioned in much of this literature. In the 1970s and '80s, a feminist critique of these models and their assumptions arose. For instance, see the edited volumes *Woman the Gatherer*, edited by Frances Dahlberg (New Haven, CT: Yale University Press, 1981) and *Engendering Archaeology: Women and Prehistory*, edited by Joan Gero and Margaret Conkey (Malden, MA: Blackwell, 1990). Later in this chapter, I discuss the idea of "man the hunter" further and present some of the critiques that moved the discussion forward.

27. As reported by Jane Goodall, *In the Shadow of Man*, 37. As mentioned in the previous note, Leakey uses "man" and "human" interchangeably here.

28. Jane Goodall, *The Chimpanzees of Gombe: Patterns of Behavior* (Cambridge, MA: Harvard University Press, 1986).

29. Craig B. Stanford, *The Hunting Apes: Meat Eating and the Origins of Human Behavior* (Princeton, NJ: Princeton University Press, 1999).

30. S. L. Washburn and Virginia Avis, "Evolution of Human Behavior," in *Behavior and Evolution*, ed. A. Roe and G. Simpson (New Haven, CT: Yale University Press, 1958), 433.

31. Raymond A. Dart, *Adventures with the Missing Link* (New York: Harper, 1959).

32. The volumes *Women in Human Evolution*, edited by Lori D. Hager (New York: Routledge, 1997) and *Woman the Gatherer* (1981) are examples of this literature. One of the seminal articles in this area is Adrienne Zihlman, "Women in Evolution Part II: Subsistence and Social Organization among Early Hominins," *Signs* 4, no. 1 (Autumn 1978): 4–20, doi.org/10.1086/493566.

33. Henry Bunn et al., "FxJj50: An Early Pleistocene Site in Northern Kenya," *World Archaeology* 12, no. 2 (1980): 109–36, doi.org/10.1080/00438243.1980.9979787.

34. Glynn Isaac, "The Food-Sharing Behaviour of Proto-Human Hominids," *Scientific American* 238, no. 4 (April 1978): 90–109, doi.org/10.1016/0278-4165(85)90009-1.

35. Lewis R. Binford, "Human Ancestors: Changing Views of Their Behavior," *Journal of Anthropological Archaeology* 4, no. 4 (December 1985): 292–327, doi.org/10.1016/0278-4165(85)90009-1.

36. A strong statement of this point can be found in Henry T. Bunn, "Meat Made Us Human," in *Evolution of the Human Diet*, ed. Peter S. Ungar (New York: Oxford University Press, 2007), 191–211.

37. Joseph V. Ferraro et al., "Earliest Archaeological Evidence of Persistent Hominin Carnivory," *PLoS One* 8, no. 4 (2013): e62174, doi.org/10.1371/journal.pone.0062174.

38. Robert J. Blumenschine and John A. Cavallo, "Scavenging and Human Evolution," *Scientific American* 267, no. 4 (October 1992): 90–97, www.jstor.org.

39. For example, see Robert Blumenschine, Karie Prassak, C. David Kreger, and Michael C. Pante, "Carnivore Tooth-Marks, Microbial Bioerosion, and the Invalidation of Domínguez-Rodrigo and Barba's (2006) Test of Oldowan Hominin Scavenging Behavior," *Journal of Human Evolution* 53, no. 4 (2007): 420–26, doi.org/10.1016/j.jhevol.2007.01.011 and Manuel Domínguez-Rodrigo and R. Barba, "Five More Arguments to Invalidate the Passive Scavenging Version of the Carnivore-Hominid-Carnivore Model: A Reply to Blumenschine et al. (2007a)," *Journal of Human Evolution* 53, no. 4 (2007): 427–33, doi.org/10.1016/j.jhevol.2007.05.010.

40. Anna Tsing, *The Mushroom at the End of the World: On the Possibility of Life in Capitalist Ruins* (Princeton, NJ: Princeton University Press, 2015).

Chapter 2

1. Alan Walker and Richard Leakey, eds., *The Nariokotome* Homo erectus *Skeleton* (Cambridge, MA: Harvard University Press, 1993).

2. As in chapter 1, here I am only giving an overview of what we know about *Homo erectus* and sidestepping a number of debates in the field of paleoanthropology. For instance, some researchers identify two distinct species, an earlier *Homo ergaster* found only in eastern Africa, and *Homo erectus*, which had a wider distribution and later dates. Others lump together *ergaster* and *erectus*. New finds, such as *Homo naledi* specimens recently found in a cave in South Africa, may rewrite the story of our genus *Homo* even by the time you read this book. Paleoanthropology is an exciting field, and our work is far from done. But to keep the focus on how food shaped us as humans, I have summarized and synthesized a lot. As before, unless otherwise specified, information on dates, sites, and specimens in this chapter comes from Conroy and Pontzer's summary in *Reconstructing Human Origins*, 3rd ed. (New York: W. W. Norton, 2012).

3. Peter E. Wheeler, "The Evolution of Bipedality and Loss of Functional Body Hair in Hominids," *Journal of Human Evolution* 13, no. 1 (January 1984): 91–98, doi.org /10.1016/S0047-2484(84)80079-2.

4. Nina G. Jablonski, "Human Skin Pigmentation as an Example of Adaptive Evolution," *Proceedings of the American Philosophical Society* 156, no. 1 (March 2012): 45–57, www.jstor.org.

5. Alan R. Rogers, David Iltis, and Stephen Wooding, "Genetic Variation at the MCIR Locus and the Time since Loss of Human Body Hair," *Current Anthropology* 45, no. 1 (February 2004): 105–8, doi.org/10.1086/381006.

6. G. Philip Rightmire, David Lordkipanidze, and Abesalom Vekua, "Anatomical Descriptions, Comparative Studies, and Evolutionary Significance of the Hominin Skulls from Dmanisi, Republic of Georgia," *Journal of Human Evolution* 50, no. 2 (February 2006): 115–41, doi.org/10.1016/j.jhev01.2005.07.009.

7. Dietrich Stout et al., "Cognitive Demands of Lower Paleolithic Toolmaking," *PLoS One* 10, no. 5 (2015): e0128256, doi.org/10.1371/journal.pone.0128256.

8. Marek Kohn and Steven Mithen, "Handaxes: Products of Sexual Selection?" *Antiquity* 73, no. 281 (September 1999): 518–26, doi.org/10.1017/S0003598X00065078. However, other paleoanthropologists have called out this "Sexy Handaxe Theory" as not well supported by the available evidence. See, for example, April Nowell and Melanie Lee Chang, "The Case against Sexual Selection as an Explanation of Handaxe Morphology," *PaleoAnthropology* (2009): 77–88, www.paleoanthro.org.

9. David Lordkipanidze et al., "The Earliest Toothless Hominin Skull," *Nature* 434, no. 7034 (April 2005): 717–18, doi.org/10.1038/434717b.

10. Peter S. Ungar and Matt Sponheimer, "The Diets of Early Hominins," *Science* 334, no. 6053 (October 2011): 190–93, doi.org/10.1126/science.1207701.

11. Conroy and Pontzer, *Reconstructing Human Origins*, 417.

12. A. Walker, M. R. Zimmerman, and Richard E. F. Leakey, "A Possible Case of Hypervitaminosis A in *Homo erectus*," *Nature* 296, no. 5854 (1982): 248–50, doi.org/10.1038 /296248a0.

13. Mark Skinner, "Bee Brood Consumption: An Alternative Explanation for Hypervitaminosis A in KNM-ER 1808 (*Homo erectus*) from Koobi Fora, Kenya,"

Journal of Human Evolution 20, no. 6 (June 1991): 493–503, doi.org/10.1016/0047-2484 (91)90022-N.

14. Frank W. Marlowe et al., "Honey, Hadza, Hunter-Gatherers, and Human Evolution," *Journal of Human Evolution* 71 (June 2014): 119–28, doi.org/10.1016/j.jhev01 .2014.03.006.

15. Mark A. Maslin et al., "East African Climate Pulses and Early Human Evolution," *Quaternary Science Reviews* 101 (October 2014): 1–17, doi.org/10.1016/j.quascirev.2014 .06.012.

16. Richard Potts, "Evolution and Environmental Change in Early Human Prehistory," *Annual Review of Anthropology* 41, no. 1 (October 2012): 151–67, doi.org/10.1146 /annurev-anthro-092611-145754.

17. Leslie C. Aiello and Peter Wheeler, "The Expensive-Tissue Hypothesis: The Brain and the Digestive System in Human and Primate Evolution," *Current Anthropology* 36, no. 2 (April 1995): 199–221, www.jstor.org.

18. In contrast, Herman Pontzer and colleagues have argued that humans do have a higher metabolic rate than closely related primates in Herman Pontzer et al., "Metabolic Acceleration and the Evolution of Human Brain Size and Life History," *Nature* 533 (May 2016): 390–92, doi.org/10.1038/nature17654.

19. Dennis Bramble and Daniel E. Lieberman, "Endurance Running and the Evolution of *Homo*," *Nature* 432, no. 7015 (November 2004): 345–52, doi.org/10.1038/nature03052.

20. Another factor in the changing shape of *Homo* bodies and brains is childbirth. *Homo* bodies became longer and narrower, changing pelvis anatomy made birth canals narrower, and brain size increased, eventually making childbirth more difficult. This so-called obstetric dilemma is reviewed by Holly Dunsworth and Leah Eccleston, "The Evolution of Difficult Childbirth and Helpless Hominin Infants," *Annual Review of Anthropology* 44, no. 1 (October 2015): 55–69, doi.org/10.1146/annurev-anthro-102214 -013918.

21. Steven J. C. Gaulin, "A Jarman/Bell Model of Primate Feeding Niches," *Human Ecology* 7, no. 1 (March 1979): 1–20, doi.org/10.1007/BF00889349.

22. Richard Wrangham, *Catching Fire: How Cooking Made Us Human* (London: Basic Books, 2009).

23. Katherine D. Zink and Daniel E. Lieberman, "Impact of Meat and Lower Palaeolithic Food Processing Techniques on Chewing in Humans," *Nature* 531 (March 2016): 500–503, doi.org/10.1038/nature16990.

24. LuAnn Wandsnider, "The Roasted and the Boiled: Food Composition and Heat Treatment with Special Emphasis on Pit-Hearth Cooking," *Journal of Anthropological Archaeology* 16, no. 1 (March 1997): 1–48, doi.org/10.1006/jaar.1997.0303.

25. Victoria Wobber, Brian Hare, and Richard Wrangham, "Great Apes Prefer Cooked Food," *Journal of Human Evolution* 55, no. 2 (August 2008): 340–48, doi.org /10.1016/j.jhev01.2008.03.003.

26. John A. J. Gowlett and Richard W. Wrangham, "Earliest Fire in Africa: Towards the Convergence of Archaeological Evidence and the Cooking Hypothesis," *Azania:*

Archaeological Research in Africa 48, no. 1 (March 2013): 5–30, doi.org/10.1080/0067270X .2012.756754.

27. Steve Weiner et al., "Evidence for the Use of Fire at Zhoukoudian, China," *Science* 281, no. 5374 (July 1998): 251–53, doi.org/10.1126/science.281.5374.251.

28. Martin Jones, *Feast: Why Humans Share Food* (Oxford: Oxford University Press, 2008).

29. C. Loring Brace, "Biocultural Interaction and the Mechanism of Mosaic Evolution in the Emergence of 'Modern' Morphology," *American Anthropologist* 97, no. 4 (December 1995): 711–21, doi.org/10.1525/aa.1995.97.4.02a00130.

30. Because of our small sample of what looks to be a very geographically diverse species, scientific opinions on *Homo erectus* sexual dimorphism are mixed; not everyone agrees with Wrangham's assertion that *Homo erectus* is less sexually dimorphic than earlier hominins (e.g., J. Michael Plavcan, "Body Size, Size Variation, and Sexual Size Dimorphism in Early *Homo*," *Current Anthropology* 53, no. S6 [December 2012]: S419, doi.org/10.1086/667605). However, there is recent support for the idea that *erectus* was between modern humans and modern primates in its level of sexual dimorphism (Brian Vilmoare, Kevin G. Hatala, and William Jungers, "Sexual Dimorphism in *Homo erectus* Inferred from 1.5 Ma Footprints Near Ileret, Kenya," *Scientific Reports* 9, no. 7867 [2019]: 1–12, doi.org/10.1038/s41598-019-44060-2).

31. Evolutionary psychologists and physical anthropologists have been able to find evidence that our reproductive behavior does change throughout the menstrual cycle, even though we are not necessarily aware of it. David Buss sums up a number of these studies in his book *The Evolution of Desire: Strategies of Human Mating* (New York: Basic Books, 1995). For instance, women seem to have different mate preferences when they are ovulating, and female strippers make more in tips when they are ovulating, making it clear that cycles of fertility do have some impact on our behavior. But this is much subtler and more unconscious than in our primate cousins.

32. Craig B. Stanford, "The Hunting Ecology of Wild Chimpanzees: Implications for the Evolutionary Ecology of Pliocene Hominids," *American Anthropologist* 98, no. 1 (March 1996): 96–113, doi.org/10.1525/aa.1996.98.1.02a00090.

33. George P. Murdock and Caterina Provost, "Factors in the Division of Labor by Sex: A Cross-Cultural Analysis," *Ethnology* 12, no. 2 (April 1973): 203–25, www.jstor.org.

34. James O'Connell, Kristen Hawkes, and Nicholas Blurton-Jones, "Meat-Eating, Grandmothering, and the Evolution of Early Human Diets," in *Human Diet: Its Origin and Evolution*, ed. P. Ungar and M. Teaford (Westport, CT: Bergin and Garvey, 2002), 49–60; James O'Connell, Kristen Hawkes, and Nicholas Blurton-Jones, "Grandmothering and the Evolution of *Homo erectus*," *Journal of Human Evolution* 36, no. 5 (May 1999): 461–85, doi.org/10.1006/jhev.1998.0285; James O'Connell et al., "Male Strategies and Plio-Pleistocene Archaeology," *Journal of Human Evolution* 43, no. 6 (December 2002): 831–72, doi.org/10.1006/jhev.2002.0604.

35. Stanford, "Hunting Ecology of Wild Chimpanzees," 8.

36. Kristen Hawkes, "The Grandmother Effect," *Nature* 428, no. 6979 (March 2004):

128–29, doi.org/10.1038%2F428128a; Kristen Hawkes et al., "Grandmothering, Menopause, and the Evolution of Human Life Histories," *Proceedings of the National Academy
of Sciences* 95, no. 3 (February 1998): 1336–39, doi.org/10.1073/pnas.95.3.1336.

37. Note that, though I present these models separately, they are not necessarily
contradictory. Kristen Hawkes has recently argued that hypotheses of mate-guarding
by males, pair bonding, and grandmothering life histories are stronger when linked together, in James E. Coxworth et al., "Grandmothering Life Histories and Human Pair
Bonding," *Proceedings of the National Academy of Sciences* 112, no. 38 (September 2015):
11806–11, doi.org/10.1073/pnas.1599993112. Wrangham states that cooking was an important dynamic in some of the changes we see in the human lifespan, in Richard Wrangham and Rachel Carmody, "Human Adaptation to the Control of Fire," *Evolutionary
Anthropology* 19, no. 5 (October 2010): 187–99, doi.org/10.1002/evan.20275. Certainly,
if tubers were useful, as both models suggest, then cooked tubers would be even more
useful. I discuss the models separately because they focus on different kinds of social
groups and interactions.

38. Michael Finkel, "The Hadza," *National Geographic* 216, no. 6 (December 2009):
94–119.

39. Hawkes, "Grandmother Effect."

40. O'Connell, Hawkes, and Blurton-Jones, "Grandmothering."

41. O'Connell, Hawkes, and Blurton-Jones, "Meat-Eating, Grandmothering, and the
Evolution of Early Human Diets."

42. O'Connell, Hawkes, and Blurton-Jones, "Grandmothering."

43. Hawkes, "Grandmother Effect."

44. Caleb E. Finch and Craig B. Stanford, "Meat-Adaptive Genes and the Evolution
of Slower Aging in Humans," *Quarterly Review of Biology* 79, no. 1 (March 2004): 3–50,
doi.org/10.1086/381662. I follow Finch and Stanford in using adolescence to describe a
stage in the human lifespan where individuals have reached close to adult size and capa-
bilities but have not yet entered sexual maturity. Like menopause, discussed above, this
is a biological stage in the human lifespan. Many different cultures give different meanings
and characteristics to adolescence and menopause, but it is impossible to speak to the
cultural meanings, if any, that were attributed to hominin adolescents or postmenopausal
women.

45. Jan Beise and Eckart Voland, "A Multilevel Event History Analysis of the Effects
of Grandmothers on Child Mortality in a Historical German Population," *Demographic
Research* 7, Article 13 (September 2002): 469–98, doi.org/10.4054/DemRes.2002.7.13.

46. O'Connell, Hawkes, and Blurton-Jones, "Meat-Eating, Grandmothering, and the
Evolution of Early Human Diets."

Chapter 3

1. These finger fragments have recently been joined by skull fragments, as reported
by Bruce Bower, "The First Known Fossil of a Denisovan Skull Has Been Found in a
Siberian Cave," *Science News*, last modified March 29, 2019, www.sciencenews.org.

2. Viviane Slon et al., "The Genome of the Offspring of a Neanderthal Mother and a Denisovan Father," *Nature* 561, no. 7721 (September 2018): 113–16, doi.org/10 .1038%2Fs41586-018-0455-x.

3. Sriram Sankararaman et al., "The Combined Landscape of Denisovan and Neanderthal Ancestry in Present-Day Humans," *Current Biology* 26, no. 9 (May 2016): 1241–47, doi.org/10.1016/j.cub.2016.03.037; Benjamin Vernot et al., "Excavating Neandertal and Denisovan DNA from the Genomes of Melanesian Individuals," *Science* 352, no. 6282 (April 2016): 235–39, doi.org/10.1126/science.aad9416.

4. Qiaomei Fu et al., "An Early Modern Human from Romania with a Recent Neanderthal Ancestor," *Nature* 524 (June 2015): 216–19, doi.org/10.1038/nature14558; Jeffrey D. Wall et al., "Higher Levels of Neanderthal Ancestry in East Asians Than in Europeans" *Genetics* 194, no. 1 (May 2013): 199–209, doi.org/10.1534/genetics.112.148213.

5. Michael Dannemann and Janet Kelso, "The Contribution of Neanderthals to Phenotypic Variation in Modern Humans," *American Journal of Human Genetics* 101, no. 4 (October 2017): 578–89, doi.org/10.1016/j.ajhg.2017.09.010.

6. Anthropologist Matthew Tocheri summarizes new hominin finds in Southeast Asia that are causing paleoanthropologists to rethink models for early hominin dispersal. Matthew Tocheri, "Previously Unknown Human Species Found in Asia Raises Questions about Early Hominin Dispersals from Africa," *Nature* 568 (April 2019): 176–78, doi.org/10.1038/d41586-019-01019-7.

7. Some scholars describe Neandertals as a distinct species (*Homo neandertalensis*), while others recognize their potential to interbreed with humans by placing them as a distinct subspecies within our species (*Homo sapiens neandertalensis*), according to Steven E. Churchill, *Thin on the Ground: Neandertal Biology, Archeology, and Ecology* (Hoboken, NJ: Wiley-Blackwell, 2014), 30.

8. Chris Stringer, *Lone Survivors: How We Came to Be the Only Humans on Earth* (New York: Times Books, 2012).

9. Churchill, *Thin on the Ground*, 11.

10. Geologists refer to the period between about 2.5 million to 11,700 years ago as the Pleistocene. The Middle Pleistocene ended about 126 million years ago, at the beginning of the last interglacial period. Neandertals were around during the end of the Middle Pleistocene and the beginning of the Upper Pleistocene. Archaeologists have divided up time into different blocks, based on artifacts not climate. In this system, the Middle Paleolithic was 300,000 to 40,000 years ago and refers to the time when Neandertals and other archaic humans were making stone tools. The Upper Paleolithic began about 40,000 years ago when modern humans began to make more complex tools. Neandertals lived in the Middle and Upper Pleistocene, and also the Middle Paleolithic.

11. Churchill, *Thin on the Ground*, 108–14.

12. Churchill, 11–13.

13. Churchill, 114–50.

14. Benjamin Vernot and Joshua M. Akey, "Resurrecting Surviving Neandertal

Lineages from Modern Human Genomes," *Science* 343, no. 6174 (February 2014): 1017–21, doi.org/10.1126/science.1245938.

15. Michael F. Holick, "Sunlight and Vitamin D for Bone Health and Prevention of Autoimmune Diseases, Cancers, and Cardiovascular Disease," *American Journal of Clinical Nutrition* 80, no. 6 (December 2004): 1678S–88S, doi.org/10.1093/ajcn/80.6.1678S.

16. M. Fiscaletti, P. Stewart, and C. F. Munns, "The Importance of Vitamin D in Maternal and Child Health: A Global Perspective," *Public Health Reviews* 38, no. 19 (September 2017): doi.org/10.1186/s40985-017-0066-3.

17. Churchill, *Thin on the Ground*, 24.

18. Information on Neandertals in this paragraph is drawn from Churchill, *Thin on the Ground*, and Stringer, *Lone Survivors*, along with John F. Hoffecker, "The Complexity of Neanderthal Technology," *Proceedings of the National Academy of Sciences* 115, no. 9 (February 2018): 1959–61, doi.org/10.1073/pnas.1800461115; Antoine Muller, Chris Clarkson, and Ceri Shipton, "Measuring Behavioural and Cognitive Complexity in Lithic Technology Throughout Human Evolution," *Journal of Anthropological Archaeology* 48 (December 2017): 166–80, doi.org/10.1016/j.jaa.2017.07.006; and Lizzie Wade, "Neandertals Made Jewelry, Proteins Confirm," *Science* 353, no. 6306 (September 2016): 1350, doi.org/10.1126/science.353.6306.1350.

19. Brian Hayden, "Neandertal Social Structure," *Oxford Journal of Archaeology* 31, no. 1 (January 2012): 1–26, doi.org/10.1111/j.1468-0092.2011.00376.x; Stringer, *Lone Survivors*, chap. 6.

20. Note that I've generally been reserving the term "human" for *Homo sapiens*. Some paleoanthropologists have argued that there is so much continuity from *Homo erectus* on that maybe we should dramatically broaden the definition of human. I use "human" to refer to anatomically modern *Homo sapiens* after about 100,000 years ago, and usually to behaviorally modern humans after about 40–50,000 years ago.

21. Svante Pääbo, "The Diverse Origins of the Human Gene Pool," *Nature Reviews* 16 (May 2015): 313–14, doi.org/10.1038/nrg3954.

22. Stringer, *Lone Survivors*, 243.

23. Michael P. Richards and Erik Trinkaus, "Isotopic Evidence for the Diets of European Neandertals and Early Modern Humans," *Proceedings of the National Academy of Sciences* 106, no. 38 (September 2009): 16034–39, doi.org/10.1073/pnas.0903821106.

24. Mark White, Paul Pettitt, and Danielle Schreve, "Shoot First, Ask Questions Later: Interpretative Narratives of Neandertal Hunting," *Quaternary Science Reviews* 140 (May 2016): 1–20, doi.org/10.1016/j.quascirev.2016.03.004.

25. Thomas D. Berger and Erik Trinkaus, "Patterns of Trauma among the Neandertals," *Journal of Archaeological Science* 22, no. 6 (November 1995): 841–52, doi.org/10.1016/0305-4403(95)90013-6.

26. Erik Trinkaus, "Neandertals, Early Modern Humans, and Rodeo Riders," *Journal of Archaeological Science* 39, no. 12 (December 2012): 3691–93, doi.org/10.1016/j.jas.2012.05.039.

27. Steven L. Kuhn and Mary C. Stiner, "What's a Mother to Do? The Division of

Labor among Neandertals and Modern Humans in Eurasia," *Current Anthropology* 47, no. 6 (December 2006): 953–81, doi.org/10.1086/507197.

28. Luca Fiorenza, "Reconstructing Diet and Behaviour of Neandertals from Central Italy through Dental Macrowear Analysis," *Journal of Anthropological Sciences* 93 (2015): 1–15, doi.org/10.4436/JASS.93002.

29. Ainara Sisitiaga et al., "The Neandertal Meal: A New Perspective Using Faecal Biomarkers" *PLoS ONE* 9, no. 6 (2014): e101045, doi.org/10.1371/journal.pone.0101045.

30. Amanda G. Henry, Alison S. Brooks, and Dolores Piperno, "Plant Foods and the Dietary Ecology of Neandertals and Early Modern Humans," *Journal of Human Evolution* 69 (April 2014): 44–54, doi.org/10.1016/j.jhevol.2013.12.014.

31. Less confident about the extent of Neandertal medical knowledge, Laura Buck and Chris Stringer propose that such plants would also have been present in herbivore stomachs, and Neandertals, like some modern foragers, ate the nutritious stomach contents of animals they killed, in "Having the Stomach for It: A Contribution to Neandertal Diets?" *Quaternary Science Reviews* 96 (July 2014): 161–67, doi.org/10.1016/j.quascirev.2013.09.003.

32. Bruce L. Hardy and Marie-Hélène Moncel, "Neandertal Use of Fish, Mammals, Birds, Starchy Plants and Wood 125–250,000 Years Ago," *PLoS One* 6, no. 8 (August 2011): e23768, doi.org/10.1371/journal.pone.0023768.

33. Hayden, "Neandertal Social Structure."

34. Almudena Estalrrich and Antonio Rosas, "Division of Labor by Sex and Age in Neandertals: An Approach through the Study of Activity-Related Dental Wear," *Journal of Human Evolution* 80 (March 2015): 51–63, doi.org/10.1016/j.jhevol.2014.07.007.

35. Churchill, *Thin on the Ground*, 333–52.

36. Recent finds in Morocco have pushed back the date for key *Homo sapiens* features to 300,000 years ago and suggested a broader regional origin for the species. Jean-Jacques Hublin et al., "New Fossils from Jebel Irhoud, Morocco and the Pan-African Origin of *Homo sapiens*," *Nature* 546 (June 2017): 289–92, doi.org/10.1038/nature22336.

37. Stringer, *Lone Survivors*, 205–44.

38. Christopher S. Henshilwood et al., "Emergence of Modern Human Behavior: Middle Stone Age Engravings from South Africa," *Science* 295, no. 5558 (February 2002): 1278–80, doi.org/10.1126/science.1067575; Christopher S. Henshilwood et al., "An Abstract Drawing from the 73,000-Year-Old Levels at Blombos Cave, South Africa" *Nature* 562 (October 2018): 115–18, doi.org/10.1038/s41586-018-0514-3.

39. Stringer, *Lone Survivors*, 205–44.

40. Michael C. Campbell and Sarah A. Tishkoff, "African Genetic Diversity: Implications for Human Demographic History, Modern Human Origins, and Complex Disease Mapping," *Annual Review of Genomics and Human Genetics* 9 (September 2008): 403–33, doi.org/10.1146/annurev.genom.9.081307.164258; Sarah A. Tishkoff et al., "The Genetic Structure and History of Africans and African Americans," *Science* 22, no. 324 (May 2009): 1035–44, doi.org/10.1126/science.1172257.

41. Huw S. Groucutt et al., "Rethinking the Dispersal of *Homo sapiens* Out of Africa,"

Evolutionary Anthropology: Issues, News, and Reviews 24, no. 4 (August 2015): 162, doi .org/10.1002/evan.21455.

42. Josephine C. A. Joordens et al., "*Homo erectus* at Trinil on Java Used Shells for Tool Production and Engraving," *Nature* 518 (February 2015): 228–31, doi.org/10.1038 /nature13962.

43. Joaquín Rodríguez-Vidal et al., "A Rock Engraving Made by Neandertals in Gibraltar," *Proceedings of the National Academy of Sciences* 111, no. 37 (September 2014): 13301–06, doi.org/10.1073/pnas.1411529111.

44. John C. Whittaker, Devin B. Pettigrew, and Ryan J. Grohsmeyer, "Atlatl Dart Velocity: Accurate Measurements and Implications for Paleoindian and Archaic Archaeology," *PaleoAmerica* 3, no. 2 (April 2017): 161–81, doi.org/10.1080%2F20555563.2017 .1301133.

45. I am indebted to my graduate advisor Marc Bermann for introducing me to this idea in the archaeology core course he taught during my first year at the University of Pittsburgh.

46. Adrian Treves and Cristian Bonacic, "Humanity's Dual Response to Dogs and Wolves," *Trends in Ecology and Evolution* 31, no. 7 (July 2016): 489–91, doi.org/10.1016/j .tree.2016.04.006.

47. Climate scientists reconstruct past climates using a number of different methods. By looking at glacial ice, seafloor sediments, tree rings, and cave formations like stalactites, which are built up in yearly intervals, scientists measure oxygen isotope ratios, which reflect global temperature at the time each layer was formed. Greenland ice cores show a rise in global temperature and decreased variability at the beginning of the Holocene about 10,000 years ago (S. O. Rasmussen et al., "A New Greenland Ice Core Chronology for Last Glacial Termination," *Journal of Geophysical Research* 111, no. D6 [March 2006]: doi.org/10.1029/2005JD006079). However, there have been periods of climatic variability within the Holocene (Paul A. Mayewski et al., "Holocene Climate Variability," *Quaternary Research* 62, no. 3 [November 2004]: 243–55, doi.org/10.1016/j.yqres.2004 .07.001).

48. Michael S. Sheehan, "Ethnographic Models, Archaeological Data, and the Applicability of Modern Foraging Theory," in *Hunter-Gatherers in History, Archaeology, and Anthropology*, ed. Alan Barnard (New York: Berg Publishers, 2004), 163–74; Eric Smith Alden et al., "Anthropological Applications of Optimal Foraging Theory: A Critical Review," *Current Anthropology* 24, no. 5 (December 1983): 625–51, doi.org/10.1086/203066.

49. Lewis R. Binford, *Nunamiut Ethnoarchaeology* (Cambridge MA: Academic Press, 1978).

50. See chapter 2.

51. Ehud Weiss et al., "Plant-Food Preparation Area on an Upper Paleolithic Brush Hut Floor at Ohalo II, Israel," *Journal of Archaeological Science* 35, no. 8 (August 2008): 2400–2414, doi.org/10.1016/j.jas.2008.03.012.

52. Weiss et al., "Plant-Food Preparation Area."

53. Britt M. Starkovich, "Optimal Foraging, Dietary Change, and Site Use during the

Paleolithic at Klissoura Cave 1 (Southern Greece)," *Journal of Archaeological Science* 52 (December 2014): 39–55, doi.org/10.1016/j.jas.2014.08.026.

54. Lawrence Guy Straus, "Recent Developments in the Study of the Upper Paleolithic of Vasco-Cantabrian Spain," *Quaternary International* 364 (April 2015): 255–71, doi.org/10.1016/j.quaint.2014.05.008.

55. Mary C. Stiner, "Thirty Years on the 'Broad Spectrum Revolution' and Paleolithic Demography," *Proceedings of the National Academy of Sciences* 98, no. 13 (June 2001): 6993–96, doi.org/10.1073/pnas.121176198; Kent V. Flannery, "Origins and Ecological Effects of Early Domestication in Iran and the Near East," in *The Domestication and Exploitation of Plants and Animals*, ed. P. J. Ucko and G. W. Dimberly (London: Gerald Duckworth, 1969), 73–100.

56. Flannery, "Origins and Ecological Effects"; see discussion of population pressure and the origins of agriculture in chapter 4.

57. Martin Jones, *Feast: Why Humans Share Food* (Oxford: Oxford University Press, 2008).

58. One interesting study on the role of myths and folklore in transmitting cultural knowledge is Michelle Scalise Sugiyama, "Food, Foragers, and Folklore: The Role of Narrative in Human Subsistence," *Evolution and Human Behavior* 22, no. 4 (July 2001): 221–40, doi.org/10.1016/S1090-5138(01)00063-0.

59. Patrick D. Nunn and Nicholas J. Reid, "Aboriginal Memories of Inundation of the Australian Coast Dating from More than 7000 Years Ago," *Australian Geographer* 47, no. 1 (January 2016): 11–47, doi.org/10.1080/00049182.2015.1077539.

60. For instance, in the next chapter I discuss evidence that some populations of humans are biologically adapted to agricultural products like milk and starchy grains.

Chapter 4

1. See Ruth Shady and Christopher Kleihege's *Caral: The First Civilization in the Americas; La primera civilización de América* (Chicago: CK Photo, 2010), or Ruth Shady, "America's First City? The Case of Late Archaic Caral," in *Andean Archaeology III: North and South*, ed. William Isbell and Helaine Silverman (New York: Springer Press, 2006), 28–66.

2. Some good sources on developments in the wider region include: Jonathan Haas and Winifred Creamer, "Crucible of Andean Civilization: The Peruvian Coast from 3000 to 1800 BC," *Current Anthropology* 47, no. 5 (October 2006): 745–75, doi.org/10.1086/506281; Matthew Piscitelli, "Pathways to Social Complexity in the Norte Chico Region of Peru," in *Feast, Famine, or Fighting?: Studies in Human Ecology and Adaptation* vol. 8, ed. Richard J. Chacon and Rubén G. Mendoza (New York: Springer International Publishing, 2017), 393–415; and Daniel H. Sandweiss et al., "Environmental Change and Economic Development in Coastal Peru between 5,800 and 3,600 Years Ago," *Proceedings of the National Academy of Sciences* 106, no. 5 (February 2009): 1359–36, doi.org/10.1073/pnas.0812645106.

3. Michael L. Ryder, "The Evolution of Fleece," *Scientific American* 256, no. 1 (1987):

112–19, www.jstor.org/stable/24979302. Melinda Zeder provides an informative overview of the process of animal domestication and the features affected by domestication
(which include brain size) in "Pathways to Animal Domestication," in *Biodiversity in
Agriculture: Domestication, Evolution, and Sustainability*, ed. Jack Rodney Harlan et al.
(Cambridge: Cambridge University Press, 2012), 227–59.

4. "Potato," International Potato Center, accessed June 4, 2019, cipotato.org.

5. Daniel Zohary, Maria Hopf, and Ehud Weiss, *Domestication of Plants in the Old
World: The Origin and Spread of Domesticated Plants in Southwest Asia, Europe, and the
Mediterranean Basin* (Oxford: Oxford University Press, 2012).

6. Michael Blake, *Maize for the Gods: Unearthing the 9,000-Year History of Corn*
(Oakland: University of California Press, 2015). The information about maize genetics
in the next few paragraphs is drawn from this text, along with John Doebley, "The Genetics of Maize Evolution," *Annual Review of Genetics* 38, no. 1 (November 2004): 37–59,
doi.org/10.1146%2Fannurev.genet.38.072902.092425.

7. Michael Pollan makes this argument about plants like apples and potatoes in *The
Botany of Desire: A Plant's-Eye View of the World* (New York: Random House, 2002) and
about corn in *The Omnivore's Dilemma: A Natural History of Four Meals* (New York:
Penguin, 2007).

8. A few examples of studies showing foragers and gardeners modifying forest
landscapes with fire include Paul Delcourt et al., "Prehistoric Human Use of Fire, the
Eastern Agricultural Complex, and Appalachian Oak-Chestnut Forests: Paleoecology
of Cliff Palace Pond, Kentucky," *American Antiquity* 63, no 2 (April 1998): 263–78, doi.
org/10.2307/2694697; R. Bliege Bird et al., "The 'Fire Stick Farming' Hypothesis: Australian Aboriginal Foraging Strategies, Biodiversity, and Anthropogenic Fire Mosaics,"
Proceedings of the National Academy of Sciences 105, no. 39 (September 2008): 14796–
801, doi.org/10.1073/pnas.0804757105; and a general view that incorporates ethnographic and historical data, Fulco Scherjon et al., "Burning the Land: An Ethnographic
Study of Off-Site Fire Use by Current and Historically Documented Foragers and Implications for the Interpretation of Past Fire Practices in the Landscape," *Current Anthropology* 56, no. 3 (June 2015): 299–326, doi.org/10.1086/681561.

9. Bruce Knauft, *The Gebusi: Lives Transformed in a Rainforest World* (Forest Grove,
IL: Waveland Press, 2015).

10. Anthropologists generally distinguish between horticulture, or small-scale, non-
intensive gardening, and agriculture, or larger-scale, intensive farming that often uses
animal or mechanical labor inputs (for example, animal-drawn plows). Here, I am focusing on the transition toward farming without explicitly emphasizing the distinctions
between horticultural and agricultural societies.

11. Childe was not the first to propose this "Oasis Theory" but became a popular
and influential proponent in his books *The Most Ancient Near East* (London: K. Paul,
Trench, Trubner, 1928) and *Man Makes Himself* (Oxford: Oxford University Press, 1936).
The term "Neolithic" refers to the first farming society in a particular region. Since farming took hold in different parts of the world at different times, the term is not attached

to a specific time period; Neolithic villages in China existed thousands of years before Neolithic villages in Britain.

12. Ofer Bar-Yosef, "Climatic Fluctuations and Early Farming in West and East Asia," *Current Anthropology* 52, no. S4 (October 2011): S175–93, doi.org/10.1086/659784.

13. Robert J. Braidwood, "The Agricultural Revolution," *Scientific American* 203, no. 3 (September 1960): 130–52, www.jstor.org.

14. For example, Ian Kuijt and Bill Finlayson, "Evidence for Food Storage and Predomestication Granaries 11,000 Years Ago in the Jordan Valley," *Proceedings of the National Academy of Sciences* 106, no. 27 (July 2009): 10966–70, doi.org/10.1073/pnas.0812764106.

15. Ester Boserup proposed population growth as a key factor in social change in *The Conditions of Agricultural Growth: The Economics of Agrarian Change under Population Pressure* (Chicago: Aldine, 1965). Lewis Binford also argued that population pressure, not a trait like cultural innovation, pushed people in the Near East toward agriculture, in "Post-Pleistocene Adaptations," in *New Perspectives in Archeology*, ed. S. Binford and L. Binford (Chicago: Aldine, 1968), 313–41.

16. Mark Nathan Cohen, *The Food Crisis in Prehistory: Overpopulation and the Origins of Agriculture* (New Haven, CT: Yale University Press, 1977). Bar-Yosef, "Climatic Fluctuations and Early Farming in West and East Asia," also discusses the interplay between foraging, decreased mobility, and habitats rich in wild grasses.

17. The interplay of these factors is discussed by Richard Lee, "Lactation, Ovulation, Infanticide, and Women's Work: A Study of Hunter-Gatherer Population Regulation," in *Biosocial Mechanisms of Population Regulation*, ed. Mark N. Cohen, Roy S. Malpass, and Harold G. Klein (New Haven, CT: Yale University Press, 1980), 321–48; and Katherine Speilmann, "A Review: Dietary Restrictions on Hunter-Gatherer Women and the Implications for Fertility and Infant Mortality," *Human Ecology* 17, no. 3 (September 1989): 321–45, doi.org/10.1007/BF00889022. Amanda Veile, "Hunter-Gatherer Diets and Human Behavioral Evolution," *Physiology and Behavior* 193, Part B (September 2018): 190–95, doi.org/10.1016/j.physbeh.2018.05.023 provides a more recent summary of work on forager diet, fertility, and child-rearing.

18. Kent Flannery, "Origins and Ecological Effects of Early Domestication in Iran and the Near East," in *The Domestication and Exploitation of Plants and Animals*, ed. Peter J. Ucko and G. W. Dimblely (Chicago: Aldine, 1969), 73–100.

19. Archaeologists working with optimal foraging theory, described in chapter 3, have studied how foragers seek to minimize risk and search cost while maximizing returns. Some examples include: Michael A. Jochim, "Optimal Foraging and the Division of Labor," *American Anthropologist* 90, no. 1 (March 1988): 130–36, doi.org/10.1525/aa.1988.90.1.02a00100; and John Yellen, "Optimization and Risk in Human Foraging Strategies," *Journal of Human Evolution* 15, no. 8 (December 1986): 733–50, doi.org/10.1016/S0047-2484(86)80007-0. Chapters in the collection *Behavioral Ecology and the Transition to Agriculture*, edited by Douglas J. Kennett and Bruce Winterhalder (Berkeley: University of California Press, 2006) apply this perspective to the origins of agriculture in various regions of the world.

20. Huw Barton and Tim Denham document Pleistocene foragers in Southeast Asia increasing productivity and reliability of key plant resources through burning and moving plants to new locations as early as 20,000 years ago. Huw Barton and Tim Denham, "Prehistoric Vegeculture and Social Life in Island Southeast Asia and Melanesia," in *Why Cultivate Anthropological and Archaeological Approaches to Foraging-Farming Transitions in Southeast Asia*, ed. Graeme Barker and Monica Janowski (Cambridge: McDonald Institute for Archaeological Research, 2011), 17–25.

21. Dolores Piperno, "The Origins of Plant Cultivation and Domestication in the New World Tropics," *Current Anthropology* 52, no. S4 (October 2011): S453–70, doi.org /10.1086/659998.

22. However, other archaeologists have argued that foragers respond to risk and climate change by intensifying their foraging strategies, not by changing them. Arlene M. Rosen and Isabel Rivera-Collazo argue that in the face of postglacial climate changes, southwestern Asian foragers adapted their foraging strategies through increased manipulation of local vegetation but did not start relying on cultivated crops until a favorable climate lowered the risk of such a shift ("Climate Change, Adaptive Cycles, and the Persistence of Foraging Economies during the Late Pleistocene/Holocene Transition in the Levant," *Proceedings of the National Academy of Sciences* 109, no. 10 [March 2012]: 3640– 45, doi.org/10.1073/pnas.1113931109).

23. Brian Hayden, "Were Luxury Foods the First Domesticates? Ethnoarchaeological Perspectives from Southeast Asia," *World Archaeology* 34, no. 3 (January 2003): 458–69, doi.org/10.1080/0043824021000026459a.

24. Brian Hayden, "Big Man, Big Heart? The Political Role of Aggrandizers in Egalitarian and Transegalitarian Societies," in *For the Greater Good of All*, ed. D. R. Forsyth and C. L. Hoyt (New York: Palgrave Macmillan, 2011), 101–18.

25. Bar-Yosef, "Climatic Fluctuations and Early Farming in West and East Asia."

26. I refer to this region as the Near East, but archaeologists also call it Southwest or West Asia, and it has also been called the Fertile Crescent. The area between the Tigris and Euphrates rivers is also called Mesopotamia and saw some of the world's first states and cities.

27. Information about Abu Hureyra comes from the report compiled by Andrew Moore, Gordon Hillman, and Anthony Legge, *Village on the Euphrates: From Foraging to Farming at Abu Hureyra* (Oxford: Oxford University Press, 2000). Abu Hureyra is not the only village to span this time period, and while the focus of plant and animal domestication was different in different communities, I use Abu Hureyra as a characteristic example in this chapter.

28. Melinda A. Zeder, "Archaeological Approaches to Documenting Animal Domestication," in *Documenting Domestication*, ed. Melinda A. Zeder et al. (Berkeley: University of California Press, 2006), 171–80.

29. Melinda A. Zeder, "The Origins of Agriculture in the Near East," *Current Anthropology* 52, no. S4 (October 2011): S221–35, doi.org/10.1086/659307.

30. Katerina Douka et al., "Dating Knossos and the Arrival of the Earliest Neolithic

in the Southern Aegean," *Antiquity* 91, no. 356 (2017): 304-21, doi:10.15184/aqy.2017.29. Douka and colleagues argue that farmers spread into Crete through existing maritime networks established during the previous Mesolithic period.

31. Much has been written on this topic. Three good open-access articles that refer to a lot of the research are B. Bramanti et al., "Genetic Discontinuity between Local Hunter-Gatherers and Central Europe's First Farmers, *Science* 326, no. 5949 (October 2009): 137–40, doi.org/10.1126/science.1176869; Rita Rasteiro and Lounes Chikhi, "Female and Male Perspectives on the Neolithic Transition in Europe: Clues from Ancient and Modern Genetic Data," *PLoS One* 8, no. 4 (2013): e60944, doi.org/10.1371/journal. pone.0060944; and Ron Pinhasi, Joaquim Form, and Albert J. Ammerman, "Tracing the Origin and Spread of Agriculture in Europe," *PLoS Biology* 3, no. 12 (2005): e410, doi.org /10.1371/journal.pbi0.0030410.

32. Joachim Juan-Cabanilles and Bernat Martí Oliver, "New Approaches to the Neolithic Transition: The Last Hunters and First Farmers of the Western Mediterranean," in *Times of Neolithic Transition along the Western Mediterranean*, ed. Oreto García Puchol and Domingo C. Salazar-García (New York: Springer, 2017), 33–65.

33. Dale Serjeantson, "Survey of Animal Remains from Southern Britain Finds No Evidence for Continuity from the Mesolithic Period," *Environmental Archaeology* 19, no. 3 (May 2014): 256–62, doi.org/10.1179/1749631414Y.0000000020.

34. Oliver E. Craig et al., "Ancient Lipids Reveal Continuity in Culinary Practices across the Transition to Agriculture in Northern Europe," *Proceedings of the National Academy of Sciences* 108, no. 44 (November 2011): 17910–15, doi.org/10.1073/pnas .1107202108.

35. Solange Rigaud, Francesco d'Errico, and Marian Vanhaeren, "Ornaments Reveal Resistance of North European Cultures to the Spread of Farming," *PLoS One* 10, no. 4 (2015): e0121166, doi.org/10.1371/journal.pone.0121166.

36. Milk and other dairy products were not initially part of the human diet, even after animals like goats and cattle were domesticated. After all, humans are the only mammal that regularly drinks milk as an adult or regularly drinks the milk of a different species.

37. Richard P. Evershed et al., "Earliest Date for Milk Use in the Near East and Southeastern Europe Linked to Cattle Herding," *Nature* 455 (August 2008): 528–31, doi.org /10.1038/nature07180; Mélanie Salque et al., "Earliest Evidence for Cheese Making in the Sixth Millennium BC in Northern Europe," *Nature* 493 (January 2013): 522–25, doi.org /10.1038/nature11698.

38. Catherine J. E. Ingram et al., "Lactose Digestion and the Evolutionary Genetics of Lactase Persistence," *Human Genetics* 124, no. 6 (January 2009): 579–91, doi.org/10.1007 /s00439-008-0593-6.

39. Geneticists have shown that lactase persistence evolved independently, based on different mutations, in Europe, sub-Saharan Africa, and other parts of the world. For instance, see Ingram et al., "Lactose Digestion," along with a summary of genetics research in Laure Ségurel and Céline Bon, "On the Evolution of Lactase Persistence in

Humans," *Annual Review of Genomics and Human Genetics* 18, no. 1 (August 2017): 297–319, doi.org/10.1146%2Fannurev-genom-091416-035340.

40. Another way that some human populations have genetically adapted to farming is by producing more amylase, an enzyme in saliva that starts to break down starch, as a response to a starch-rich farming diet. George H. Perry et al., "Diet and the Evolution of Human Amylase Gene Copy Number Variation," *Nature Genetics* 39 (2007): 1256–60, doi.org/10.1038/ng2123.

41. Some scholars argue that lactase persistence is an example of human niche construction. Niche construction refers to the ways in which some organisms construct components of their environment, which then create the conditions under which natural selection operates. The advantages of digesting milk in the context of animal domestication might have done just that: Pascale Gerbault et al., "Evolution of Lactase Persistence: An Example of Human Niche Construction," *Philosophical Transactions of the Royal Society B: Biological Sciences* 366, no. 1566 (March 2011): 863–77, doi.org/10.1098/rstb.2010.0268.

42. The peopling of the Americas is a huge question for research and debate among archaeologists. New dates from Monte Verde, in Chile, could show human activity between 18,500 and 14,500 BP (Tom D. Dillehay et al., "New Archaeological Evidence for Early Human Presence at Monte Verde, Chile," *PLoS One* 10, no. 11 [December 2015]: e0145471, doi.org/10.1371/journal.pone.0145471). At the same time, new research is questioning the idea that humans could use the ice-free corridor to travel south through Canada before about 12,600 years ago (Mikkel W. Pederson et al., "Postglacial Viability and Colonization in North America's Ice-Free Corridor," *Nature* 537 [September 2016]: 45–49, doi.org/10.1038/nature19085). Clearly, there is still much work to do on this question.

43. Douglas J. Kennett, "Archaic-Period Foragers and Farmers in Mesoamerica," in *The Oxford Handbook of Mesoamerican Archaeology*, ed. Deborah L. Nichols and Christopher A. Pool (New York: Oxford University Press, 2012), 141–50.

44. Bruce Benz, "Archaeological Evidence of Teosinte Domestication from Guilá Naquitz, Oaxaca," *Proceedings of the National Academy of Sciences* 98, no. 4 (February 2001): 2104–06, doi.org/10.1073/pnas.98.4.2104; Blake, *Maize for the Gods*. Guilá Naquitz was excavated by a team of archaeologists including Kent Flannery and became the basis for his thinking about the role of domestication in forager strategies I discussed earlier in this chapter. Kent V. Flannery, ed., *Guilá Naquitz* (Orlando, FL: Academic Press, 1986).

45. Bruce D. Smith, "The Initial Domestication of Cucurbita Pepo in the Americas 10,000 Years Ago," *Science* 276, no. 5314 (May 1997): 932–34, doi.org/10.1126/science.276.5314.932.

46. Dolores R. Piperno et al., "Starch Grain and Phytolith Evidence for Early Ninth Millennium B.P. Maize from the Central Balsas River Valley, Mexico," *Proceedings of the National Academy of Sciences* 106, no. 13 (March 2009): 5019–24, doi.org/10.1073/pnas.0812525106. An interactive database created by Michael Blake, Bruce Benz, and their

team at en.ancientmaize.com reports dates from corn samples throughout the Americas and is worth browsing.

47. Joyce Marcus and Kent Flannery, *Zapotec Civilization: How Urban Society Evolved in Mexico's Oaxaca Valley* (New York: Thames and Hudson, 1996). My descriptions of Guilá Naquitz and San José Mogote in this section come from this comprehensive synthesis of two lifetimes of archaeological research in central Mexico.

48. Blake, *Maize for the Gods.*

49. Data on Kentucky is synthesized from R. Barry Lewis, ed., *Kentucky Archaeology* (Lexington: University Press of Kentucky, 1996).

50. Gary D. Crites, "Domesticated Sunflower in Fifth Millennium B.P. Temporal Context: New Evidence from Middle Tennessee," *American Antiquity* 58, no. 1 (January 1993): 146–48, doi.org/10.2307/281459; Kristen J. Gremillion, "Changing Roles of Wild and Cultivated Plant Resources among Early Farmers of Eastern Kentucky," *Southeastern Archaeology* 12, no. 1 (1998): 140–57, www.jstor.org; G. William Monaghan, William A. Lovis, and Kathryn C. Egan-Bruhy, "Earliest *Cucurbita* from the Great Lakes, Northern USA," *Quaternary Research* 65, no. 2 (March 2006): 216–22, doi.org/10.1016/j.yqres.2005.12.002; Bruce D. Smith, "Eastern North America as an Independent Center of Plant Domestication," *Proceedings of the National Academy of Sciences* 103, no. 33 (2006): 12223–28, doi.org/10.1073/pnas.0604335103.

51. Natalie G. Mueller, "The Earliest Occurrence of a Newly Described Domesticate in Eastern North America: Adena/Hopewell Communities and Agricultural Innovation," *Journal of Anthropological Archaeology* 49 (March 2018): 39–50, doi.org/10.1016/j.jaa.2017.12.001.

52. Jeffrey Pilcher, ¡*Que vivan los tamales! Food and the Making of Mexican Identity* (Albuquerque: University of New Mexico Press, 1998); Enrique Rodríguez-Alegría, "From Grinding Corn to Dishing Out Money: A Long-Term History of Cooking in Xaltocan, Mexico," in *The Menial Art of Cooking: Archaeological Studies of Cooking and Food Preparation*, ed. Sarah R. Graff and Enrique Rodríguez-Alegría (Boulder: University Press of Colorado, 2012), 99–118.

53. Benefits include higher calcium and other mineral contents and better bioavailability of niacin, allowing prehispanic populations to avoid the nutritional deficiency pellagra (Rodríguez-Alegría, "From Grinding Corn to Dishing Out Money"; and Martin Biskowski, "Maize Preparation and the Aztec Subsistence Economy," *Ancient Mesoamerica* 11, no. 2 [Fall 2000]: 293–306, www.jstor.org).

54. Robert A. Cook and T. Douglas Price, "Maize, Mounds, and the Movement of People: Isotope Analysis of a Mississippian/Fort Ancient Region," *Journal of Archaeological Science* 61 (September 2015): 112–28, doi.org/10.1016/j.jas.2015.03.022; Mary L. Simon, "Reevaluating the Evidence for Middle Woodland Maize from the Holding Site," *American Antiquity* 82, no. 1 (January 2017): 140–50, doi.org/10.1017/aaq.2016.2.

55. Gayle J. Fritz, *Feeding Cahokia: Early Agriculture in the North American Heartland* (Tuscaloosa: University of Alabama Press, 2019); Amber M. VanDerwarker, Dana N. Bardolph, and C. Margaret Scarry, "Maize and Mississippian Beginnings," in

Mississippian Beginnings, ed. Gregory D. Wilson (Gainesville: University Press of Florida, 2017), 29–70.

56. For example, Elic M. Weitzel and Brian Codding ("Population Growth as a Driver of Initial Domestication in Eastern North America," *Royal Society Open Science* 3, no. 8 [August 2016]: doi.org/10.1098/rsos.160319) use statistical modeling to find support for population pressure in eastern North America, while Bruce D. Smith and Richard A. Yarnell ("Initial Formation of an Indigenous Crop Complex in Eastern North America at 3800 B.P.," *Proceedings of the National Academy of Sciences* 106, no. 16 [April 2009]: 6561–66, doi.org/10.1073/pnas.0901846106) argue that crops were developed as an expansion of forager adaptation to and cultural modification of the landscape, in the absence of resource pressure.

57. George J. Armelagos and Mark Nathan Cohen, "Preface to the 2013 Edition," in *Paleopathology at the Origins of Agriculture*, ed. George J. Armelagos and Mark Nathan Cohen (Orlando: University Press of Florida, 2013), xxii. See also Mark Nathan Cohen, *Health and the Rise of Civilization* (New Haven, CT: Yale University Press, 1989), and Clark Spencer Larsen, "The Agricultural Revolution as Environmental Catastrophe: Implications for Health and Lifestyle in the Holocene," *Quaternary International* 150, no. 1 (June 2006): 12–20, doi.org/10.1016/j.quaint.2006.01.004.

58. Marshall Sahlins, *Stone Age Economics* (Chicago: Aldine, 1972).

59. For example, Rodríguez-Alegría cites ethnographic accounts of Mesoamerican women in the twentieth-century spending at least four hours, and sometimes up to eight hours a day grinding maize ("From Grinding Corn to Dishing Out Money," 102).

60. Richard Lee recounts a wonderful example of this in his article "Eating Christmas in the Kalahari," *Natural History* 78, no. 10 (December 1969): 14–22, 60–64.

61. Some foragers, like those who fished intensively along the central coast of Peru or the northwest coast of the United States, regularly amassed and stored surplus fish and other marine resources; these groups are an exception to this rule.

62. Ian Kuijt, "Negotiating Equality through Ritual: A Consideration of Late Natufian and Prepottery Neolithic A Period Mortuary Practices," *Journal of Anthropological Archaeology* 15, no. 4 (December 1996): 313–36, doi.org/10.1006/jaar.1996.0012.

63. Ian Hodder, "Çatalhöyük in the Context of the Middle Eastern Neolithic," *Annual Review of Anthropology* 36 (October 2007): 105–20, doi.org/10.1146/annurev.anthr0.36.081406.094308.

64. Ian Hodder and Craig Cessford, "Daily Practice and Social Memory at Çatalhöyük," *American Antiquity* 69, no. 1 (January 2004): 17–40, doi.org/10.2307/4128346.

65. For example, Smith and Yarnell, "Initial Formation of an Indigenous Crop Complex."

66. For example, Mary D. Pohl et al., "Early Agriculture in the Maya Lowlands," *Latin American Antiquity* 7, no. 4 (December 1996): 355–72, doi.org/10.2307/972264.

67. Martin Jones, *Feast: Why Humans Share Food* (Oxford: Oxford University Press, 2008).

Chapter 5

1. Michael E. Moseley et al., "Burning Down the Brewery: Establishing and Evacuating an Ancient Imperial Colony at Cerro Baúl, Peru," *Proceedings of the National Academy of Sciences* 102, no. 48 (November 2005): 17264–71, doi.org/10.1073/pnas.0508673102.

2. This quote appears in the title of Justin Jennings et al., "Drinking Beer in a Blissful Mood: Alcohol Production, Operational Chains, and Feasting in the Ancient World," *Current Anthropology* 46, no. 2 (April 2005): 275–303, doi.org/10.1086/427119.

3. Monica Smith, "Feasts and Their Failures," *Journal of Archaeological Method and Theory* 22, no. 4 (December 2015): 1215–37, doi.org/10.1007/s10816-014-9222-y.

4. Brian Hayden, "A Prolegomenon to the Importance of Feasting," in *Feasts: Archaeological and Ethnographic Perspectives on Food, Politics, and Power*, ed. M. Dietler and B. Hayden (Washington, DC: Smithsonian Institution Press, 2001), 23–64.

5. Michael Dietler, "Theorizing the Feast: Rituals of Consumption, Commensal Politics, and Power in African Contexts," in Dietler and Hayden, *Feasts*, 65–114.

6. Hayden and Dietler lay out these different perspectives in their introduction to Dietler and Hayden, *Feasts*, 1–21. The same debate was present in the different theoretical perspectives discussed in the introduction to this book.

7. Brian Hayden and Suzanne Villeneuve, "A Century of Feasting Studies," *Annual Review of Anthropology* 40 (October 2011): 433–49, doi.org/10.1146/annurev-anthro-081309-145740.

8. Hayden, "A Prolegomenon to the Importance of Feasting."

9. Dietler, "Theorizing the Feast."

10. Charlie Nairn, *Kawelka: Ongka's Big Moka* (1974; Watertown, MA: Documentary Educational Resources, 2010), DVD.

11. Franz Boas and Helen F. Codere, *Kwakiutl Ethnography* (Chicago: University of Chicago Press, 1966).

12. Peggy Brock, "Moveable Feasts: Chronicles of 'Potlatching' among the Tsimshian, 1860s–1900s," *Ethnohistory* 59, no. 2 (2012): 387–405, doi.org/10.1215/00141801-1536921; Stuart Piddocke, "The Potlatch System of the Southern Kwakiutl: A New Perspective," *Southwestern Journal of Anthropology* 21, no. 3 (Autumn 1965): 244–64, doi.org/10.1086/soutjanth.21.3.3629231.

13. Laura Junker, "The Evolution of Ritual Feasting Systems in Prehispanic Philippine Chiefdoms," in Dietler and Hayden, *Feasts*, 267–310.

14. Frances M. Hayashida, "Ancient Beer and Modern Brewers: Ethnoarchaeological Observations of *Chicha* Production in Two Regions of the North Coast of Peru," *Journal of Anthropological Archaeology* 27, no. 2 (June 2008): 161–74, doi.org/10.1016/j.jaa.2008.03.003; Jerry D. Moore, "Pre-Hispanic Beer in Coastal Peru: Technology and Social Context of Prehistoric Production," *American Anthropologist* 91, no. 3 (September 1989): 682–96, doi.org/10.1525/aa.1989.91.3.02a00090.

15. Gary Urton and Alejandro Chu, "The Invention of Taxation in the Inka Empire," *Latin American Antiquity* 30, no. 1 (March 2019), 1–16, doi.org/10.1017/laq.2018.64.

16. Information about the Inca Empire in this section is distilled from several

sources, including Tamara Bray, "The Role of Chicha in Inca State Expansion," in *Drink, Power, and Society in the Andes*, ed. Justin Jennings and Brenda Bowser (Gainesville: University Press of Florida, 2008), 108–32; Terence D'Altroy and Timothy Earle, "Staple Finance, Wealth Finance, and Storage in the Inka Political Economy," *Current Anthropology* 26, no. 2 (April 1985): 187–206, doi.org/10.1086/203249; Craig Morris, "Maize Beer in the Economics, Politics, and Religion of the Inca Empire," in *Fermented Food Beverages in Nutrition*, ed. Clifford Gastineau (New York: Academic Press, 1979), 21–34; and Charles Stanish, "Nonmarket Imperialism in the Prehispanic Americas: The Inka Occupation of the Titicaca Basin," *Latin American Antiquity* 8, no. 3 (September 1997): 195–216, doi.org/10.2307/971652.

17. Two deep ethnographic descriptions of *ayni* and other forms of reciprocity in Andean communities can be found in Catherine J. Allen, *The Hold Life Has: Coca and Cultural Identity in an Andean Community* (Washington, DC: Smithsonian Institution Press, 1988); and Enrique Mayer, *The Articulated Peasant: Household Economies in the Andes* (New York: Routledge, 2002). Descriptions in this section are drawn from both texts.

18. Allen, *The Hold Life Has*.

19. Peter Gose, "The State as a Chosen Woman: Brideservice and the Feeding of Tributaries in the Inka Empire," *American Anthropologist* 102, no. 1 (March 2000): 84–97, doi.org/10.1525/aa.2000.102.1.84.

20. D'Altroy and Earle, "Staple Finance, Wealth Finance, and Storage in the Inka Political Economy."

21. Allen, *The Hold Life Has*.

22. Tamara Bray, "Inka Pottery as Culinary Equipment: Food, Feasting, and Gender in Imperial State Design," *Latin American Antiquity* 14, no. 1 (March 2003): 3–28, doi .org/10.2307/972233.

23. Terence D'Altroy and Christine Hastorf, eds., *Empire and Domestic Economy* (New York: Springer, 2001). This volume collects several studies on the impact of Inca conquest on local households in the Mantaro Valley.

24. Cathy Lynne Costin and Timothy Earle, "Status Distinction and Legitimation of Power as Reflected in Changing Patterns of Consumption in Late Prehispanic Peru," *American Antiquity* 54, no. 4 (October 1989): 691–714, doi.org/10.2307/280677.

25. I discuss how archaeologists define luxury foods in chapter 6.

26. Information on feasts at the Royal Tombs of Ur is from Louise Steel, "Sumptuous Feasting in the Ancient Near East: Exploring the Materiality of the Royal Tombs of Ur," in *Exploring the Materiality of Food "Stuffs": Transformations, Symbolic Consumption, and Embodiments*, ed. L. Steel and K. Zinn (New York: Routledge, 2016), 189–204.

27. Steel, "Sumptuous Feasting in the Ancient Near East," 191; Susan Pollock, "Feasts, Funerals, and Fast Food in Early Mesopotamian States," in *The Archaeology and Politics of Food and Feasting in Early States and Empires*, ed. Tamara Bray (New York: Springer, 2003), 24.

28. Pollock, "Feasts, Funerals, and Fast Food in Early Mesopotamian States."

29. J. Cameron Monroe and Anneke Janzen, "The Dahomean Feast: Royal Women,

Private Politics, and Culinary Practices in Atlantic West Africa," *African Archaeological Review* 31, no. 2 (June 2014): 299–337, doi.org/10.1007/s10437-014-9156-5.

30. Kimberley J. Hockings et al., "Tools to Tipple: Ethanol Ingestion by Wild Chimpanzees Using Leaf Sponges," *Royal Society Open Science* 2, no. 6 (June 2015): 1–6, doi .org/10.1098/rsos.150150.

31. Matthew A. Carrigan et al., "Hominids Adapted to Metabolize Ethanol Long before Human-Directed Fermentation," *Proceedings of the National Academy of Sciences* 112, no. 2 (January 2015): 458–63, doi.org/10.1073/pnas.1404167111.

32. Robert Dudley, *The Drunken Monkey: Why We Drink and Abuse Alcohol* (Berkeley: University of California Press, 2014).

33. Jennings et al., "Drinking Beer in a Blissful Mood."

34. See Jennings et al., "Drinking Beer in a Blissful Mood" and Hayashida, "Ancient Beer and Modern Brewers" for more technical explanations of the process.

35. Justin Jennings, "La Chichera y el Patrón: Chicha and the Energetics of Feasting in the Prehistoric Andes," *Archaeological Papers of the American Anthropological Association* 14, no. 1 (June 2004): 241–59, doi.org/10.1525/ap3a.2004.14.241.

36. Jennings et al., "Drinking Beer in a Blissful Mood."

37. Alexander H. Joffe, "Alcohol and Social Complexity in Ancient Western Asia," *Current Anthropology* 39, no. 3 (June 1998): 297–322, doi.org/10.1086/204736.

38. Peter Damerow, "Sumerian Beer: The Origins of Brewing Technology in Ancient Mesopotamia," *Cuneiform Digital Library Journal* 2 (January 2012): www.cdli.ucla.edu. The Hymn to Ninkasi essentially provides a recipe for making beer.

39. Margaret A. Murray, *The Splendor That Was Egypt* (Mineola, NY: Dover Publications, 1963), 87.

40. Miguel Civil, "A Hymn to the Beer Goddess and a Drinking Song," in *Studies Presented to A. Leo Oppenheim* (Chicago: Oriental Institute, 1964), 67–69, quoted in Solomon H. Katz and Mary M. Voight, "Bread and Beer: The Early Use of Cereals in the Human Diet," *Expedition* 28, no. 2 (1986): 29.

41. Oliver Dietrich et al., "Establishing a Radiocarbon Sequence for Göbekli Tepe: State of Research and New Data," *Neo-Lithics* 1 (October 2013): 36–41.

42. Tristam R. Kidder, "Transforming Hunter-Gatherer History at Poverty Point," in *Hunter-Gatherer Archaeology as Historical Process*, ed. Kenneth E. Sassaman and Donald H. Holly (Tucson: University of Arizona Press, 2011), 95–119.

43. Oliver Dietrich et al., "The Role of Cult and Feasting in the Emergence of Neolithic Communities: New Evidence from Göbekli Tepe, South-Eastern Turkey," *Antiquity* 86, no. 333 (September 2012): 674–95, doi.org/10.1017/S0003598X00047840.

44. Brian Hayden, "Were Luxury Foods the First Domesticates?" *World Archaeology* 34, no. 3 (January 2003): 458–69, doi.org/10.1080/0043824021000026459a.

45. Dietrich et al., "Role of Cult and Feasting in the Emergence of Neolithic Communities."

46. The next several paragraphs are synthesized from Yannis Hamilakis, "Food Technologies/Technologies of the Body: The Social Context of Wine and Oil Production

and Consumption in Bronze Age Crete," *World Archaeology* 31, no. 1 (June 1999): 38–54, doi.org/10.1080%2F00438243.1999.9980431; and Yannis Hamilakis and Susan Sherratt, "Feasting and the Consuming Body in Bronze Age Crete and Early Iron Age Cyprus," *British School at Athens Studies* 20, *Parallel Lives: Ancient Island Societies in Crete and Cyprus* (2012): 187–207, www.jstor.org.

47. Hamilakis and Sherratt, "Feasting and the Consuming Body," 192.

Chapter 6

1. Sophie Coe, *America's First Cuisines* (Austin: University of Texas Press, 1994). Descriptions of Aztec cuisine and specific references to texts come from Coe's thorough summary.

2. Michael Smith, *At Home with the Aztecs: An Archaeologist Uncovers Their Daily Life* (New York: Routledge, 2016).

3. Randolph J. Widmer and Rebecca Storey, "The Cuisine of Prehispanic Central Mexico Reconsidered: The 'Omnivore's Dilemma' Revisited," in *New Directions in Biocultural Anthropology*, ed. Molly K. Zuckerman and Debra L. Martin (Hoboken, NJ: Wiley, 2017), 259–78.

4. Jack Goody, *Cooking, Cuisine, and Class: A Study in Comparative Sociology* (Cambridge: Cambridge University Press, 1982).

5. In addition to Goody's descriptions, I reference here Melitta Weiss Adamson, ed., *Regional Cuisines of Medieval Europe, A Book of Essays* (New York: Routledge, 2002); Phyllis Pray Bober, *Art, Culture, and Cuisine: Ancient and Medieval Gastronomy* (Chicago: University of Chicago Press, 1999); and Stephen Mennell, *All Manners of Food: Eating and Taste in England and France from the Middle Ages to the Present*, 2nd ed. (Urbana: University of Illinois Press, 1996).

6. A good summary of some of this work is provided by Marijke van der Veen, "When Is Food a Luxury?" *World Archaeology* 34, no. 3 (January 2003): 405–27, doi.org/10.1080/0043824021000026422, from which I draw this definition.

7. Michael E. Smith, Jennifer B. Wharton, and Jan Marie Olson, "Aztec Feasts, Rituals, and Markets: Political Uses of Ceramic Vessels in a Commercial Economy," in *The Archaeology and Politics of Food and Feasting in Ancient States and Empires*, ed. Tamara Bray (New York: Kluwer Academic/Plenum Publishers, 2003), 235–68.

8. Smith, Wharton, and Olson, "Aztec Feasts, Rituals, and Markets," 245.

9. Elizabeth M. Brumfiel, "Consumption and Politics at Aztec Huexotla," *American Anthropologist* 89, no. 3 (September 1987): 676–86, doi.org/10.1525/aa.1987.89.3.02a00090.

10. A great description of this feast can be found here at the University of Pennsylvania's website, "The Funerary Feast of King Midas," Penn Museum, accessed June 5, 2019, www.penn.museum.

11. Patrick E. McGovern et al., "A Funerary Feast Fit for King Midas," *Nature* 402, no. 6764 (December 1999): 863–64, doi.org/10.1038/47217.

12. In chapter 5, I discuss research on alcohol production and consumption in the ancient world that supports this assertion.

13. Julie Rauer, "The Last Feast of Lady Dai," Asianart.com, accessed June 27, 2017, asianart.com/articles/ladydai/index.html.

14. Kwang-Chih Chang, introduction to *Food in Chinese Culture: Anthropological and Historical Perspectives*, ed. K. C. Chang (New Haven, CT: Yale University Press, 1977), 1–21.

15. "Systematic Inequality: How America's Structural Racism Helped Create the Black-White Wealth Gap," Center for American Progress, last modified February 21, 2018, www.americanprogress.org.

16. Susan C. Andres and James P. Fenton, "Archaeology and the Invisible Man: The Role of Slavery in the Production of Wealth and Social Class in the Bluegrass Region of Kentucky, 1820 to 1870," *World Archaeology* 33, no. 1 (January 2001): 115–36, doi.org /10.1080/00438240126649.

17. James McWilliams, *A Revolution in Eating: How the Quest for Food Shaped America* (New York: Columbia University Press, 2005), along with many of the sources cited from here on.

18. McWilliams, *Revolution in Eating*.

19. Michael Trinkley, Natalie Adams, and Debi Hacker, *Archaeological Studies Associated with the Nineteenth Century Owens-Thomas Carriage House, Savannah, Georgia* (Columbia, SC: Chicora Foundation Research Series 38, 1993).

20. Free Africans and African Americans also had important histories in the United States. Mark S. Wagner's book, *Eating in the Side Room: Food, Archaeology, and African American Identity* (Gainesville: University Press of Florida, 2015), recounts 140 years of one free Maryland family's foodways.

21. See the studies referenced from here on for specific examples of these patterns.

22. Elizabeth M. Scott, "Food and Social Relations at Nina Plantation," *American Anthropologist* 103, no. 3 (September 2001): 671–91, www.jstor.org.

23. Tanya M. Peres, "Foodways, Economic Status, and the Antebellum Upland South in Central Kentucky," *Historical Archaeology* 42, no. 4 (December 2008): 88–104, doi .org/10.1007/BF03377156.

24. Diana C. Crader, "Slave Diet at Monticello," *American Antiquity* 55, no. 4 (October 1990): 690–717, doi.org/10.2307/281246.

25. Brian W. Thomas, "Power and Community: The Archaeology of Slavery at the Hermitage Plantation," *American Antiquity* 63, no. 4 (October 1998): 531–51, doi.org /10.2307/2694107.

26. Larry McKee, "Food Supply and Plantation Order," in *"I, Too, Am America": Archaeological Studies of African-American Life*, ed. Theresa A. Singleton (Charlottesville: University of Virginia Press, 1999), 218–39.

27. Culinary historian Michael Twitty's response to southern celebrity chef Paula Deen points out a few relevant critiques: "An Open Letter to Paula Deen," Afroculinaria, last modified June 25, 2013, afroculinaria.com.

28. James McCann, "Maize and Grace: History, Corn, and Africa's New Landscapes, 1500–1999," *Comparative Studies in Society and History* 43, no. 2 (April 2001): 250, www.jstor.org.

29. Leland Ferguson, *Uncommon Ground: Archaeology and Early African America, 1650–1800* (Washington, DC: Smithsonian Institution Press, 1992).

30. Judith Carney, *Black Rice: The African Origins of Rice Cultivation in the Americas* (Cambridge, MA: Harvard University Press, 2002).

31. McWilliams, *A Revolution in Eating*.

32. Ferguson, *Uncommon Ground*.

33. Colono ware pottery seems to be a truly hybrid tradition. It incorporated Native American and African influences and also varied across Spanish and British colonial territories. Mark D. Groover, "Evidence for Folkways and Cultural Exchange in the 18th Century South Carolina Backcountry," *Historical Archaeology* 28, no. 1 (March 1994): 41–64, doi.org/10.1007/BF03374180; Richard Vernon, "17th Century Apalachee Colono-Ware as a Reflection of Demography, Economics, and Acculturation," *Historical Archaeology* 22, no. 1 (January 1988): 76–82, doi.org/10.1007/BF03374502.

34. Maria Franklin, "The Archaeological Dimensions of Soul Food: Interpreting Race, Culture, and Afro-Virginian Identity," in *Race and the Archaeology of Identity*, ed. Charles Orser (Salt Lake City: University of Utah Press, 2001), 88–107.

35. Wilbur Cross, *Gullah Culture in America* (Winston-Salem, NC: John E. Blair, 2008).

36. Mark Groover, "Creolization and the Archaeology of Multiethnic Households in the American South," *Historical Archaeology* 34, no. 3 (September 2000): 102, doi.org/10.1007/BF03373645.

37. Ferguson, *Uncommon Ground*.

38. Michael W. Twitty, *The Cooking Gene: A Journey through African-American Culinary History in the Old South* (New York: HarperCollins, 2017).

39. Michael W. Twitty, "Barbecue Is an American Tradition—of Enslaved Africans and Native Americans," *The Guardian*, last modified July 4, 2015, www.theguardian.com.

40. Hominy is made by soaking corn in an alkaline solution of wood ash and water. This is another version of the nixtamalization process discussed in chapter 4. It changes the texture of the corn and makes the niacin (vitamin B) easier to absorb.

41. Dinner menu from July 3, 2017, husknashville.com, accessed July 3, 2017.

42. Alfred Crosby, *The Columbian Exchange: The Biological and Cultural Consequences of 1492* (Westport, CT: Praeger Press, 2003).

43. Sidney W. Mintz, *Sweetness and Power: The Place of Sugar in Modern History* (New York: Viking-Penguin, 1985).

44. Mintz, *Sweetness and Power*, 96.

45. Hayden, "Were Luxury Foods the First Domesticates?"; Van der Veen ("When Is Food a Luxury?") describes this as the "trickle-down effect."

46. Sophie D. Coe and Michael D. Coe, *The True History of Chocolate* (New York: Thames and Hudson, 2013).

47. Jeffrey Pilcher, *¡Que vivan los tamales! Food and the Making of Mexican Identity* (Albuquerque: University of New Mexico Press, 1998).

48. Crosby, *Columbian Exchange*.

49. Robyn E. Cutright, "Eating Empire in the Jequetepeque: A Local View of Chimú

Expansion on the North Coast of Peru," *Latin American Antiquity* 26, no. 1 (March 2015): 64–86, doi.org/10.7183/1045-6635.26.1.64.

50. Carol J. Mackey, "Chimú Statecraft in the Provinces," in *Andean Civilization: A Tribute to Michael E. Moseley*, ed. Joyce Marcus and P. Ryan Williams (Los Angeles: Cotsen Institute, 2009), 325–49.

51. Robyn E. Cutright, "Between the Kitchen and the State: Domestic Practice and Chimú Expansion in the Jequetepeque Valley, Peru" (PhD diss., University of Pittsburgh, 2009), d-scholarship.pitt.edu.

52. In chapter 5, I describe the role of corn beer and feasts in Inca political hospitality.

53. D'Altroy and Hastorf, *Empire and Domestic Economy*.

54. Christine Hastorf, "Gender, Space, and Food in Prehistory," in *Engendering Archaeology: Women and Prehistory*, ed. J. Gero and M. Conkey (Oxford: Blackwell Publishers, 1991), 132–59.

55. Sarah A. Kennedy and Parker VanValkenburgh, "Zooarchaeology and Changing Food Practices at Carrizales, Peru Following the Spanish Invasion," *International Journal of Historical Archaeology* 20, no. 1 (March 2016): 73–104, doi.org/10.1007/s10761-015 -0319-0.

56. For example, Charlotte Coté, "'Indigenizing' Food Sovereignty: Revitalizing Indigenous Food Practices and Ecological Knowledges in Canada and the United States," *Humanities* 5, no. 3 (July 2016): 57, doi.org/10.3390/h5030057. You can read about the work of one chef involved in revitalizing indigenous foodways in Sean Sherman and Beth Dooley, *The Sioux Chef's Indigenous Kitchen* (Minneapolis: University of Minnesota Press, 2017).

Chapter 7

1. Christopher B. Donnan, "The Thematic Approach to Moche Iconography," *Journal of Latin American Lore* 1, no. 2 (1975): 147–62.

2. Steve Bourget, *Sacrifice, Violence, and Ideology among the Moche: The Rise of Social Complexity in Ancient Peru* (Austin: University of Texas Press, 2016); Richard C. Sutter and Rosa J. Cortez, "The Nature of Moche Human Sacrifice: A Bioarchaeological Perspective," *Current Anthropology* 46, no. 4 (August/October 2005): 521–49, doi. org/10.1086/431527; Edward Swenson, "Cities of Violence: Sacrifice, Power, and Urbanization in the Andes," *Journal of Social Archaeology* 3, no. 2 (June 2003): 256–96, doi.org /10.1177/1469605303003002006.

3. Steve Bourget, "Rituals of Sacrifice: Its Practice at Huaca de la Luna and Its Representation in Moche Iconography," in *Moche Art and Archaeology in Ancient Peru*, ed. Joanne Pillsbury (New Haven, CT: Yale University Press, 2001), 89–109.

4. Christine Hastorf, "Andean Luxury Foods: Special Food for the Ancestors, Deities, and the Elite," *Antiquity* 77, no. 297 (September 2003): 545–54, doi.org/10.1017 /S0003598X00092607.

5. Elizabeth Morán, *Sacred Consumption: Food and Ritual in Aztec Art and Culture* (Austin: University of Texas Press, 2016).

6. Hastorf, "Andean Luxury Foods," 549.

7. Hastorf, 550.

8. Egyptian and Irish examples from Joan P. Alcock, *Food in the Ancient World* (Westport, CT: Greenwood Press, 2006).

9. Christine D. White, "Gendered Food Behaviour among the Maya," *Journal of Social Archaeology* 5, no. 3 (October 2005): 356–82, doi.org/10.1177/1469605305057572.

10. Hastorf, "Andean Luxury Foods," 551.

11. *Ulluchu* is mysterious because scholars are not exactly sure what it is. The term "ulluchu" was invented by one of the earliest archaeologists to describe ancient drawings of the fruit. Rainer W. Bussman and Douglas Sharon, "Naming a Phantom—The Quest to Find the Identity of *Ulluchu*, an Unidentified Ceremonial Plant of the Moche Culture," *Journal of Ethnobiology and Ethnomedicine* 5, no. 8 (2009): doi.org/10.1186 /1746-4269-5-8.

12. Morán, *Sacred Consumption*.

13. Mary Glowacki, "Food of the Gods or Mere Mortals? Hallucinogenic *Spondylus* and Its Interpretive Implications for Early Andean Society," *Antiquity* 79, no. 304 (June 2005): 257–68, doi.org/10.1017/S0003598X00114061.

14. Miriam Hospodar, "Aphrodisiac Foods: Bringing Heaven to Earth," *Gastronomica* 4, no. 4 (Fall 2004): 82–93, doi.org/10.1525/gfc.2004.4.4.82.

15. Morán, *Sacred Consumption*.

16. Michael Dietler, "Feasting and Fasting," in *The Oxford Handbook of the Archaeology of Ritual and Religion*, ed. Timothy Insoll (Oxford: Oxford University Press, 2011), 180–94.

17. Bernabé Cobo, *Inca Religion and Customs*, trans. Roland Hamilton (Austin: University of Texas Press, 1990), 151.

18. Severin M. Fowles, "Steps toward an Archaeology of Taboo," in *Religion, Archaeology, and the Material World*, ed. Lars Fogelin (Carbondale: Southern Illinois University Press, 2008), 15–37.

19. Gustavo Politis and Nicholas Saunders, "Archaeological Correlates of Ideological Activity: Food Taboos and Spirit-Animals in an Amazonian Hunter-Gatherer Society," in *Consuming Passions and Patterns of Consumption*, ed. Preston Miracle (Cambridge: McDonald Institute for Archaeological Research, University of Cambridge, 2002), 113–30.

20. Recall from the introduction that anthropologist Marvin Harris has argued strongly that the Hindu taboo against beef and the Muslim and Jewish taboo against pork help to regulate human ecological behavior in their respective environments.

21. M. D. Merlin, "Archaeological Evidence for the Tradition of Psychoactive Plant Use in the Old World," *Economic Botany* 57, no. 3 (September 2003): 295–323, doi.org /10.1663/0013-0001(2003)057[0295:AEFTTO]2.0.CO;2.

22. Elisa Guerra-Doce, "Psychoactive Substances in Prehistoric Times: Examining the Archaeological Evidence," *Time and Mind* 8, no. 1 (2015): 91–112, doi.org/10.1080/1751 696X.2014.993244; Elisa Guerra-Doce, "The Origins of Inebriation: Archaeological Evidence of the Consumption of Fermented Beverages and Drugs in Prehistoric Eurasia,"

Journal of Archaeological Method and Theory 22, no. 3 (September 2015): 751–82, doi .org/10.1007/s10816-014-9205-z.

23. Yannis Hamilakis, "Food Technologies/Technologies of the Body: The Social Context of Wine and Oil Production and Consumption in Bronze Age Crete," *World Archaeology* 31, no. 1 (June 1999): 38–54, doi.org/10.1080/00438243.1999.9980431.

24. Richard L. Burger, "What Kind of Hallucinogenic Snuff Was Used at Chavín de Huántar?" *Ñawpa Pacha* 31, no. 2 (December 2011): 123–40, doi.org/10.1179/naw.2011 .31.2.123.

25. Bonnie Glass-Coffin, "Shamanism and San Pedro through Time: Some Notes on the Archaeology, History, and Continued Use of an Entheogen in Northern Peru," *Anthropology of Consciousness* 21, no. 1 (March 2010): 58–83, doi.org/10.1111/j.1556-3537 .2010.01021.x.

26. Robyn E. Cutright, "Food for the Dead, Cuisine of the Living: Mortuary Food Offerings from the Jequetepeque Valley, Perú," in *From State to Empire in the Prehistoric Jequetepeque Valley, Peru*, ed. Colleen Zori and Ilana Johnson (Oxford: Archaeopress, 2011), 83–92. Scholars have used two terms, *Lambayeque* and *Sicán*, to refer to this culture. Following the archaeologist who led the project at Farfán, Carol Mackey, I use the term "Lambayeque" to refer to the people who lived in the Jequetepeque during this time. Later in this book, I use "Sicán" to refer to the state centered farther to the north in the Lambayeque and La Leche Valleys.

27. George Gumerman IV, "Corn for the Dead: The Significance of *Zea mays* in Moche Burial Offerings," in *Corn and Culture in the Prehistoric New World*, ed. Sissel Johansen and Christine Hastorf (Boulder, CO: Westview Press, 1994), 399–410.

28. During a Paleokitchen seminar in 2016, then-sophomore Jessie Hale wrote her final paper on the role of food in Viking funerals. This section is based on her exemplary work.

29. Jan Bill, "Ambiguous Mobility in the Viking Age Ship Burial from Oseberg," in *Materialities of Passing: Explorations in Transformation, Transition, and Transience*, ed. P. Bjerregaard, A. E. Rasmussen, and T. F. Sørensen (New York: Routledge, 2016), 207–20.

30. Thomas Dubois, *Nordic Religions in the Viking Age* (Philadelphia: University of Pennsylvania Press, 1999), 69–92.

31. Christina Lee, *Feasting the Dead: Food and Drink in Anglo-Saxon Burial Rituals* (Suffolk, UK: Boydell Press, 2007).

32. Elisabeth Arwill-Nordbladh, "A Reigning Queen or the Wife of a King—Only? Gender Politics in the Scandinavian Viking Age," in *Ancient Queens: Archaeological Explorations*, ed. S. M. Nelson (Walnut Creek, CA: AltaMira Press, 2003), 19–40.

33. Allen J. Frantzen, *Food, Eating, and Identity in Early Medieval England* (Suffolk, UK: Boydell Press, 2014).

34. Christopher Fung, "The Drinks Are on Us: Ritual, Social Status, and Practice in Dawenkou Burials, North China," *Journal of East Asian Archaeology* 2, no. 1 (January 2000): 67–92, doi.org/10.1163/156852300509808.

35. Sara Milledge Nelson, "Feasting the Ancestors in Early China," in *The*

Archaeology and Politics of Food and Feasting in Early States and Empires, ed. Tamara Bray (New York: Kluwer Academic/Plenum Publishers, 2003), 65–89.

36. Christy G. Turner and Jacqueline A. Turner, *Man Corn: Cannibalism and Violence in the Prehistoric American Southwest* (Salt Lake City: University of Utah Press, 1999).

37. You can find an excellent summary of archaeological research on the Chaco phenomenon and the deep history of the Ancestral Pueblo people in David E. Stuart, *Anasazi America: Seventeen Centuries on the Road from Center Place*, 2nd ed. (Albuquerque: University of New Mexico Press, 2014).

38. Brian R. Billman, Patricia M. Lambert, and Banks L. Leonard, "Cannibalism, Warfare, and Drought in the Mesa Verde Region during the Twelfth Century A.D.," *American Antiquity* 65, no. 1 (January 2000): 145–78, doi.org/10.2307/2694812.

39. Beth Conklin, *Consuming Grief: Compassionate Cannibalism in an Amazonian Society* (Austin: University of Texas Press, 2001).

40. Yannis Hamilakis and Eleni Konsolaki, "Pigs for the Gods: Burnt Animal Sacrifices as Embodied Rituals at a Mycenean Sanctuary," *Oxford Journal of Archaeology* 23, no. 2 (June 2004): 135–52, doi.org/10.1111/j.1468-0092.2004.00206.x.

41. Amber M. VanDerwarker and Bruce Idol, "Rotten Food and Ritual Behavior: Late Woodland Plant Foodways and Special Purpose Features at Buzzard Rock II, Virginia (44RN2/70)," *Southeastern Archaeology* 27, no. 1 (Summer 2008): 61–77, www.jstor.org.

42. Morán, *Sacred Consumption*.

43. Robyn E. Cutright, "Household *Ofrendas* and Community Feasts: Ritual at a Late Intermediate Period Village in the Jequetepeque Valley, Peru," *Ñawpa Pacha* 33, no. 1 (2013): 1–21, doi.org/10.1179/0077629713Z.0000000001.

Chapter 8

1. While the full burial data excavated by Carol Mackey awaits publication, my analysis of the food remains from this cemetery can be found in Robyn E. Cutright, "Food for the Dead, Cuisine of the Living: Mortuary Food Offerings from the Jequetepeque Valley, Perú," in *From State to Empire in the Prehistoric Jequetepeque Valley, Peru*, ed. Colleen Zori and Ilana Johnson (Oxford: Archaeopress, 2011), 83–92.

2. The Early Archaic stretched from 8000 to 6000 BC, the Middle Archaic from 6000 to 3000 BC, and the Late Archaic from 3000 to 1000 BC, a total of seven thousand years.

3. Recent collections of papers in *The Menial Art of Cooking: Archaeological Studies of Cooking and Food Preparation*, edited by Sarah R. Graff and Enrique Rodríguez-Alegría (Boulder: University Press of Colorado, 2012) and *Inside Ancient Kitchens: New Directions in the Study of Daily Meals and Feasts*, edited by Elizabeth Klarich (Boulder: University Press of Colorado, 2010) explicitly consider food in the everyday lives of commoners—some case studies in this chapter come from these collections. Earlier work, such as the classic *The Early Mesoamerican Village*, edited by Kent Flannery (Cambridge, MA: Academic Press, 1976) considered the empirical evidence from these kinds of houses but without a theoretical focus on the lives of individuals.

4. L. P. Hartley, *The Go-Between* (London: H. Hamilton, 1953).

5. Cynthia Robin, *Everyday Life Matters: Maya Farmers at Chan* (Gainesville: University Press of Florida, 2013).

6. Monica Smith, *A Prehistory of Ordinary People* (Tucson: University of Arizona Press, 2010).

7. Smith, *Prehistory of Ordinary People*, 53.

8. For example, Sonya Atalay and Christine Hastorf, "Food, Meals, and Daily Activities: Food Habitus at Neolithic Çatalhöyük," *American Antiquity* 71, no. 2 (April 2006): 283–319, www.jstor.org; and Ian Hodder and Craig Cessford, "Daily Practice and Social Memory at Çatalhöyük," *American Antiquity* 69, no. 1 (January 2004): 17–40, doi.org /10.2307/4128346.

9. Hastorf makes this argument specifically in Christine Hastorf, "The Habitus of Cooking Practices at Neolithic Çatalhöyük: What Was the Place of the Cook?" in *The Menial Art of Cooking*, ed. Sarah R. Graff and Enrique Rodríguez-Alegría (Boulder: University Press of Colorado, 2012), 65–86. Her recent book, *The Social Archaeology of Food: Thinking about Eating from Prehistory to the Present* (New York: Cambridge University Press, 2016), makes a broader argument for the social life of food.

10. Drew Desilver, "What's on Your Table? How America's Diet Has Changed over the Decades," Pew Research Center Fact Tank, last modified December 13, 2016, www .pewresearch.org.

11. Nineteenth-century factoid from Digital History, "Food in America," accessed July 13, 2017, www.digitalhistory.uh.edu/topic_display.cfm?tcid=92. Contemporary data from the World Health Organization, "Appendix 1," *Global Status Report on Alcohol and Health, 2014*, accessed July 13, 2017, www.who.int.

12. Hastorf, "Habitus of Cooking Practices."

13. Atalay and Hastorf, "Food, Meals, and Daily Activities," 293. Descriptions in the next few paragraphs of the shift from clay balls to clay pots come from this article.

14. Patricia Crown, "Women's Role in Changing Cuisine," in *Women and Men in the Prehispanic Southwest: Labor, Power, and Prestige*, ed. Patricia Crown (Santa Fe: School for Advanced Research Press, 2000), 221–66.

15. Michael Pollan, *Cooked: A Natural History of Transformation* (New York: Penguin Press, 2013), 3.

16. Hastorf, "Habitus of Cooking Practices," 80.

17. Richard Wrangham, discussed in chapter 2, used both to relate cooking to pair-bonding in *Homo erectus*.

18. George P. Murdock and Caterina Provost, "Factors in the Division of Labor by Sex: A Cross-Cultural Analysis," *Ethnology* 12, no. 2 (April 1973): 203–25, www.jstor.org.

19. Marjorie Shostak, *Nisa: The Life and Words of a !Kung Woman* (Cambridge, MA: Harvard University Press, 2000).

20. Debra Martin, "Bodies and Lives: Biological Indicators of Health Differentials and Division of Labor by Sex," in *Women and Men in the Prehispanic Southwest: Labor, Power, and Prestige*, ed. Patricia Crown (Santa Fe: School for Advanced Research Press, 2000), 266–300.

21. Frances F. Berdan and Patricia Rieff Anawalt, eds., *The Codex Mendoza*, vol. 4 (Berkeley: University of California Press, 1992), fol. 60r.

22. Felipe Guaman Poma de Ayala, *Nueva Corónica y Buen Gobierno* (1615), Dibujo 83, June 20, 2019, www.kb.dk.

23. Lynn Meskell, *Private Life in New Kingdom Egypt* (Princeton, NJ: Princeton University Press, 2004), 109.

24. Mary Weismantel, *Food, Gender, and Poverty in the Ecuadorian Andes* (Long Grove, IL: Waveland Press, 1988).

25. Joan M. Gero and M. Christina Scattolin, "Beyond Complementarity and Hierarchy: New Definitions for Archaeological Gender Relations," in *In Pursuit of Gender: Worldwide Archaeological Approaches*, ed. S. Nelson and M. Rosen-Ayalon (Walnut Creek, CA: AltaMira Press, 2002), 155–71.

26. Tracy Sweely, "Gender, Space, People, and Power at Cerén, El Salvador," in *Manifesting Power: Gender and the Interpretation of Power in Archaeology*, ed. Tracy Sweely (New York: Routledge, 1999), 155–72.

27. Alan Farahani et al., "Exploring Culinary Practices through GIS Modeling at Joya de Cerén, El Salvador," in *Social Perspectives on Ancient Lives from Paleoethnobotanical Data*, ed. Matthew Sayre and Maria Bruno (New York: Springer, 2017), 101–20.

28. Delwyn Samuel, "Bread Making and Social Interactions at the Amarna Workmen's Village, Egypt," *World Archaeology* 31, no. 1 (June 1999): 121–44, doi.org/10.1080/00438243.1999.9980435.

29. For example, John W. Janusek, "Of Pots and People: Ceramic Style and Social Identity in the Tiwanaku State," in *Us and Them: Archaeology and Ethnicity in the Andes*, ed. Richard M. Reycraft (Los Angeles: Cotsen Institute of Archaeology, 2005), 34–53.

30. Pierre Bourdieu, *Outline of the Theory of Practice* (Cambridge: Cambridge University Press, 1977).

31. Gil Stein, "Food Preparation, Social Context, and Ethnicity in a Prehistoric Mesopotamian Colony," in *The Menial Art of Cooking*, ed. Sarah R. Graff and Enrique Rodríguez-Alegría (Boulder: University Press of Colorado, 2012), 47–63.

32. Kathleen Deagan, "Colonial Transformation: Euro-American Cultural Genesis in the Early Spanish-American Colonies," *Journal of Anthropological Research* 52, no. 2 (Summer 1996): 135–60, doi.org/10.1086/jar.52.2.3630198.

33. Deagan, "Colonial Transformation," 144.

34. Kent Lightfoot, Antoinette Martinez, and Ann M. Schiff, "Daily Practice and Material Culture in Pluralistic Social Settings: An Archaeological Study of Culture Change and Persistence from Fort Ross, California," *American Antiquity* 63, no. 2 (April 1998): 199–222, doi.org/10.2307/2694694.

35. Barbara L. Voss, "Domesticating Imperialism: Sexual Politics and the Archaeology of Empire," *American Anthropologist* 110, no. 2 (July 2008): 191–203, doi.org/10.1111/j.1548-1433.2008.00025.x.

36. Barbara L. Voss, "From *Casta* to *Californio*: Social Identity and the Archaeology

of Culture Contact," *American Anthropologist* 107, no. 3 (January 2008): 461–74, doi.org
/10.1525/aa.2005.107.3.461.

37. Voss, "From *Casta* to *Californio*," 465–67.

38. Voss, 471.

39. Robyn E. Cutright, "Continuity and Change in Late Intermediate Period
Households on the North Coast of Peru," in *Ancient Households on the North Coast of
Peru*, ed. Ilana Johnson, David Pacifico, and Robyn Cutright (Boulder: University Press
of Colorado, 2020); Robyn E. Cutright and Carlos Osores Mendives, "A Tale of Two Cities: Neighborhood Identity and Integration at Ventanillas, Peru," in *Sociopolitical Integration in Prehispanic Neighborhoods*, ed. Gabriela Cervantes and John Walden (under
review at University of Pittsburgh Press).

40. William Sapp, "Lambayeque Norte and Lambayeque Sur: Evidence for the Devel-
opment of an Indigenous Lambayeque Polity in the Jequetepeque Valley, Peru," in *From
State to Empire in the Prehistoric Jequetepeque Valley, Peru*, ed. Colleen M. Zori and
Ilana Johnson (Oxford: Archaeopress, 2011), 93–104.

41. Howard Tsai, *Las Varas: Ritual and Ethnicity in the Ancient Andes* (Tuscaloosa:
University of Alabama Press, 2020).

42. Cutright and Osores Mendives, "A Tale of Two Cities."

Conclusion

1. Claude Lévi-Strauss's well-known quote, from *Totemism* (Boston: Beacon Press,
1963), 89.

2. National Corn Growers Association, "World Corn Production 2016–17," accessed
July 26, 2017, www.worldofcorn.com.

3. Vaclav Smil, "Harvesting the Biosphere: The Human Impact," *Population and Development Review* 37, no. 4 (December 2011): 613–37, doi.org/10.1111/j.1728-4457.2011
.00450.x.

4. Kevin N. Laland, John Odling-Smee, and Marcus W. Feldman, "Niche Construction,
Biological Evolution, and Cultural Change," *Behavioral and Brain Sciences* 23, no. 1 (February 2000): 131–46, doi.org/10.1017/S0140525X00002417.

5. This echoes Martin Jones's discussion of deep temporal trends in *Feast* (Oxford:
Oxford University Press, 2008).

6. Michael Pollan, *The Omnivore's Dilemma* (New York: Penguin Press, 2006).

7. The World Bank, "Employment in Agriculture," accessed July 26, 2017, data
.worldbank.org.

8. "The past is a foreign country" is the first line of L. P. Hartley, *The Go-Between*
(London: Hamish Hamilton, 1953) and is a favorite quote of archaeologists and
historians.

BIBLIOGRAPHY

Adamson, Melitta Weiss, ed. *Regional Cuisines of Medieval Europe: A Book of Essays*.
New York: Routledge, 2002.

Aiello, Leslie C., and Peter Wheeler. "The Expensive-Tissue Hypothesis: The Brain and
the Digestive System in Human and Primate Evolution." *Current Anthropology* 36,
no. 2 (April 1995): 199–221. www.jstor.org.

Alcock, Joan P. *Food in the Ancient World*. Westport, CT: Greenwood Press, 2006.

Allen, Catherine J. *The Hold Life Has: Coca and Cultural Identity in an Andean Community*. Washington, DC: Smithsonian Institution Press, 1988.

Andres, Susan C., and James P. Fenton. "Archaeology and the Invisible Man: The Role
of Slavery in the Production of Wealth and Social Class in the Bluegrass Region of
Kentucky, 1820 to 1870." *World Archaeology* 33, no. 1 (January 2001): 115–36. doi.org
/10.1080/00438240126649.

Armelagos, George J., and Mark Nathan Cohen. "Preface to the 2013 Edition." In *Paleopathology at the Origins of Agriculture*, edited by George J. Armelagos and Mark
Nathan Cohen, xvii–xxxv. Orlando: University Press of Florida, 2013.

Arranz-Otaegui, Amaia, Lara Gonzalez Carretero, Monica N. Ramsey, Dorian Q. Fuller,
and Tobias Richter. "Archaeobotanical Evidence Reveals the Origins of Bread
14,400 Years Ago in Northeastern Jordan." *Proceedings of the National Academy of
Science* 115, no. 31 (July 2018): 7925–30. doi.org/10.1073/pnas.1801071115.

Arwill-Nordbladh, Elisabeth. "A Reigning Queen or the Wife of a King—Only? Gender
Politics in the Scandinavian Viking Age." In *Ancient Queens: Archaeological Ex-
plorations*, edited by Sarah Milledge Nelson, 19–40. Walnut Creek, CA: AltaMira
Press, 2003.

Atalay, Sonya, and Christine Hastorf. "Food, Meals, and Daily Activities: Food Habitus at Neolithic Çatalhöyük." *American Antiquity* 71, no. 2 (April 2006): 283–319.
www.jstor.org.

Barton, Huw, and Tim Denham. "Prehistoric Vegeculture and Social Life in Island
Southeast Asia and Melanesia." In *Why Cultivate? Anthropological and Archaeo-
logical Approaches to Foraging-Farming Transitions in Southeast Asia*, edited by
Graeme Barker and Monica Janowski, 17–25. Cambridge: McDonald Institute for
Archaeological Research, 2011.

Bar-Yosef, Ofer. "Climatic Fluctuations and Early Farming in West and East Asia."
Current Anthropology 52, no. S4 (October 2011): S175–93. doi.org/10.1086/659784.

Beise, Jan, and Eckart Voland. "A Multilevel Event History Analysis of the Effects of Grandmothers on Child Mortality in a Historical German Population." *Demographic Research* 7, Article 13 (September 2002): 469–98. doi.org/10.4054 /DemRes.2002.7.13.

Benz, Bruce. "Archaeological Evidence of Teosinte Domestication from Guilá Naquitz, Oaxaca." *Proceedings of the National Academy of Sciences* 98, no. 4 (February 2001): 2104–6. doi.org/10.1073/pnas.98.4.2104.

Berdan, Frances F., and Patricia Rieff Anawalt, eds. *The Codex Mendoza*. Vol. 4. Berkeley: University of California Press, 1992.

Berger, Thomas D., and Erik Trinkaus. "Patterns of Trauma among the Neandertals." *Journal of Archaeological Science* 22, no. 6 (November 1995): 841–52.

Bill, Jan. "Ambiguous Mobility in the Viking Age Ship Burial from Oseberg." In *Materialities of Passing: Explorations in Transformation, Transition, and Transience*, edited by Peter Bjerregaard, Anders Emil Rasmussen, and Tim Flohr Sørensen, 207–20. New York: Routledge, 2016.

Billman, Brian R., Patricia M. Lambert, and Banks L. Leonard. "Cannibalism, Warfare, and Drought in the Mesa Verde Region during the Twelfth Century A.D." *American Antiquity* 65, no. 1 (January 2000): 145–78. doi.org/10.2307/2694812.

Binford, Lewis R. "Human Ancestors: Changing Views of Their Behavior." *Journal of Anthropological Archaeology* 4, no. 4 (December 1985): 292–327. doi.org/10.1016 /0278-4165(85)90009-1.

———. *Nunamiut Ethnoarchaeology*. Cambridge, MA: Academic Press, 1978.

———. "Post-Pleistocene Adaptations." In *New Perspectives in Archeology*, edited by Sally Binford and Lewis R. Binford, 313–41. Chicago: Aldine, 1968.

Bird, R. Bliege, D. W. Bird, B. F. Codding, C. H. Parker, and J. H. Jones. "The 'Fire Stick Farming' Hypothesis: Australian Aboriginal Foraging Strategies, Biodiversity, and Anthropogenic Fire Mosaics." *Proceedings of the National Academy of Sciences* 105, no. 39 (September 2008): 14796–801. doi.org/10.1073/pnas.0804757105.

Biskowski, Martin. "Maize Preparation and the Aztec Subsistence Economy." *Ancient Mesoamerica* 11, no. 2 (Fall 2000): 293–306. www.jstor.org.

Blake, Michael. *Maize for the Gods: Unearthing the 9,000-Year History of Corn*. Oakland: University of California Press, 2015.

Blumenschine, Robert J., and John A. Cavallo. "Scavenging and Human Evolution." *Scientific American* 267, no. 4 (October 1992): 90–7. www.jstor.org.

Blumenschine, Robert J., Karie Prassak, C. David Kreger, and Michael C. Pante. "Carnivore Tooth-Marks, Microbial Bioerosion, and the Invalidation of Domínguez-Rodrigo and Barba's (2006) Test of Oldowan Hominin Scavenging Behavior." *Journal of Human Evolution* 53, no. 4 (2007): 420–26. doi.org/10.1016/j.jhev01.2007.01.011.

Boas, Franz, and Helen F. Codere. *Kwakiutl Ethnography*. Chicago: University of Chicago Press, 1966.

Bober, Phyllis Pray. *Art, Culture, and Cuisine: Ancient and Medieval Gastronomy*. Chicago: University of Chicago Press, 1999.

Boserup, Ester. *The Conditions of Agricultural Growth: The Economics of Agrarian Change under Population Pressure*. Chicago: Aldine, 1965.

Bourdieu, Pierre. *Outline of the Theory of Practice*. Cambridge: Cambridge University Press, 1977.

Bourget, Steve. "Rituals of Sacrifice: Its Practice at Huaca de la Luna and Its Representation in Moche Iconography." In *Moche Art and Archaeology in Ancient Peru*, edited by Joanne Pillsbury, 88–109. New Haven, CT: Yale University Press, 2001.

———. *Sacrifice, Violence, and Ideology among the Moche: The Rise of Social Complexity in Ancient Peru*. Austin: University of Texas Press, 2016.

Bower, Bruce. "The First Known Fossil of a Denisovan Skull Has Been Found in a Siberian Cave." *Science News*. Last modified March 29, 2019. www.sciencenews.org.

Brace, C. Loring. "Biocultural Interaction and the Mechanism of Mosaic Evolution in the Emergence of 'Modern' Morphology." *American Anthropologist* 97, no. 4 (December 1995): 711–21. doi.org/10.1525/aa.1995.97.4.02a00130.

Braidwood, Robert J. "The Agricultural Revolution." *Scientific American* 203, no. 3 (September 1960): 130–52. www.jstor.org.

Bramanti, B., M. G. Thomas, W. Haak, M. Unterlaender, P. Jores, K. Tambets, I. Antanaitis-Jacobs, et al. "Genetic Discontinuity between Local Hunter-Gatherers and Central Europe's First Farmers." *Science* 326, no. 5949 (October 2009): 137–40. doi.org/10.1126/science.1176869.

Bramble, Dennis, and Daniel E. Lieberman. "Endurance Running and the Evolution of *Homo*." *Nature* 432, no. 7015 (November 2004): 345–52. doi.org/10.1038/nature03052.

Bray, Tamara. "Inka Pottery as Culinary Equipment: Food, Feasting, and Gender in Imperial State Design." *Latin American Antiquity* 14, no. 1 (March 2003): 3–28. doi.org/10.2307/972233.

———. "The Role of Chicha in Inca State Expansion." In *Drink, Power, and Society in the Andes*, edited by Justin Jennings and Brenda Bowser, 108–32. Gainesville: University Press of Florida, 2008.

Brock, Peggy. "Moveable Feasts: Chronicles of 'Potlatching' among the Tsimshian, 1860s–1900s." *Ethnohistory* 59, no. 2 (2012): 387–405. doi.org/10.1215/00141801-1536921.

Brumfiel, Elizabeth M. "Consumption and Politics at Aztec Huexotla." *American Anthropologist* 89, no. 3 (September 1987): 676–86. doi.org/10.1525/aa.1987.89.3.02a00090.

Buck, Laura, and Chris Stringer. "Having the Stomach for It: A Contribution to Neandertal Diets?" *Quaternary Science Reviews* 96 (July 2014): 161–67. doi.org/10.1016/j.quascirev.2013.09.003.

Bunn, Henry T. "Meat Made Us Human." In *Evolution of the Human Diet*, edited by Peter S. Ungar, 191–211. New York: Oxford University Press, 2007.

Bunn, Henry T., John W. K. Harris, Glynn Isaac, Zefe Kaufulu, Ellen Kroll, Kathy Schick, Nicholas Toth, and Anna K. Behrensmyer. "FxJj50: An Early Pleistocene Site in Northern Kenya." *World Archaeology* 12, no. 2 (1980): 109–36. doi.org/10.1080/00438243.1980.9979787.

Burger, Richard L. "What Kind of Hallucinogenic Snuff Was Used at Chavín de Huántar?" *Ñawpa Pacha* 31, no. 2 (December 2011): 123–40. doi.org/10.1179/naw.2011
  .31.2.123.

Buss, David. *The Evolution of Desire: Strategies of Human Mating.* New York: Basic
  Books, 1995.

Bussman, Rainer W., and Douglas Sharon. "Naming a Phantom—The Quest to Find the
  Identity of *Ulluchu*, an Unidentified Ceremonial Plant of the Moche Culture." *Journal of Ethnobiology and Ethnomedicine* 5, no. 8 (2009). doi.org/10.1186/1746
  -4269-5-8.

Campbell, Michael C., and Sarah A. Tishkoff. "African Genetic Diversity: Implications
  for Human Demographic History, Modern Human Origins, and Complex Disease
  Mapping." *Annual Review of Genomics and Human Genetics* 9 (September 2008):
  403–33. doi.org/10.1146/annurev.genom.9.081307.164258.

Carney, Judith. *Black Rice: The African Origins of Rice Cultivation in the Americas.* Cambridge, MA: Harvard University Press, 2002.

Carrigan, Matthew A., Oleg Urasev, Carole B. Frye, Blair L. Eckman, Candace R. Myers,
  Thomas D. Hurley, and Steven A. Benner. "Hominids Adapted to Metabolize Ethanol Long Before Human-Directed Fermentation." *Proceedings of the National Academy of Sciences* 112, no. 2 (January 2015): 458–63. doi.org/10.1073/pnas.1404167111.

Center for American Progress. "Systematic Inequality: How America's Structural Racism Helped Create the Black-White Wealth Gap." Last modified February 21, 2018.
  www.americanprogress.org.

Chang, Kwang-Chih. Introduction to *Food in Chinese Culture: Anthropological and Historical Perspectives*, edited by K. C. Chang, 1–21. New Haven, CT: Yale University
  Press, 1977.

Childe, V. Gordon. *Man Makes Himself.* Oxford: Oxford University Press, 1936.

———. *The Most Ancient Near East.* London: K. Paul, Trench, Trubner, 1928.

Churchill, Steven E. *Thin on the Ground: Neandertal Biology, Archeology, and Ecology.*
  Hoboken, NJ: Wiley-Blackwell, 2014.

Civil, Miguel. "A Hymn to the Beer Goddess and a Drinking Song." In *Studies Presented
  to A. Leo Oppenheim*, edited by R. D. Biggs and J. A. Brinkman, 67–69. Chicago:
  Oriental Institute, 1964.

Cobo, Bernabé. *Inca Religion and Customs.* Translated by Roland Hamilton. Austin:
  University of Texas Press, 1990.

Coe, Sophie. *America's First Cuisines.* Austin: University of Texas Press, 1994.

Coe, Sophie D., and Michael D. Coe. *The True History of Chocolate.* New York: Thames
  and Hudson, 2013.

Cohen, Mark Nathan. *The Food Crisis in Prehistory: Overpopulation and the Origins of
  Agriculture.* New Haven, CT: Yale University Press, 1977.

———. *Health and the Rise of Civilization.* New Haven, CT: Yale University Press, 1989.

Conklin, Beth. *Consuming Grief: Compassionate Cannibalism in an Amazonian Society.*
  Austin: University of Texas Press, 2001.

Conroy, Glenn C., and Herman Pontzer, eds. *Reconstructing Human Origins*. 3rd ed. New York: W. W. Norton, 2012.

Cook, Robert A., and T. Douglas Price. "Maize, Mounds, and the Movement of People: Isotope Analysis of a Mississippian/Fort Ancient Region." *Journal of Archaeological Science* 61 (September 2015): 112–28. doi.org/10.1016/j.jas.2015.03.022.

Cordain, Loren. *The Paleo Diet: Lose Weight and Get Healthy by Eating the Food You Were Designed to Eat*. Hoboken, NJ: John Wiley and Sons, 2002.

Costin, Cathy Lynne, and Timothy Earle. "Status Distinction and Legitimation of Power as Reflected in Changing Patterns of Consumption in Late Prehispanic Peru." *American Antiquity* 54, no. 4 (October 1989): 691–714. doi.org/10.2307/280677.

Coté, Charlotte. "'Indigenizing' Food Sovereignty: Revitalizing Indigenous Food Practices and Ecological Knowledges in Canada and the United States." *Humanities* 5, no. 3 (July 2016): 57. doi.org/10.3390/h5030057.

Coxworth, James E., Peter S. Kim, John S. McQueen, and Kristen Hawkes. "Grandmothering Life Histories and Human Pair Bonding." *Proceedings of the National Academy of Sciences* 112, no. 38 (September 2015): 11806–11. doi.org/10.1073/pnas.1599993112.

Crader, Diana C. "Slave Diet at Monticello." *American Antiquity* 55, no. 4 (October 1990): 690–717. doi.org/10.2307/281246.

Craig, Oliver E., Val J. Steele, Anders Fischer, Sönke Hartz, Søren H. Andersen, Paul Donohoe, Aikaterini Glykou, et al. "Ancient Lipids Reveal Continuity in Culinary Practices across the Transition to Agriculture in Northern Europe." *Proceedings of the National Academy of Sciences* 108, no. 44 (November 2011): 17910–15. doi.org/10.1073/pnas.1107202108.

Crites, Gary D. "Domesticated Sunflower in Fifth Millennium B.P. Temporal Context: New Evidence from Middle Tennessee." *American Antiquity* 58, no. 1 (January 1993): 146–48. doi.org/10.2307/281459.

Crosby, Alfred. *The Columbian Exchange: The Biological and Cultural Consequences of 1492*. Westport, CT: Praeger Press, 2003.

Cross, Wilbur. *Gullah Culture in America*. Winston-Salem, NC: John E. Blair, Publisher, 2008.

Crown, Patricia. "Women's Role in Changing Cuisine." In *Women and Men in the Prehispanic Southwest: Labor, Power, and Prestige*, edited by Patricia Crown, 221–66. Santa Fe: School for Advanced Research Press, 2000.

Cutright, Robyn E. "Between the Kitchen and the State: Domestic Practice and Chimú Expansion in the Jequetepeque Valley, Peru." PhD diss., University of Pittsburgh, 2009. d-scholarship.pitt.edu.

———. "Continuity and Change in Late Intermediate Period Households on the North Coast of Peru." In *Ancient Households on the North Coast of Peru*, edited by Ilana Johnson, David Pacifico, and Robyn Cutright (Boulder: University Press of Colorado, 2020).

———. "Eating Empire in the Jequetepeque: A Local View of Chimú Expansion on the

North Coast of Peru." *Latin American Antiquity* 26, no. 1 (March 2015): 64–86. doi.org/10.7183/1045-6635.26.1.64.

———. "Food for the Dead, Cuisine of the Living: Mortuary Food Offerings from the Jequetepeque Valley, Perú." In *From State to Empire in the Prehistoric Jequetepeque Valley, Peru*, edited by Colleen Zori and Ilana Johnson, 83–92. Oxford: Archaeopress, 2011.

———. "Household *Ofrendas* and Community Feasts: Ritual at a Late Intermediate Period Village in the Jequetepeque Valley, Peru." *Ñawpa Pacha* 33, no. 1 (November 2013): 1–21. doi.org/10.1179/0077629713Z.0000000001.

Cutright, Robyn E., and Carlos Osores Mendives. "A Tale of Two Cities: Neighborhood Identity and Integration at Ventanillas, Peru." In *Sociopolitical Integration in Prehispanic Neighborhoods*, edited by Gabriela Cervantes and John Walden. Under review at University of Pittsburgh Press.

Cylinder seal of Pu-abi. Ur, Early Dynastic III (2600 BC). Item 121544. British Museum, London.

Dahlberg, Frances, ed. *Woman the Gatherer*. New Haven, CT: Yale University Press, 1981.

D'Altroy, Terence, and Christine Hastorf, eds. *Empire and Domestic Economy*. New York: Springer, 2001.

D'Altroy, Terence, and Timothy Earle. "Staple Finance, Wealth Finance, and Storage in the Inka Political Economy." *Current Anthropology* 26, no. 2 (April 1985): 187–206. doi.org/10.1086/203249.

Damerow, Peter. "Sumerian Beer: The Origins of Brewing Technology in Ancient Mesopotamia." *Cuneiform Digital Library Journal* 2 (January 2012). www.cdli.ucla.edu.

Dannemann, Michael, and Janet Kelso. "The Contribution of Neanderthals to Phenotypic Variation in Modern Humans." *American Journal of Human Genetics* 101, no. 4 (October 2017): 578–89. doi.org/10.1016/j.ajhg.2017.09.010.

Dart, Raymond A. *Adventures with the Missing Link*. New York: Harper, 1959.

———. "Australopithecus africanus: The Man-Ape of South Africa." *Nature* 115, no. 2884 (February 1925): 195–99. doi.org/10.1038%2F115195a0.

Deagan, Kathleen. "Colonial Origins and Colonial Transformations in Spanish America." *Historical Archaeology* 37, no. 4 (December 2003): 3–13. doi.org/10.1007/BF03376619.

———. "Colonial Transformation: Euro-American Cultural Genesis in the Early Spanish-American Colonies." *Journal of Anthropological Research* 52, no. 2 (Summer 1996): 135–60. doi.org/10.1086/jar.52.2.3630198.

Delcourt, Paul A., Hazel R. Delcourt, Cecil R. Ison, William E. Sharp, and Kristen J. Gremillion. "Prehistoric Human Use of Fire, the Eastern Agricultural Complex, and Appalachian Oak-Chestnut Forests: Paleoecology of Cliff Palace Pond, Kentucky." *American Antiquity* 63, no. 2 (April 1998): 263–78. doi.org/10.2307/2694697.

Desilver, Drew. "What's On Your Table? How America's Diet Has Changed over the Decades." Pew Research Center Fact Tank. Last modified December 13, 2016. www.pewresearch.org.

Dietler, Michael. "Feasting and Fasting." In *The Oxford Handbook of the Archaeology of Ritual and Religion*, edited by Timothy Insoll, 180–94. Oxford: Oxford University Press, 2011.

———. "Theorizing the Feast: Rituals of Consumption, Commensal Politics, and Power in African Contexts." In *Feasts: Archaeological and Ethnographic Perspectives on Food, Politics, and Power*, edited by M. Dietler and B. Hayden, 65–114. Washington, DC: Smithsonian Institution Press, 2001.

Dietler, Michael, and Brian Hayden, eds. *Feasts: Archaeological and Ethnographic Perspectives on Food, Politics, and Power*. Washington, DC: Smithsonian Institution Press, 2001.

Dietrich, Oliver, M. Heun, Jens Notroff, Klaus Schmidt, and M. Zarnkow. "The Role of Cult and Feasting in the Emergence of Neolithic Communities: New Evidence from Göbekli Tepe, South-Eastern Turkey." *Antiquity* 86, no. 333 (September 2012): 674–95. doi.org/10.1017/S0003598X00047840.

Dietrich, Oliver, Çiğdem Köksal-Schmidt, Jens Notroff, and Klaus Schmidt. "Establishing a Radiocarbon Sequence for Göbekli Tepe: State of Research and New Data." *Neo-Lithics* 1 (October 2013): 36–41.

Digital History. "Food in America." Accessed July 13, 2017. www.digitalhistory.uh.edu.

Dillehay, Tom D., Carlos Ocampo, José Saavedra, Andre Oliveira Sawakuchi, Rodrigo M. Vega, Mario Pino, Michael B. Collins, et al. "New Archaeological Evidence for Early Human Presence at Monte Verde, Chile." *PLoS One* 10, no. 11 (December 2015): e0145471. doi.org/10.1371/journal.pone.0145471.

Doebley, John. "The Genetics of Maize Evolution." *Annual Review of Genetics* 38, no. 1 (November 2004): 37–59. doi.org/10.1146%2Fannurev.genet.38.072902.092425.

Domínguez-Rodrigo, Manuel, and R. Barba. "Five More Arguments to Invalidate the Passive Scavenging Version of the Carnivore-Hominid-Carnivore Model: A Reply to Blumenschine et al. (2007a)." *Journal of Human Evolution* 53, no. 4 (2007): 427–33. doi.org/10.1016/j.jhevol.2007.05.010.

Donnan, Christopher B. "The Thematic Approach to Moche Iconography." *Journal of Latin American Lore* 1, no. 2 (1975): 147–62.

Douglas, Mary. "Deciphering a Meal." In *Food and Culture: A Reader*, edited by Carole Counihan and Penny van Esterik, 36–54. New York: Routledge, 2008.

———. *Purity and Danger: An Analysis of Concepts of Pollution and Taboo*. New York: Routledge, 1966.

Douka, Katerina, Nikos Efstratiou, Mette Marie Hald, Peter Steen Henricksen, and Alexandra Karetsou. "Dating Knossos and the Arrival of the Earliest Neolithic in the Southern Aegean." *Antiquity* 91, no. 356 (2017): 304–21. doi:10.15184/aqy.2017.29.

Dubois, Thomas. *Nordic Religions in the Viking Age*. Philadelphia: University of Pennsylvania Press, 1999.

Dudley, Robert. *The Drunken Monkey: Why We Drink and Abuse Alcohol*. Berkeley: University of California Press, 2014.

Dunsworth, Holly, and Leah Eccleston. "The Evolution of Difficult Childbirth and

Helpless Hominin Infants." *Annual Review of Anthropology* 44, no. 1 (October 2015): 55–69. doi.org/10.1146/annurev-anthro-102214-013918.

Duvall, Chris. "Chimpanzee Diet in the Bafing Area, Mali." *African Journal of Ecology* 46 (2008): 679–83. doi.org/10.1111/j.1365-2028.2007.00883.x.

Ember, Carol, Melvin Ember, and Peter Peregrine. *Physical Anthropology and Archaeology*. 2nd ed. New York: Pearson, 2007.

Estalrrich, Almudena, and Antonio Rosas. "Division of Labor by Sex and Age in Neandertals: An Approach through the Study of Activity-Related Dental Wear." *Journal of Human Evolution* 80 (March 2015): 51–63. doi.org/10.1016/j.jhevol.2014.07.007.

Evershed, Richard P., Sebastian Payne, Andrew G. Sherratt, Mark S. Copley, Jennifer Coolidge, Duska Urem-Kotsu, Kostas Kotsakis, et al. "Earliest Date for Milk Use in the Near East and Southeastern Europe Linked to Cattle Herding." *Nature* 455 (August 2008): 528–31. doi.org/10.1038/nature07180.

Falconer, Steven. "Rural Responses to Early Urbanism: Bronze Age Household and Village Economy at Tell el-Hayyat, Jordan." *Journal of Field Archaeology* 22, no. 4 (1995): 399–419. doi.org/10.1179/009346995791974107.

Farahani, Alan, Katherine L. Chiou, Rob Q. Cuthrell, Annay Harkey, Shanti Morell-Hart, Christine A. Hastorf, and Payson D. Sheets. "Exploring Culinary Practices through GIS Modeling at Joya de Cerén, El Salvador." In *Social Perspectives on Ancient Lives from Paleoethnobotanical Data*, edited by Matthew Sayre and Maria Bruno, 101–20. New York: Springer, 2017.

Ferguson, Leland. *Uncommon Ground: Archaeology and Early African America, 1650–1800*. Washington, DC: Smithsonian Institution Press, 1992.

Fernández, Manuel Hernández, and Elisabeth S. Vrba. "Plio-Pleistocene Climatic Change in the Turkana Basin (East Africa): Evidence from Large Mammal Faunas." *Journal of Human Evolution* 50, no. 6 (June 2006): 595–626. doi.org/10.1016/j.jhevol.2005.11.004.

Ferraro, Joseph V., Thomas W. Plummer, Briana L. Pobiner, James S. Oliver, Laura C. Bishop, David R. Braun, Peter W. Ditchfield, et al. "Earliest Archaeological Evidence of Persistent Hominin Carnivory." *PLoS One* 8, no. 4 (2013): e62174. doi.org/10.1371/journal.pone.0062174.

Finch, Caleb E., and Craig B. Stanford. "Meat-Adaptive Genes and the Evolution of Slower Aging in Humans." *Quarterly Review of Biology* 79, no. 1 (March 2004): 3–50. doi.org/10.1086/381662.

Finkel, Michael. "The Hadza." *National Geographic* 216, no. 6 (December 2009): 94–119.

Fiorenza, Luca. "Reconstructing Diet and Behaviour of Neandertals from Central Italy through Dental Macrowear Analysis." *Journal of Anthropological Sciences* 93 (2015): 1–15. doi.org/10.4436/JASS.93002.

Fiscaletti, M., P. Stewart, and C. F. Munns. "The Importance of Vitamin D in Maternal and Child Health: A Global Perspective." *Public Health Reviews* 38, no. 19 (September 2017). doi.org/10.1186/s40985-017–0066-3.

Flannery, Kent. *The Early Mesoamerican Village*. Cambridge, MA: Academic Press, 1976.

———. "Origins and Ecological Effects of Early Domestication in Iran and the Near East." In *The Domestication and Exploitation of Plants and Animals*, edited by Peter J. Ucko and G. W. Dimbleby, 73–100. Chicago: Aldine, 1969.

Food and Agriculture Organization of the United Nations. "Staple Foods: What Do People Eat?" Accessed August 3, 2018. www.fao.org.

Fowles, Severin M. "Steps toward an Archaeology of Taboo." In *Religion, Archaeology, and the Material World*, edited by Lars Fogelin, 15–37. Carbondale: Southern Illinois University Press, 2008.

Franklin, Maria. "The Archaeological Dimensions of Soul Food: Interpreting Race, Culture, and Afro-Virginian Identity." In *Race and the Archaeology of Identity*, edited by Charles Orser, 88–107. Salt Lake City: University of Utah Press, 2001.

Frantzen, Allen J. *Food, Eating, and Identity in Early Medieval England*. Suffolk, UK: Boydell Press, 2014.

Fritz, Gayle J. *Feeding Cahokia: Early Agriculture in the North American Heartland*. Tuscaloosa: University of Alabama Press, 2019.

Fu, Qiaomei, Mateja Hajdinjak, Oana Teodora Moldovan, Silviu Constantin, Swapan Mallick, Pontus Skoglund, Nick Patterson, et al. "An Early Modern Human from Romania with a Recent Neanderthal Ancestor." *Nature* 524 (June 2015): 216–19. doi .org/10.1038/nature14558.

Fung, Christopher. "The Drinks Are on Us: Ritual, Social Status, and Practice in Dawenkou Burials, North China." *Journal of East Asian Archaeology* 2, no. 1 (January 2000): 67–92. doi.org/10.1163/156852300509808.

Garrod, Dorothy. "Palaeolithic Spear-Throwers." *Proceedings of the Prehistoric Society* 21 (July 1956): 21–35. doi.org/10.1017/S0079497X00017370.

Gaulin, Steven J. C. "A Jarman/Bell Model of Primate Feeding Niches." *Human Ecology* 7, no. 1 (March 1979): 1–20. doi.org/10.1007/BF00889349.

Gerbault, Pascale, Anke Liebert, Yuval Itan, Adam Powell, Mathias Currat, Joachim Burger, Dallas M. Swallow, and Mark G. Thomas. "Evolution of Lactase Persistence: An Example of Human Niche Construction." *Philosophical Transactions of the Royal Society B: Biological Sciences* 366, no. 1566 (March 2011): 863–77. doi.org/10.1098 /rstb.2010.0268.

Gero, Joan, and Margaret Conkey, eds. *Engendering Archaeology*. Malden, MA: Blackwell, 1990.

Gero, Joan M., and M. Christina Scattolin. "Beyond Complementarity and Hierarchy: New Definitions for Archaeological Gender Relations." In *In Pursuit of Gender: Worldwide Archaeological Approaches*, edited by Sarah Milledge Nelson and Myriam Rosen-Ayalon, 155–71. Walnut Creek, CA: AltaMira Press, 2002.

Glass-Coffin, Bonnie. "Shamanism and San Pedro through Time: Some Notes on the Archaeology, History, and Continued Use of an Entheogen in Northern Peru." *Anthropology of Consciousness* 21, no. 1 (March 2010): 58–83. doi.org/10.1111/j .1556–3537.2010.01021.x.

Glowacki, Mary. "Food of the Gods or Mere Mortals? Hallucinogenic *Spondylus* and

Its Interpretive Implications for Early Andean Society." *Antiquity* 79, no. 304 (June 2005): 257–68. doi.org/10.1017/S0003598X00114061.

Goldstone, Lucas, Volker Sommer, Niina Nurmi, Colleen Stephens, and Barbara Fruth. "Food Begging and Sharing in Wild Bonobos (*Pan paniscus*): Assessing Relationship Quality." *Primates* 57, no 3 (July 2016): 367–76. doi.org/10.1007/s10329-016-0522-6.

Gomes, Cristina M., Christophe Boesch, and Colin Allen. "Wild Chimpanzees Exchange Meat for Sex on a Long-Term Basis." *PLoS One* 4, no. 4 (2009): e5116. doi.org /10.1371/journal.pone.0005116.

Goodall, Jane. *The Chimpanzees of Gombe: Patterns of Behavior*. Cambridge, MA: Harvard University Press, 1986.

———. *In the Shadow of Man*. Boston: Houghton Mifflin, 1971.

Goody, Jack. *Cooking, Cuisine, and Class: A Study in Comparative Sociology*. Cambridge: Cambridge University Press, 1982.

Gose, Peter. "The State as a Chosen Woman: Brideservice and the Feeding of Tributaries in the Inka Empire." *American Anthropologist* 102, no. 1 (March 2000): 84–97. doi .org/10.1525/aa.2000.102.1.84.

Gowlett, John A. J., and Richard W. Wrangham. "Earliest Fire in Africa: Towards the Convergence of Archaeological Evidence and the Cooking Hypothesis." *Azania: Archaeological Research in Africa* 48, no. 1 (March 2013): 5–30. doi.org/10.1080 /0067270X.2012.756754.

Graff, Sarah R., and Enrique Rodríguez-Alegría, eds. *The Menial Art of Cooking: Archaeological Studies of Cooking and Food Preparation*. Boulder: University Press of Colorado, 2012.

Gremillion, Kristen J. "Changing Roles of Wild and Cultivated Plant Resources among Early Farmers of Eastern Kentucky." *Southeastern Archaeology* 12, no. 1 (1998): 140– 57. www.jstor.org.

Groover, Mark D. "Creolization and the Archaeology of Multiethnic Households in the American South." *Historical Archaeology* 34, no. 3 (September 2000): 99–106. doi. org/10.1007/BF03373645.

———. "Evidence for Folkways and Cultural Exchange in the 18th Century South Carolina Backcountry." *Historical Archaeology* 28, no. 1 (March 1994): 41–64. doi.org /10.1007/BF03374180.

Groucutt, Huw S., Michael D. Petraglia, Geoff Bailey, Eleanor M. L. Scerri, Ash Parton, Laine Clark-Balzan, Richard P. Jennings, et al. "Rethinking the Dispersal of *Homo sapiens* Out of Africa." *Evolutionary Anthropology: Issues, News, and Reviews* 24, no. 4 (August 2015): 149–64. doi.org/10.1002/evan.21455.

Guaman Poma de Ayala, Felipe. *Nueva Corónica y Buen Gobierno* (1615), Dibujo 83. Accessed June 20, 2019. www.kb.dk.

Guerra-Doce, Elisa. "The Origins of Inebriation: Archaeological Evidence of the Consumption of Fermented Beverages and Drugs in Prehistoric Eurasia." *Journal of Archaeological Method and Theory* 22, no. 3 (September 2015): 751–82. doi.org /10.1007/s10816-014-9205-z.

Guerra-Doce, Elisa. "Psychoactive Substances in Prehistoric Times: Examining the Archaeological Evidence." *Time and Mind* 8, no. 1 (2015): 91–112. doi.org/10.1080/1751696X.2014.993244.

Gumerman, George, IV. "Corn for the Dead: The Significance of *Zea mays* in Moche Burial Offerings." In *Corn and Culture in the Prehistoric New World*, edited by Sissel Johansen and Christine Hastorf, 399–410. Boulder, CO: Westview Press, 1994.

Haas, Jonathan, and Winifred Creamer. "Crucible of Andean Civilization: The Peruvian Coast from 3000 to 1800 BC." *Current Anthropology* 47, no. 5 (October 2006): 745–75. doi.org/10.1086/506281.

Hager, Lori D., ed. *Women in Human Evolution*. New York: Routledge, 1997.

Hamienkowski, Nicolás M., and Pastor Arenas. "'Bitter' Manioc (*Manihot esculenta*): Its Consumption and the Grater Used by the Indigenous Peoples of the Gran Chaco in Its Preparation." *Journal de la Société des Américanistes* 103, no. 2 (2017): 205–28. doi.org/10.4000/jsa.15230.

Hamilakis, Yannis. "Food Technologies/Technologies of the Body: The Social Context of Wine and Oil Production and Consumption in Bronze Age Crete." *World Archaeology* 31, no. 1 (June 1999): 38–54. doi.org/10.1080%2F00438243.1999.9980431.

Hamilakis, Yannis, and Eleni Konsolaki. "Pigs for the Gods: Burnt Animal Sacrifices as Embodied Rituals at a Mycenean Sanctuary." *Oxford Journal of Archaeology* 23, no. 2 (June 2004): 135–52. doi.org/10.1111/j.1468-0092.2004.00206.x.

Hamilakis, Yannis, and Susan Sherratt. "Feasting and the Consuming Body in Bronze Age Crete and Early Iron Age Cyprus." *British School at Athens Studies* 20, *Parallel Lives: Ancient Island Societies in Crete and Cyprus* (2012): 187–207. www.jstor.org.

Harcourt-Smith, William E. H. "The Origins of Bipedal Locomotion." In *Handbook of Paleoanthropology*, edited by Winfried Henke and Ian Tattersall, 1–36. Berlin: Springer, 2014.

Hardy, Bruce L., and Marie-Hélène Moncel. "Neandertal Use of Fish, Mammals, Birds, Starchy Plants, and Wood, 125–250,000 Years Ago." *PLoS One* 6, no. 8 (August 2011): e23768. doi.org/10.1371/journal.pone.0023768.

Harris, Marvin. "The Abominable Pig." In *Food and Culture: A Reader*, edited by Carole Counihan and Penny van Esterik, 67–79. New York: Routledge, 1988.

Hartley, L. P. *The Go-Between*. London: H. Hamilton, 1953.

Hastorf, Christine. "Andean Luxury Foods: Special Food for the Ancestors, Deities, and the Elite." *Antiquity* 77, no. 297 (September 2003): 545–54. doi.org/10.1017/S0003598X00092607.

———. "Gender, Space, and Food in Prehistory." In *Engendering Archaeology: Women and Prehistory*, edited by Joan Gero and Margaret Conkey, 132–59. Oxford: Blackwell Publishers, 1991.

———. "The Habitus of Cooking Practices at Neolithic Çatalhöyük: What Was the Place of the Cook?" In *The Menial Art of Cooking: Archaeological Studies of Cooking and Food Preparation*, edited by Sarah R. Graff and Enrique Rodríguez-Alegría, 65–86. Boulder: University Press of Colorado, 2012.

———. *The Social Archaeology of Food: Thinking about Eating from Prehistory to the Present*. New York: Cambridge University Press, 2016.

Hawkes, Kristen. "The Grandmother Effect." *Nature* 428, no. 6979 (March 2004): 128–29. doi.org/10.1038%2F428128a.

Hawkes, Kristen, J. F. O'Connell, N. G. Blurton Jones. H. Alvarez, and E. L. Charnov. "Grandmothering, Menopause, and the Evolution of Human Life Histories." *Proceedings of the National Academy of Sciences* 95, no. 3 (February 1998): 1336–39. doi.org/10.1073/pnas.95.3.1336.

Hayashida, Frances M. "Ancient Beer and Modern Brewers: Ethnoarchaeological Observations of *Chicha* Production in Two Regions of the North Coast of Peru." *Journal of Anthropological Archaeology* 27, no. 2 (June 2008): 161–74. doi.org/10.1016/j.jaa.2008.03.003.

Hayden, Brian. "Big Man, Big Heart? The Political Role of Aggrandizers in Egalitarian and Transegalitarian Societies." In *For the Greater Good of All*, edited by D. R. Forsyth and C. L. Hoyt, 101–18. New York: Palgrave Macmillan, 2011.

———. "Neandertal Social Structure." *Oxford Journal of Archaeology* 31, no. 1 (January 2012): 1–26. doi.org/10.1111/j.1468-0092.2011.00376.x.

———. "A Prolegomenon to the Importance of Feasting." In *Feasts: Archaeological and Ethnographic Perspectives on Food, Politics, and Power*, edited by M. Dietler and B. Hayden, 23–64. Washington, DC: Smithsonian Institution Press, 2001.

———. "Were Luxury Foods the First Domesticates? Ethnoarchaeological Perspectives from Southeast Asia." *World Archaeology* 34, no. 3 (January 2003): 458–69. doi.org/10.1080/0043824021000026459a.

Hayden, Brian, and Suzanne Villeneuve. "A Century of Feasting Studies." *Annual Review of Anthropology* 40 (October 2011): 433–49. doi.org/10.1146/annurev-anthro-081309-145740.

Henry, Amanda G., Alison S. Brooks, and Dolores R. Piperno. "Microfossils in Calculus Demonstrate Consumption of Plants and Cooked Foods in Neandertal Diets (Shanidar III, Iraq; Spy I and II, Belgium." *Proceedings of the National Academy of Sciences* 108, no. 2 (January 2011): 486–91. doi.org/10.1073/pnas.1016868108.

———. "Plant Foods and the Dietary Ecology of Neandertals and Early Modern Humans." *Journal of Human Evolution* 69 (April 2014): 44–54. doi.org/10.1016/j.jhev01.2013.12.014.

Henshilwood, Christopher S., Francesco d'Errico, Karen L. van Niekirk, Laure Dayet, Alain Queffelec, and Luca Pollarolo. "An Abstract Drawing from the 73,000-Year-Old Levels at Blombos Cave, South Africa." *Nature* 562 (October 2018): 115–18. doi.org/10.1038/s41586-018-0514-3.

Henshilwood, Christopher S., Francesco d'Errico, Royden Yates, Zenobia Jacobs, Chantal Tribolo, Geoff A. T. Duller, Norbert Mercier, et al. "Emergence of Modern Human Behavior: Middle Stone Age Engravings from South Africa." *Science* 295, no. 5558 (February 2002): 1278–80. doi.org/10.1126/science.1067575.

Hockings, Kimberley J., Nicola Bryson-Morrison, Susana Carvalho, Michiko Fujisawa,

Tatyana Humle, William C. McGrew, Miho Nakamura, et al. "Tools to Tipple: Ethanol Ingestion by Wild Chimpanzees Using Leaf Sponges." *Royal Society Open Science* 2, no. 6 (June 2015): 1–6. doi.org/10.1098/rsos.150150.

Hodder, Ian. "Çatalhöyük in the Context of the Middle Eastern Neolithic." *Annual Review of Anthropology* 36 (October 2007): 105–20. doi.org/10.1146/annurev.anthr0 .36.081406.094308.

Hodder, Ian, and Craig Cessford. "Daily Practice and Social Memory at Çatalhöyük." *American Antiquity* 69, no. 1 (January 2004): 17–40. doi.org/10.2307/4128346.

Hoffecker, John F. "The Complexity of Neanderthal Technology." *Proceedings of the National Academy of Sciences* 115, no. 9 (February 2018): 1959–61. doi.org/10.1073/pnas .1800461115.

Holick, Michael F. "Sunlight and Vitamin D for Bone Health and Prevention of Autoimmune Diseases, Cancers, and Cardiovascular Disease." *American Journal of Clinical Nutrition* 80, no. 6 (December 2004): 1678S–88S. doi.org/10.1093/ajcn/80.6.1678S.

Hospodar, Miriam. "Aphrodisiac Foods: Bringing Heaven to Earth." *Gastronomica* 4, no. 4 (Fall 2004): 82–93. doi.org/10.1525/gfc.2004.4.4.82.

Hublin, Jean-Jacques, Abdelouahed Ben-Ncer, Shara E. Bailey, Sarah E. Freidline, Simon Neubauer, Matthew M. Skinner, Inga Bergmann, et al. "New Fossils from Jebel Irhoud, Morocco and the Pan-African Origin of *Homo sapiens*." *Nature* 546 (June 2017): 289–92. doi.org/10.1038/nature22336.

Husk Restaurant. "Today's Menu." Accessed July 3, 2017. husknashville.com.

Ingram, Catherine J. E., Charlotte A. Mulcare, Yuval Itan, Mark G. Thomas, and Dallas M. Swallow. "Lactose Digestion and the Evolutionary Genetics of Lactase Persistence." *Human Genetics* 124, no. 6 (January 2009): 579–91. doi.org/10.1007/ s00439-008-0593-6.

International Potato Center. "Potato." Accessed June 4, 2019. cipotato.org.

Isaac, Glynn. "The Food-Sharing Behaviour of Proto-Human Hominids." *Scientific American* 238, no. 4 (April 1978): 90–109. doi.org/10.1016/0278-4165(85)90009-1.

Jablonski, Nina G. "Human Skin Pigmentation as an Example of Adaptive Evolution." *Proceedings of the American Philosophical Society* 156, no. 1 (March 2012): 45–57. www.jstor.org.

Janusek, John W. "Of Pots and People: Ceramic Style and Social Identity in the Tiwanaku State." In *Us and Them: Archaeology and Ethnicity in the Andes*, edited by Richard M. Reycraft, 34–53. Los Angeles: Cotsen Institute of Archaeology, 2005.

Jennings, Justin. "La Chichera y el Patrón: Chicha and the Energetics of Feasting in the Prehistoric Andes." *Archaeological Papers of the American Anthropological Association* 14, no. 1 (June 2004): 241–59. doi.org/10.1525/ap3a.2004.14.241.

Jennings, Justin, Kathleen L. Antrobus, Sam J. Atencio, Erin Glavich, Rebecca Johnson, German Loffler, and Christine Luu. "Drinking Beer in a Blissful Mood: Alcohol Production, Operational Chains, and Feasting in the Ancient World." *Current Anthropology* 46, no. 2 (April 2005): 275–303. doi.org/10.1086/427119.

Jochim, Michael A. "Optimal Foraging and the Division of Labor." *American*

Anthropologist 90, no. 1 (March 1988): 130–36. doi.org/10.1525/aa.1988.90.1
.02a00100.

Joffe, Alexander. "Alcohol and Social Complexity in Ancient Western Asia." *Current Anthropology* 39, no. 3 (June 1998): 297–322. doi.org/10.1086/204736.

Johanson, Donald C. "Lucy, Thirty Years Later: An Expanded View of Australopithecus afarensis." *Journal of Anthropological Research* 60, no. 4 (Winter 2004): 465–86. doi.org/10.1086/jar.60.4.3631138.

Jones, Martin. *Feast: Why Humans Share Food*. Oxford: Oxford University Press, 2008.

Joordens, Josephine C. A., Francesco d'Errico, Frank P. Wesselingh, Stephen Munro, John de Vos, Jakob Wallinga, Christina Ankjærgaard, et al. "*Homo erectus* at Trinil on Java Used Shells for Tool Production and Engraving." *Nature* 518 (February 2015): 228–31. doi.org/10.1038/nature13962.

Juan-Cabanilles, Joachim, and Bernat Martí Oliver. "New Approaches to the Neolithic Transition: The Last Hunters and First Farmers of the Western Mediterranean." In *Times of Neolithic Transition along the Western Mediterranean*, edited by Oreto García Puchol and Domingo C. Salazar-García, 33–65. New York: Springer, 2017.

Junker, Laura. "The Evolution of Ritual Feasting Systems in Prehispanic Philippine Chiefdoms." In *Feasts: Archaeological and Ethnographic Perspectives on Food, Politics, and Power*, edited by Michael Dietler and Brian Hayden, 267–310. Washington, DC: Smithsonian Institution Press, 2001.

Katz, Solomon H., and Mary M. Voight. "Bread and Beer: The Early Use of Cereals in the Human Diet." *Expedition* 28, no. 2 (1986): 23–34.

Kennedy, Sarah A., and Parker VanValkenburgh. "Zooarchaeology and Changing Food Practices at Carrizales, Peru Following the Spanish Invasion." *International Journal of Historical Archaeology* 20, no. 1 (March 2016): 73–104. doi.org/10.1007/s10761 -015-0319-0.

Kennett, Douglas J. "Archaic-Period Foragers and Farmers in Mesoamerica." In *The Oxford Handbook of Mesoamerican Archaeology*, edited by Deborah L. Nichols and Christopher A. Pool, 141–50. New York: Oxford University Press, 2012.

Kennett, Douglas J., and Bruce Winterhalder, eds. *Behavioral Ecology and the Transition to Agriculture*. Berkeley: University of California Press, 2006.

Kidder, Tristam R. "Transforming Hunter-Gatherer History at Poverty Point." In *Hunter-Gatherer Archaeology as Historical Process*, edited by Kenneth E. Sassaman and Donald H. Holly, 95–119. Tucson: University of Arizona Press, 2011.

Klarich, Elizabeth, ed. *Inside Ancient Kitchens: New Directions in the Study of Daily Meals and Feasts*. Boulder: University Press of Colorado, 2010.

Knauft, Bruce. *The Gebusi: Lives Transformed in a Rainforest World*. Forest Grove, IL: Waveland Press, 2015.

Kohn, Marek, and Steven Mithen. "Handaxes: Products of Sexual Selection?" *Antiquity* 73, no. 281 (September 1999): 518–26. doi.org/10.1017/S0003598X00065078.

Kuhn, Steven L., and Mary C. Stiner. "What's a Mother to Do? The Division of Labor among Neandertals and Modern Humans in Eurasia." *Current Anthropology* 47, no. 6 (December 2006): 953–81. doi.org/10.1086/507197.

Kuijt, Ian. "Negotiating Equality through Ritual: A Consideration of Late Natufian and Prepottery Neolithic A Period Mortuary Practices." *Journal of Anthropological Archaeology* 15, no. 4 (December 1996): 313–36. doi.org/10.1006/jaar.1996.0012.

Kuijt, Ian, and Bill Finlayson. "Evidence for Food Storage and Predomestication Granaries 11,000 Years Ago in the Jordan Valley." *Proceedings of the National Academy of Sciences* 106, no. 27 (July 2009): 10966–70. doi.org/10.1073/pnas.0812764106.

Lab of Archaeology at UBC and Culture Code. "Ancient Maize Map." Last modified February 20, 2017. en.ancientmaize.com.

Laland, Kevin N., John Odling-Smee, and Marcus W. Feldman. "Niche Construction, Biological Evolution, and Cultural Change." *Behavioral and Brain Sciences* 23, no. 1 (February 2000): 131–46. doi.org/10.1017/S0140525X00002417.

Larsen, Clark Spencer. "The Agricultural Revolution as Environmental Catastrophe: Implications for Health and Lifestyle in the Holocene." *Quaternary International* 150, no. 1 (June 2006): 12–20. doi.org/10.1016/j.quaint.2006.01.004.

Lauter, Nick, and John Doebley. "Genetic Variation for Phenotypically Invariant Traits Detected in Teosinte: Implications for the Evolution of Novel Forms." *Genetics* 160, no. 1 (January 2002). www.genetics.org.

Lee, Christina. *Feasting the Dead: Food and Drink in Anglo-Saxon Burial Rituals.* Suffolk, UK: Boydell Press, 2007.

Lee, Richard. "Eating Christmas in the Kalahari." *Natural History* 78, no. 10 (December 1969): 14–22, 60–64.

———. "Lactation, Ovulation, Infanticide, and Women's Work: A Study of Hunter-Gatherer Population Regulation." In *Biosocial Mechanisms of Population Regulation*, edited by Mark N. Cohen, Roy S. Malpass, and Harold G. Klein, 321–48. New Haven, CT: Yale University Press, 1980.

Leonard, William R. "The Global Diversity of Eating Patterns: Human Nutritional Health in Comparative Perspective." *Physiology and Behavior* 134 (July 2014): 5–14. dx.doi.org/10.1016/j.physbeh.2014.02.050.

Lévi-Strauss, Claude. "The Culinary Triangle." In *Food and Culture: A Reader*, edited by Carole Counihan and Penny van Estrile, 28–35. New York: Routledge, 2008.

———. *The Savage Mind* [*La Pensée sauvage*]. Chicago: University of Chicago Press, 1966.

———. *Totemism* [*Le Totémisme aujourd'hui*]. Translated by Rodney Needham. Boston: Beacon Press, 1963.

Lewis, R. Barry. *Kentucky Archaeology.* Lexington: University Press of Kentucky, 1996.

Lightfoot, Kent, Antoinette Martinez, and Ann M. Schiff. "Daily Practice and Material Culture in Pluralistic Social Settings: An Archaeological Study of Culture Change and Persistence from Fort Ross, California." *American Antiquity* 63, no. 2 (April 1998): 199–222. doi.org/10.2307/2694694.

Lordkipanidze, David, Abesalom Vekua, Reid Ferring, G. Philip Rightmire, Jordi Agusti,

Gocha Kiladze, Alexander Mouskhelishvili, et al. "The Earliest Toothless Hominin Skull." *Nature* 434, no. 7034 (April 2005): 717–18. doi.org/10.1038/434717b.

Mackey, Carol J. "Chimú Statecraft in the Provinces." In *Andean Civilization: A Tribute to Michael E. Moseley*, edited by Joyce Marcus and P. Ryan Williams, 325–49. Los Angeles: Cotsen Institute, 2009.

Marcus, Joyce, and Kent Flannery. *Zapotec Civilization: How Urban Society Evolved in Mexico's Oaxaca Valley*. New York: Thames and Hudson, 1996.

Marlowe, Frank W., J. Colette Berbesque, Brian Wood, Alyssa Crittenden, Claire Porter, and Audax Mabulla. "Honey, Hadza, Hunter-Gatherers, and Human Evolution." *Journal of Human Evolution* 71 (June 2014): 119–28. doi.org/10.1016/j.jhev01.2014.03.006.

Martin, Debra. "Bodies and Lives: Biological Indicators of Health Differentials and Division of Labor by Sex." In *Women and Men in the Prehispanic Southwest: Labor, Power, and Prestige*, edited by Patricia Crown, 266–300. Santa Fe: School for Advanced Research Press, 2000.

Maslin, Mark A., Chris M. Brierley, Alice M. Milner, Susanne Shultz, Martin H. Trauth, and Katy E. Wilson. "East African Climate Pulses and Early Human Evolution." *Quaternary Science Reviews* 101 (October 2014): 1–17. doi.org/10.1016/j.quascirev.2014.06.012.

Mayer, Enrique. *The Articulated Peasant: Household Economies in the Andes*. New York: Routledge, 2002.

Mayewski, Paul A., Eelco E. Rohling, J. Curt Stager, Wibjörn Karlén, Kirk A. Maasch, L. David Meeker, Eric A Meyerson, et al. "Holocene Climate Variability." *Quaternary Research* 62, no. 3 (November 2004): 243–55. doi.org/10.1016/j.yqres.2004.07.001.

McCann, James. "Maize and Grace: History, Corn, and Africa's New Landscapes, 1500–1999." *Comparative Studies in Society and History* 43, no. 2 (April 2001): 246–72. www.jstor.org.

McGovern, Patrick E., Donald L. Glusker, Robert A. Moreau, Alberto Nuñez, Curt W. Beck, Elizabeth Simpson, Eric D. Butrym, Lawrence J. Exner, and Edith C. Stout. "A Funerary Feast Fit for King Midas." *Nature* 402, 6764 (December 1999): 863–64. doi.org/10.1038/47217.

McKee, Larry. "Food Supply and Plantation Order." In *"I, Too, Am America": Archaeological Studies of Afro-American Life*, edited by Theresa A. Singleton, 218–39. Charlottesville: University of Virginia Press, 1999.

McWilliams, James. *A Revolution in Eating: How the Quest for Food Shaped America*. New York: Columbia University Press, 2005.

Mennell, Stephen. *All Manners of Food: Eating and Taste in England and France from the Middle Ages to the Present*. 2nd ed. Urbana: University of Illinois Press, 1996.

Menzel, Peter, and Faith D'Aluisio. *Hungry Planet: What the World Eats*. New York: Material World, 2007.

Merlin, M. D. "Archaeological Evidence for the Tradition of Psychoactive Plant Use in the Old World." *Economic Botany* 57, no. 3 (September 2003): 295–323. doi.org /10.1663/0013-0001(2003)057[0295:AEFTTO]2.0.CO;2.

Meskell, Lynn. *Private Life in New Kingdom Egypt.* Princeton, NJ: Princeton University Press, 2004.

Mintz, Sidney W. *Sweetness and Power: The Place of Sugar in Modern History.* New York: Viking-Penguin, 1985.

Monaghan, G. William, William A. Lovis, and Kathryn C. Egan-Bruhy. "Earliest *Cucurbita* from the Great Lakes, Northern USA." *Quaternary Research* 65, no. 2 (March 2006): 216–22. doi.org/10.1016/j.yqres.2005.12.002.

Monroe, J. Cameron, and Anneke Janzen. "The Dahomean Feast: Royal Women, Private Politics, and Culinary Practices in Atlantic West Africa." *African Archaeological Review* 31, no. 2 (June 2014): 299–337. doi.org/10.1007/s10437-014-9156-5.

Moore, Andrew, Gordon Hillman, and Anthony Legge. *Village on the Euphrates: From Foraging to Farming at Abu Hureyra.* Oxford: Oxford University Press, 2000.

Moore, Jerry D. "Pre-Hispanic Beer in Coastal Peru: Technology and Social Context of Prehistoric Production." *American Anthropologist* 91, no. 3 (September 1989): 682– 96. doi.org/10.1525/aa.1989.91.3.02a00090.

Morán, Elizabeth. *Sacred Consumption: Food and Ritual in Aztec Art and Culture.* Austin: University of Texas Press, 2016.

Morris, Craig. "Maize Beer in the Economics, Politics, and Religion of the Inca Empire." In *Fermented Food Beverages in Nutrition*, edited by Clifford Gastineau, 21–34. New York: Academic Press, 1979.

Moseley, Michael E., Donna J. Nash, Patrick Ryan Williams, Susan D. deFrance, Ana Miranda, and Mario Ruales. "Burning Down the Brewery: Establishing and Evacuating an Ancient Imperial Colony at Cerro Baúl, Peru." *Proceedings of the National Academy of Sciences* 102, no. 48 (November 2005): 17264–71. doi.org/10.1073/pnas .0508673102.

Mueller, Natalie G. "The Earliest Occurrence of a Newly Described Domesticate in Eastern North America: Adena/Hopewell Communities and Agricultural Innovation." *Journal of Anthropological Archaeology* 49 (March 2018): 39–50. doi.org/10.1016/j .jaa.2017.12.001.

Muller, Antoine, Chris Clarkson, and Ceri Shipton. "Measuring Behavioural and Cognitive Complexity in Lithic Technology Throughout Human Evolution." *Journal of Anthropological Archaeology* 48 (December 2017): 166–80. doi.org/10.1016/j.jaa .2017.07.006.

Murdock, George P., and Caterina Provost. "Factors in the Division of Labor by Sex: A Cross-Cultural Analysis." *Ethnology* 12, no. 2 (April 1973): 203–25. www.jstor.org.

Murray, Margaret A. *The Splendor That Was Egypt.* Mineola, NY: Dover Publications, 1963.

Nairn, Charlie. *Kawelka: Ongka's Big Moka.* 1974; Watertown, MA: Documentary Educational Resources, 2010. DVD.

National Corn Growers Association. "World Corn Production 2016–17." Accessed July 26, 2017. www.worldofcorn.com.

Nelson, Sarah Milledge. "Feasting the Ancestors in Early China." In *The Archaeology and Politics of Food and Feasting in Early States and Empires*, edited by Tamara Bray, 65–89. New York: Kluwer Academic/Plenum Publishers, 2003.

Nowell, April, and Melanie Lee Chang. "The Case against Sexual Selection as an Explanation of Handaxe Morphology." *PaleoAnthropology* (2009): 77–88. www.paleoanthro .org.

Nunn, Patrick D., and Nicholas J. Reid. "Aboriginal Memories of Inundation of the Australian Coast Dating from More than 7000 Years Ago." *Australian Geographer* 47, no. 1 (January 2016): 11–47. doi.org/10.1080/00049182.2015.1077539.

O'Connell, James, Kristen Hawkes, and Nicholas Blurton-Jones. "Grandmothering and the Evolution of *Homo erectus*." *Journal of Human Evolution* 36, no. 5 (May 1999): 461–85. doi.org/10.1006/jhev.1998.0285.

———. "Meat-Eating, Grandmothering, and the Evolution of Early Human Diets." In *Human Diet: Its Origin and Evolution*, edited by P. Ungar and M. Teaford, 49–60. Westport, CT: Bergin and Garvey, 2002.

O'Connell, James, Kristen Hawkes, K. D. Lupo, and Nicholas Blurton-Jones. "Male Strategies and Plio-Pleistocene Archaeology." *Journal of Human Evolution* 43, no. 6 (December 2002): 831–72. doi.org/10.1006/jhev.2002.0604.

Pääbo, Svante. "The Diverse Origins of the Human Gene Pool." *Nature Reviews* 16 (May 2015): 313–14. doi.org/10.1038/nrg3954.

Pederson, Mikkel W., Anthony Ruter, Charles Schweger, Harvey Friebe, Richard A. Staff, Kristian K. Kjeldsen, Marie L. Z. Mendoza, et al. "Postglacial Viability and Colonization in North America's Ice-Free Corridor." *Nature* 537 (September 2016): 45–49. doi.org/10.1038/nature19085.

Penn Museum. "The Funerary Feast of King Midas." Accessed June 5, 2019. www.penn .museum.

Peres, Tanya M. "Foodways, Economic Status, and the Antebellum Upland South in Central Kentucky." *Historical Archaeology* 42, no. 4 (December 2008): 88–104. doi .org/10.1007/BF03377156.

Perry, George H., Nathaniel J. Dominy, Katrina G. Claw, Arthur S. Lee, Heike Fiegler, Richard Redon, John Werner, et al. "Diet and the Evolution of Human Amylase Gene Copy Number Variation." *Nature Genetics* 39 (2007): 1256–60. doi.org /10.1038/ng2123.

Pettitt, Paul. "The Rise of Modern Humans." In *The Human Past: World Prehistory and the Development of Human Societies*, edited by Chris Scarre, 124–73. New York: Thames and Hudson, 2009.

Piddocke, Stuart. "The Potlatch System of the Southern Kwakiutl: A New Perspective." *Southwestern Journal of Anthropology* 21, no. 3 (Autumn 1965): 244–64. doi.org /10.1086/soutjanth.21.3.3629231.

Pilcher, Jeffrey. *¡Que vivan los tamales! Food and the Making of Mexican Identity*. Albuquerque: University of New Mexico Press, 1998.

Pinhasi, Ron, Joaquim Form, and Albert J. Ammerman. "Tracing the Origin and Spread

of Agriculture in Europe." *PLoS Biology* 3, no. 12 (2005): e410. doi.org/10.1371
/journal.pbi0.0030410.

Piperno, Dolores. "The Origins of Plant Cultivation and Domestication in the New
World Tropics." *Current Anthropology* 52, no. S4 (October 2011): S453–70. doi.org
/10.1086/659998.

Piperno, Dolores R., Anthony J. Ranere, Irene Holst, Jose Iriarte, and Ruth Dickau.
"Starch Grain and Phytolith Evidence for Early Ninth Millennium B.P. Maize from
the Central Balsas River Valley, Mexico." *Proceedings of the National Academy of
Sciences* 106, no. 13 (March 2009): 5019–24. doi.org/10.1073/pnas.0812525106.

Piscitelli, Matthew. "Pathways to Social Complexity in the Norte Chico Region of Peru."
In *Feast, Famine, or Fighting?: Studies in Human Ecology and Adaptation*, vol. 8, ed-
ited by Richard J. Chacon and Rubén G. Mendoza, 393–415. New York: Springer
International Publishing, 2017.

Plavcan, J. Michael. "Body Size, Size Variation, and Sexual Size Dimorphism in Early
Homo." *Current Anthropology* 53, no. S6 (December 2012): S409–23. doi.org
/10.1086/667605.

Plummer, Thomas W., and Emma M. Finestone. "Archaeological Sites from 2.6–2.0 Ma:
Toward a Deeper Understanding of the Early Oldowan." In *Rethinking Human Evolution*, edited by Jeffrey Schwartz, 267–96. Cambridge, MA: MIT Press, 2017.

Pobiner, Briana L., Michael J. Rogers, Christopher M. Monahan, and John W. K. Harris.
"New Evidence for Hominin Carcass Processing Strategies at 1.5 Ma., Koobi Fora,
Kenya." *Journal of Human Evolution* 55, no. 1 (July 2008): 103–30. doi.org/10.1016/j
.jhev01.2008.02.001.

Pohl, Mary D., Kevin O. Pop, John G. Jones, John S. Jacob, Dolores R. Piperno, Susan D.
deFrance, David L. Lentz, John A. Gifford, Marie E. Danforth, and J. Kathryn Jos-
serand. "Early Agriculture in the Maya Lowlands." *Latin American Antiquity* 7, no.
4 (December 1996): 355–72. doi.org/10.2307/972264.

Politis, Gustavo, and Nicholas Saunders. "Archaeological Correlates of Ideological Activity: Food Taboos and Spirit-Animals in an Amazonian Hunter-Gatherer Society."
In *Consuming Passions and Patterns of Consumption*, edited by Preston Miracle,
113–30. Cambridge: McDonald Institute for Archaeological Research, University of
Cambridge, 2002.

Pollan, Michael. *The Botany of Desire: A Plant's-Eye View of the World*. New York: Random House, 2002.

———. *Cooked: A Natural History of Transformation*. New York: Penguin, 2013.

———. *The Omnivore's Dilemma: A Natural History of Four Meals*. New York: Penguin,
2006.

Pollock, Susan. "Feasts, Funerals, and Fast Food in Early Mesopotamian States." In *The
Archaeology and Politics of Food and Feasting in Early States and Empires*, edited by
Tamara Bray, 17–38. New York: Springer, 2003.

Pontzer, Herman. "Economy and Endurance in Human Evolution." *Current Biology* 27,
no. 12 (June 2017): R613–21. doi.org/10.1016/j.cub.2017.05.031.

Pontzer, Herman, Mary H. Brown, David A. Raichlen, Holly Dunsworth, Brian Hare, Kara Walker, Amy Luke, et al. "Metabolic Acceleration and the Evolution of Human Brain Size and Life History." *Nature* 533 (May 2016): 390–92. doi.org/10.1038/nature17654.

Potts, Richard. "Environmental and Behavioral Evidence Pertaining to the Evolution of Early *Homo.*" *Current Anthropology* 53, no. S6 (December 2012): S299–S317. doi.org/10.1086/667704.

———. "Evolution and Environmental Change in Early Human Prehistory." *Annual Review of Anthropology* 41, no. 1 (October 2012): 151–67. doi.org/10.1146/annurev-anthro-092611-145754.

Raichlen, David, Herman Pontzer, and Michael D. Sockol. "The Laetoli Footprints and Early Hominin Locomotor Kinematics." *Journal of Human Evolution* 54, no. 1 (January 2008): 112–17. doi.org/10.1016/j.jhevol.2007.07.005.

Rappaport, Roy. *Pigs for the Ancestors: Ritual in the Ecology of a New Guinea People.* New Haven, CT: Yale University Press, 1968.

Rasmussen, S. O., K. K. Anderson, A. M. Svensson, J. P. Steffensen, B. M. Vinther, H. B. Clausen, and M. L. Siggaard-Andersen. "A New Greenland Ice Core Chronology for Last Glacial Termination." *Journal of Geophysical Research* 111, no. D6 (March 2006). doi.org/10.1029/2005JD006079.

Rasteiro, Rita, and Lounes Chikhi. "Female and Male Perspectives on the Neolithic Transition in Europe: Clues from Ancient and Modern Genetic Data." *PLoS One* 8, no. 4 (2013): e60944. doi.org/10.1371/journal.pone.0060944.

Rauer, Julie. "The Last Feast of Lady Dai." Asianart.com. Accessed June 27, 2017.

Richards, Michael P., and Erik Trinkaus. "Isotopic Evidence for the Diets of European Neandertals and Early Modern Humans." *Proceedings of the National Academy of Sciences* 106, no. 38 (September 2009): 16034–39. doi.org/10.1073/pnas.0903821106.

Rigaud, Solange, Francesco d'Errico, and Marian Vanhaeren. "Ornaments Reveal Resistance of North European Cultures to the Spread of Farming." *PLoS One* 10, no. 4 (2015): e0121166. doi.org/10.1371/journal.pone.0121166.

Rightmire, G. Philip, David Lordkipanidze, and Abesalom Vekua. "Anatomical Descriptions, Comparative Studies, and Evolutionary Significance of the Hominin Skulls from Dmanisi, Republic of Georgia." *Journal of Human Evolution* 50, no. 2 (February 2006): 115–41. doi.org/10.1016/j.jhevol.2005.07.009.

Robin, Cynthia. *Everyday Life Matters: Maya Farmers at Chan.* Gainesville: University Press of Florida, 2013.

Rodríguez-Alegría, Enrique. "From Grinding Corn to Dishing Out Money: A Long-Term History of Cooking in Xaltocan, Mexico." In *The Menial Art of Cooking: Archaeological Studies of Cooking and Food Preparation*, edited by Sarah R. Graff and Enrique Rodríguez-Alegría, 99–118. Boulder: University Press of Colorado, 2012.

Rodríguez-Vidal, Joaquín, Francesco d'Errico, Francisco Giles Pacheco, Ruth Blasco, Jordi Rosell, Richard P. Jennings, Alain Queffelec, et al. "A Rock Engraving Made by Neandertals in Gibraltar." *Proceedings of the National Academy of Sciences* 111, no. 37 (September 2014): 13301–06. doi.org/10.1073/pnas.1411529111.

Rogers, Alan R., David Iltis, and Stephen Wooding. "Genetic Variation at the MCIR Locus and the Time since Loss of Human Body Hair." *Current Anthropology* 45, no. 1 (February 2004): 105–8. doi.org/10.1086/381006.

Rosen, Arlene M., and Isabel Rivera-Collazo. "Climate Change, Adaptive Cycles, and the Persistence of Foraging Economies during the Late Pleistocene/Holocene Transition in the Levant." *Proceedings of the National Academy of Sciences* 109, no. 10 (March 2012): 3640–45. doi.org/10.1073/pnas.1113931109.

Rozin, Paul. "Psychobiological Perspectives on Food Preferences and Avoidances." In *Food and Culture: Toward a Theory of Human Habits*, edited by Marvin Harris and Eric Ross, 181–201. Philadelphia: Temple University Press, 1987.

Ryder, Michael L. "The Evolution of Fleece." *Scientific American* 256, no. 1 (1987): 112–19. www.jstor.org.

Sahlins, Marshall. *Stone Age Economics.* Chicago: Aldine, 1972.

Sahrhage, Dietrich, and Johannes Lundbeck. *A History of Fishing.* New York: Springer, 1992.

Salque, Mélanie, Peter I. Bogucki, Joanna Pyzel, Iwona Sobkowiak-Tabaka, Ryszard Grygiel, Marzena Szmyt, and Richard P. Evershed. "Earliest Evidence for Cheese Making in the Sixth Millennium BC in Northern Europe." *Nature* 493 (January 2013): 522–25. doi.org/10.1038/nature11698.

Samuel, Delwyn. "Bread Making and Social Interactions at the Amarna Workmen's Village, Egypt." *World Archaeology* 31, no. 1 (June 1999): 121–44. doi.org/10.1080/00438243.1999.9980435.

Sandweiss, Daniel H., Ruth Shady Solís, Michael E. Moseley, David K. Keefer, and Charles R. Ortloff. "Environmental Change and Economic Development in Coastal Peru between 5,800 and 3,600 Years Ago." *Proceedings of the National Academy of Sciences* 106, no. 5 (February 2009): 1359–36. doi.org/10.1073/pnas.0812645106.

Sankararaman, Sriram, Swapan Mallick, Nick Patterson, and David Reich. "The Combined Landscape of Denisovan and Neanderthal Ancestry in Present-Day Humans." *Current Biology* 26, no. 9 (May 2016): 1241–47. doi.org/10.1016/j.cub.2016.03.037.

Sapp, William. "Lambayeque Norte and Lambayeque Sur: Evidence for the Development of an Indigenous Lambayeque Polity in the Jequetepeque Valley, Peru." In *From State to Empire in the Prehistoric Jequetepeque Valley, Peru*, edited by Colleen M. Zori and Ilana Johnson, 93–104. Oxford: Archaeopress, 2011.

Scherjon, Fulco, Corrie Bakels, Katharine MacDonald, and Wil Roebroeks. "Burning the Land: An Ethnographic Study of Off-Site Fire Use by Current and Historically Documented Foragers and Implications for the Interpretation of Past Fire Practices in the Landscape." *Current Anthropology* 56, no. 3 (June 2015): 299–326. doi.org/10.1086/681561.

Scott, Elizabeth M. "Food and Social Relations at Nina Plantation." *American Anthropologist* 103, no. 3 (September 2001): 671–91. www.jstor.org.

Ségurel, Laure, and Céline Bon. "On the Evolution of Lactase Persistence in Humans." *Annual Review of Genomics and Human Genetics* 18, no. 1 (August 2017): 297–319, doi.org/10.1146%2Fannurev-genom-091416-035340.

Serjeantson, Dale. "Survey of Animal Remains from Southern Britain Finds No Evidence for Continuity from the Mesolithic Period." *Environmental Archaeology* 19, no. 3 (May 2014): 256–62. doi.org/10.1179/1749631414Y.0000000020.

Shady, Ruth. "America's First City? The Case of Late Archaic Caral." in *Andean Archaeology III: North and South*, edited by William Isbell and Helaine Silverman, 28–66. New York: Springer Press, 2006.

Shady, Ruth, and Christopher Kleihege. *Caral: The First Civilization in the Americas; La primera civilización de América*. Chicago: CK Photo, 2010.

Sheehan, Michael S. "Ethnographic Models, Archaeological Data, and the Applicability of Modern Foraging Theory." In *Hunter-Gatherers in History, Archaeology, and Anthropology*, edited by Alan Barnard, 163–74. New York: Berg Publishers, 2004.

Sherman, Sean, and Beth Dooley. *The Sioux Chef's Indigenous Kitchen*. Minneapolis: University of Minnesota Press, 2017.

Shostak, Marjorie. *Nisa: The Life and Words of a !Kung Woman*. Cambridge, MA: Harvard University Press, 2000.

Simon, Mary L. "Reevaluating the Evidence for Middle Woodland Maize from the Holding Site." *American Antiquity* 82, no. 1 (January 2017): 140–50. doi.org/10.1017/aaq.2016.2.

Sisitiaga, Ainara, Carolina Mallol, Bertila Galván, and Roger Everett Summons. "The Neandertal Meal: A New Perspective Using Faecal Biomarkers." *PLoS One* 9, no. 6 (2014): e101045. doi.org/10.1371/journal.pone.0101045.

Skinner, Mark. "Bee Brood Consumption: An Alternative Explanation for Hypervitaminosis A in KNM-ER 1808 (*Homo erectus*) from Koobi Fora, Kenya." *Journal of Human Evolution* 20, no. 6 (June 1991): 493–503. doi.org/10.1016/0047-2484(91)90022-N.

Slon, Viviane, Fabrizio Mafessoni, Benjamin Vernot, Cesare de Filippo, Steffi Grote, Bence Viola, Mateja Hajdinjak, et al. "The Genome of the Offspring of a Neanderthal Mother and a Denisovan Father." *Nature* 561, no. 7721 (September 2018): 113–16. doi.org/10.1038%2Fs41586-018-0455-x.

Smil, Vaclav. "Harvesting the Biosphere: The Human Impact." *Population and Development Review* 37, no. 4 (December 2011): 613–37. doi.org/10.1111/j.1728-4457.2011.00450.x.

Smith, Bruce D. "Eastern North America as an Independent Center of Plant Domestication." *Proceedings of the National Academy of Sciences* 103, no. 33 (2006): 12223–28. doi.org/10.1073/pnas.0604335103.

———. "The Initial Domestication of *Cucurbita pepo* in the Americas 10,000 Years Ago." *Science* 276, no. 5314 (May 1997): 932–34. doi.org/10.1126/science.276.5314.932.

Smith, Bruce D., and Richard A. Yarnell. "Initial Formation of an Indigenous Crop Complex in Eastern North America at 3800 B.P." *Proceedings of the National*

Academy of Sciences 106, no. 16 (April 2009): 6561–66. doi.org/10.1073/pnas
.0901846106.

Smith, Eric Alden, Robert L. Bettinger, Charles A. Bishop, Valda Blundell, Elizabeth
Cashdan, Michael J. Casimir, Andrew L. Christenson, et al. "Anthropological Applications of Optimal Foraging Theory: A Critical Review." *Current Anthropology*
24, no. 5 (December 1983): 625–51. doi.org/10.1086/203066.

Smith, Michael. *At Home with the Aztecs: An Archaeologist Uncovers Their Daily Life.*
New York: Routledge, 2016.

Smith, Michael E., Jennifer B. Wharton, and Jan Marie Olson. "Aztec Feasts, Rituals,
and Markets: Political Uses of Ceramic Vessels in a Commercial Economy." In
The Archaeology and Politics of Food and Feasting in Ancient States and Empires,
edited by Tamara Bray, 235–68. New York: Kluwer Academic/Plenum Publishers,
2003.

Smith, Monica. "The Archaeology of Food Preference." *American Anthropologist* 108, no.
3 (September 2006): 480–93. doi.org/10.1525/aa.2006.108.3.480.

———. "Feasts and Their Failures." *Journal of Archaeological Method and Theory* 22, no.
4 (December 2015): 1215–37. doi.org/10.1007/s10816-014-9222-y.

———. *A Prehistory of Ordinary People.* Tucson: University of Arizona Press, 2010.

Speilmann, Katherine. "A Review: Dietary Restrictions on Hunter-Gatherer Women and
the Implications for Fertility and Infant Mortality." *Human Ecology* 17, no. 3 (September 1989): 321–45. doi.org/10.1007/BF00889022.

Sponheimer, Matt, Benjamin H. Passey, Darryl J. de Ruiter, Debbie Guatelli-Steinberb,
Thure E. Cerling, and Julia A. Lee-Thorp. "Isotopic Evidence for Dietary Variability in the Early Hominin *Paranthropus robustus.*" *Science* 314, no. 5801 (November
2006): 980–82. doi.org/10.1126/science.1133827.

Stanford, Craig B. *The Hunting Apes: Meat Eating and the Origins of Human Behavior.*
Princeton, NJ: Princeton University Press, 1999.

———. "The Hunting Ecology of Wild Chimpanzees: Implications for the Evolutionary
Ecology of Pliocene Hominids." *American Anthropologist* 98, no. 1 (March 1996):
96–113. doi.org/10.1525/aa.1996.98.1.02a00090.

Stanford, Craig B., and Henry T. Bunn, eds. *Meat-Eating and Human Evolution.* New
York: Oxford University Press, 2001.

Stanish, Charles. "Nonmarket Imperialism in the Prehispanic Americas: The Inka Occupation of the Titicaca Basin." *Latin American Antiquity* 8, no. 3 (September 1997):
195–216. doi.org/10.2307/971652.

Starkovich, Britt M. "Optimal Foraging, Dietary Change, and Site Use during the Paleolithic at Klissoura Cave 1 (Southern Greece)." *Journal of Archaeological Science* 52
(December 2014): 39–55. doi.org/10.1016/j.jas.2014.08.026.

Steel, Louise. "Sumptuous Feasting in the Ancient Near East: Exploring the Materiality
of the Royal Tombs of Ur." In *Exploring the Materiality of Food "Stuffs": Transformations, Symbolic Consumption, and Embodiments*, edited by L. Steel and K. Zinn,
189–204. New York: Routledge, 2016.

Stein, Gil. "Food Preparation, Social Context, and Ethnicity in a Prehistoric Mesopota-
    mian Colony." In *The Menial Art of Cooking: Archaeological Studies of Cooking and
    Food Preparation*, edited by Sarah R. Graff and Enrique Rodríguez-Alegría, 47–63.
    Boulder: University Press of Colorado, 2012.
Stiner, Mary C. "Thirty Years on the 'Broad Spectrum Revolution' and Paleolithic De-
    mography." *Proceedings of the National Academy of Sciences* 98, no. 13 (June 2001):
    6993–96. doi.org/10.1073/pnas.121176198.
Stout, Dietrich, Erin Hecht, Nada Khreisheh, Bruce Bradley, and Thierry Chaminade.
    "Cognitive Demands of Lower Paleolithic Toolmaking." *PLoS One* 10, no. 5 (2015):
    e0128256. doi.org/10.1371/journal.pone.0128256.
Straus, Lawrence Guy. "Recent Developments in the Study of the Upper Paleolithic of
    Vasco-Cantabrian Spain." *Quaternary International* 364 (April 2015): 255–71. doi
    .org/10.1016/j.quaint.2014.05.008.
Stringer, Chris. *Lone Survivors: How We Came to Be the Only Humans on Earth*. New
    York: Times Books, 2012.
Stuart, David E. *Anasazi America: Seventeen Centuries on the Road from Center Place*.
    2nd ed. Albuquerque: University of New Mexico Press, 2014.
Sugiyama, Michelle Scalise. "Food, Foragers, and Folklore: The Role of Narrative in Hu-
    man Subsistence." *Evolution and Human Behavior* 22, no. 4 (July 2001): 221–40. doi
    .org/10.1016/S1090-5138(01)00063-0.
Sutter, Richard C., and Rosa J. Cortez. "The Nature of Moche Human Sacrifice: A Bioar-
    chaeological Perspective." *Current Anthropology* 46, no. 4 (August/October 2005):
    521–49. doi.org/10.1086/431527.
Sweely, Tracy. "Gender, Space, People, and Power at Cerén, El Salvador." In *Manifest-
    ing Power: Gender and the Interpretation of Power in Archaeology*, edited by Tracy
    Sweely, 155–72. New York: Routledge, 1999.
Swenson, Edward. "Cities of Violence: Sacrifice, Power, and Urbanization in the Andes."
    Journal of Social Archaeology 3, no. 2 (June 2003): 256–96. doi.org/10.1177/1469605
    303003002006.
Tan, Jingzhi, and Brian Hare. "Bonobos Share with Strangers." *PLoS One* 8, no. 1 (Janu-
    ary 2013): e51922. doi.org/10.1371/journal.pone.0051922.
Thomas, Brian W. "Power and Community: The Archaeology of Slavery at the Hermit-
    age Plantation." *American Antiquity* 63, no. 4 (October 1998): 531–51. doi.org
    /10.2307/2694107.
Tishkoff, Sarah A., Floyd A. Reed, François R. Friedlaender, Christopher Ehret, Alessia
    Ranciaro, Alain Froment, Jibril B. Hirbo, et al. "The Genetic Structure and History
    of Africans and African Americans." *Science* 22, no. 324 (May 2009): 1035–44. doi
    .org/10.1126/science.1172257.
Tocheri, Matthew. "Previously Unknown Human Species Found in Asia Raises Ques-
    tions about Early Hominin Dispersals from Africa." *Nature* 568 (April 2019): 176–
    78. doi.org/10.1038/d41586-019-01019-7.
Treves, Adrian, and Cristian Bonacic. "Humanity's Dual Response to Dogs and Wolves."

Trends in Ecology and Evolution 31, no. 7 (July 2016): 489–91. doi.org/10.1016/j
.tree.2016.04.006.

Trinkaus, Erik. "Neandertals, Early Modern Humans, and Rodeo Riders." *Journal of
Archaeological Science* 39, no. 12 (December 2012): 3691–93. doi.org/10.1016/j.jas
.2012.05.039.

Trinkley, Michael, Natalie Adams, and Debi Hacker. *Archaeological Studies Associated
with the Nineteenth Century Owens-Thomas Carriage House, Savannah, Georgia.*
Columbia, SC: Chicora Foundation Research Series 38, 1993.

Tsai, Howard. *Las Varas: Ritual and Ethnicity in the Ancient Andes.* Tuscaloosa: University of Alabama Press, 2020.

Tsing, Anna. *The Mushroom at the End of the World: On the Possibility of Life in Capitalist Ruins.* Princeton, NJ: Princeton University Press, 2015.

Turner, Christy G., and Jacqueline A. Turner. *Man Corn: Cannibalism and Violence in
the Prehistoric American Southwest.* Salt Lake City: University of Utah Press, 1999.

Twitty, Michael. "An Open Letter to Paula Deen." Afroculinaria. Last modified June 25,
2013. afroculinaria.com.

Twitty, Michael W. "Barbecue is an American Tradition—of Enslaved Africans and Native Americans." *The Guardian.* Last modified July 4, 2015. www.theguardian.com.

———. *The Cooking Gene: A Journey through African-American Culinary History in the
Old South.* New York: HarperCollins, 2017.

Ungar, Peter S., and Matt Sponheimer. "The Diets of Early Hominins." *Science* 334, no.
6053 (October 2011): 190–93. doi.org/10.1126/science.1207701.

Urton, Gary, and Alejandro Chu. "The Invention of Taxation in the Inka Empire." *Latin
American Antiquity* 30, no. 1 (March 2019): 1–16. doi.org/10.1017/laq.2018.64.

van der Veen, Marijke. "When Is Food a Luxury?" *World Archaeology* 34, no 3 (January
2003): 405–27. doi.org/10.1080/0043824021000026422.

VanDerwarker, Amber M., Dana N. Bardolph, and C. Margaret Scarry. "Maize and Mississippian Beginnings." In *Mississippian Beginnings*, edited by Gregory D. Wilson,
29–70. Gainesville: University Press of Florida, 2017.

VanDerwarker, Amber M., and Bruce Idol. "Rotten Food and Ritual Behavior: Late
Woodland Plant Foodways and Special Purpose Features at Buzzard Rock II, Virginia (44RN2/70)." *Southeastern Archaeology* 27, no. 1 (Summer 2008): 61–77.
www.jstor.org.

Veile, Amanda. "Hunter-Gatherer Diets and Human Behavioral Evolution." *Physiology
and Behavior* 193, Part B (September 2018): 190–95. doi.org/10.1016/j.physbeh
.2018.05.023.

Vernon, Richard. "17th Century Apalachee Colono-Ware as a Reflection of Demography, Economics, and Acculturation." *Historical Archaeology* 22, no. 1 (January
1988): 76–82. doi.org/10.1007/BF03374502.

Vernot, Benjamin, and Joshua M. Akey. "Resurrecting Surviving Neandertal Lineages
from Modern Human Genomes." *Science* 343, no. 6174 (February 2014): 1017–21.
doi.org/10.1126/science.1245938.

Vernot, Benjamin, Serena Tucci, Janet Kelso, Joshua G. Schraiber, Aaron B. Wolf, Rachel M. Gittleman, Michael Dannemann, et al. "Excavating Neandertal and Denisovan DNA from the Genomes of Melanesian Individuals." *Science* 352, no. 6282 (April 2016): 235–39. doi.org/10.1126/science.aad9416.

Vilmoare, Brian, Kevin G. Hatala, and William Jungers. "Sexual Dimorphism in *Homo erectus* Inferred from 1.5 Ma Footprints Near Ileret, Kenya." *Scientific Reports* 9, no. 7867 (2019): 1–12. doi.org/10.1038/s41598-019-44060-2.

Voss, Barbara L. "Domesticating Imperialism: Sexual Politics and the Archaeology of Empire." *American Anthropologist* 110, no. 2 (July 2008): 191–203. doi.org/10.1111/j.1548-1433.2008.00025.x.

———. "From *Casta* to *Californio*: Social Identity and the Archaeology of Culture Contact." *American Anthropologist* 107, no. 3 (January 2008): 461–74. doi.org/10.1525/aa.2005.107.3.461.

Wade, Lizzie. "Neandertals Made Jewelry, Proteins Confirm." *Science* 353, no. 6306 (September 2016): 1350. doi.org/10.1126/science.353.6306.1350.

Wall, Jeffrey D., Melinda A. Yang, Flora Jay, Sung K. Kim, Eric Y. Durand, Laurie S. Stevison, Christopher Gignoux, August Woerner, Michael F. Hammer, and Montgomery Slatkin. "Higher Levels of Neanderthal Ancestry in East Asians Than in Europeans." *Genetics* 194, no. 1 (May 2013): 199–209. doi.org/10.1534/genetics.112.148213.

Walker, Alan, M. R. Zimmerman, and Richard E. F. Leakey. "A Possible Case of Hypervitaminosis A in *Homo erectus*." *Nature* 296, no. 5854 (1982): 248–50. doi.org/10.1038/296248a0.

Walker, Alan, and Richard Leakey, eds. *The Nariokotome* Homo erectus *Skeleton*. Cambridge, MA: Harvard University Press, 1993.

Wandsnider, LuAnn. "The Roasted and the Boiled: Food Composition and Heat Treatment with Special Emphasis on Pit-Hearth Cooking." *Journal of Anthropological Archaeology* 16, no. 1 (March 1997): 1–48. doi.org/10.1006/jaar.1997.0303.

Warner, Mark S. *Eating in the Side Room: Food, Archaeology, and African American Identity*. Gainesville: University Press of Florida, 2015.

Washburn, S. L., and Virginia Avis. "Evolution of Human Behavior." In *Behavior and Evolution*, edited by A. Roe and G. Simpson, 421–36. New Haven, CT: Yale University Press, 1958.

Weiner, Jonathan. *Beak of the Finch: A Story of Evolution in Our Time*. New York: Penguin Random House, 1995.

Weiner, Steve, Qinqi Xu, Paul Goldberg, Jinyi Liu, and Ofer Bar-Yosef. "Evidence for the Use of Fire at Zhoukoudian, China." *Science* 281, no. 5374 (July 1998): 251–53. doi.org/10.1126/science.281.5374.251.

Weismantel, Mary. *Food, Gender, and Poverty in the Ecuadorian Andes*. Long Grove, IL: Waveland Press, 1988.

Weiss, Ehud, Mordechai E. Kislev, Orit Simchoni, Dani Nadel, and Hartmut Tschauner. "Plant-Food Preparation Area on an Upper Paleolithic Brush Hut Floor at Ohalo

II, Israel." *Journal of Archaeological Science* 35, no. 8 (August 2008): 2400–2414. doi
.org/10.1016/j.jas.2008.03.012.

Weitzel, Elic M., and Brian Codding. "Population Growth as a Driver of Initial Domestication in Eastern North America." *Royal Society Open Science* 3, no. 8 (August
2016). doi.org/10.1098/rsos.160319.

Wheeler, Peter E. "The Evolution of Bipedality and Loss of Functional Body Hair in
Hominids." *Journal of Human Evolution* 13, no. 1 (January 1984): 91–98. doi.org
/10.1016/S0047-2484(84)80079-2.

White, Christine D. "Gendered Food Behaviour among the Maya." *Journal of Social
Archaeology* 5, no. 3 (October 2005): 356–82. doi.org/10.1177/1469605305057572.

White, Mark, Paul Pettitt, and Danielle Schreve. "Shoot First, Ask Questions Later: Interpretative Narratives of Neandertal Hunting." *Quaternary Science Reviews* 140
(May 2016): 1–20. doi.org/10.1016/j.quascirev.2016.03.004.

Whiten, Andrew, Jane Goodall, W. C. McGrew, T. Nishida, V. Reynolds, Y. Sugiyama,
C. E. G. Tutin, Richard Wrangham, and C. Boesch. "Charting Cultural Variation
in Chimpanzees." *Behaviour* 138, no. 11 (January 2001): 1481–516. www.jstor.org.

Whittaker, John C., Devin B. Pettigrew, and Ryan J. Grohsmeyer. "Atlatl Dart Velocity: Accurate Measurements and Implications for Paleoindian and Archaic Archaeology." *PaleoAmerica* 3, no. 2 (April 2017): 161–81. doi.org/10.1080
%2F20555563.2017.1301133.

Widmer, Randolph J., and Rebecca Storey. "The Cuisine of Prehispanic Central Mexico
Reconsidered: The 'Omnivore's Dilemma' Revisited." In *New Directions in Biocul-
tural Anthropology*, edited by Molly K. Zuckerman and Debra L. Martin, 259–78.
Hoboken, NJ: Wiley, 2017.

Wobber, Victoria, Brian Hare, and Richard Wrangham. "Great Apes Prefer Cooked
Food." *Journal of Human Evolution* 55, no. 2 (August 2008): 340–48. doi.org/10
.1016/j.jhevol.2008.03.003.

The World Bank. "Employment in Agriculture." Accessed July 26, 2017. data.worldbank.
org.

World Health Organization. "Appendix 1." *Global Status Report on Alcohol and Health,
2014.* Accessed July 13, 2017. www.who.int.

World History for Us All. "Key Theme 1: Patterns of Population." Accessed July 10, 2017.
worldhistoryforusall.ss.ucla.edu.

Wrangham, Richard. *Catching Fire: How Cooking Made Us Human.* London: Profile
Books, 2009.

Wrangham, Richard, and Rachel Carmody. "Human Adaptation to the Control of Fire."
Evolutionary Anthropology 19, no. 5 (October 2010): 187–99. doi.org/10.1002
/evan.20275.

Wynn, Jonathan, Matt Sponheimer, William H. Kimbel, Zeresenay Alemseged, Kaye
Reed, Zelalem K. Bedaso, and Jessica N. Wilson. "Diet of *Australopithecus afarensis*
from the Pliocene Hadar Formation, Ethiopia." *Proceedings of the National Academy of Sciences* 110, no. 26 (2013): 10495–500. doi.org/10.1073/pnas.1222559110.

Yellen, John. "Optimization and Risk in Human Foraging Strategies." *Journal of Human Evolution* 15, no. 8 (December 1986): 733–50. doi.org/10.1016/S0047-2484 (86)80007-0.

Zeder, Melinda A. "Archaeological Approaches to Documenting Animal Domestication." In *Documenting Domestication*, edited by Melinda A. Zeder, Daniel G. Bradley, Bruce D. Smith, and Eve Emshwiller, 171–80. Berkeley: University of California Press, 2006.

———. "The Origins of Agriculture in the Near East." *Current Anthropology* 52, no. S4 (October 2011): S221–35. doi.org/10.1086/659307.

———. "Pathways to Animal Domestication." In *Biodiversity in Agriculture: Domestication, Evolution, and Sustainability*, edited by Paul Gepts, Thomas R. Famula, Robert L. Bettinger, Stephen B. Brush, Ardeshir B. Damania, Patrick E. McGuire, and Calvin O. Qualset, 227–59. Cambridge: Cambridge University Press, 2012.

Zihlman, Adrienne. "Women in Evolution Part II: Subsistence and Social Organization among Early Hominins." *Signs* 4, no. 1 (Autumn 1978): 4–20. doi.org/10.1086/493566.

Zink, Katherine D., and Daniel E. Lieberman. "Impact of Meat and Lower Palaeolithic Food Processing Techniques on Chewing in Humans." *Nature* 531 (March 2016): 500–503. doi.org/10.1038/nature16990.

Zohary, Daniel, Maria Hopf, and Ehud Weiss. *Domestication of Plants in the Old World: The Origin and Spread of Domesticated Plants in Southwest Asia, Europe, and the Mediterranean Basin*. Oxford: Oxford University Press, 2012.

INDEX

A + 2B structure, 11–12
Abu Hureyra (village; Syria), 101–2
abundance, of food, 139–43, 163
access, to food, 143
acorns, 175
adaptation: environmental, 52–54; and food/cooking, 14–15, 182
addiction, in contemporary Western culture, 167
adolescence, 62, 215n44
aesthetics, 139–43, 163
Africa, 68, 78–79, 110, 112; Angola, 148; Dahomey (kingdom), 127–28; East Africa, 34, 36, 43, 212n2; Gombe reserve (Tanzania), 38; Hadar site (Ethiopia), 33; Hadza people (Tanzania), 60–63, 65, 82, 110; Kalahari Desert, 110, 112, 186–87; Kanjera South (Kenya), 42; Koobi Fora (Kenya), 39, 53–54; Maasai people, 44; Middle Awash Valley (Ethiopia), 33; Nariokotome site (Kenya), 48; Senegal, 28; Sierra Leone, 148; South Africa, 36, 78, 212n2; West Africa, 127, 149–50, 158
African Americans, 2, 148, 158. *See also* enslaved people, in antebellum South; plantation diets; slavery
age, and cook's role, 186
"agriculture," use of term, 95, 221n10
agricultural development, 21, 89–114, 185, 202
agricultural subsidies, 17
Aiello, Leslie, 54
Akha people (Southeast Asia), 99
Alabama, Moundville site, 109
alcohol, 129–34, 162, 167–69. *See also* beer and beer drinking; corn beer (*chicha*); wine
Allen, Catherine, 124
alliance feasts, 119–21

alpacas, 106
altered sensory perceptions, 133–34, 167–69. *See also* alcohol; hallucinogens; plants: psychoactive
amaranth, 163
Amarna (village; Egypt), 1–2, 190–91
Amazon region, 110; Nukak people (northern Amazon), 166–67; Warí people, 110, 115–19, 174
ambrosia, 162, 165
amrita, 165
amylase (enzyme), 225n40
ancestors, dead family members as, 172–73
Ancestral Puebloan people (Southwest US), 173
Andean societies, 8, 121–25, 165, 188–90; at Cerro Baúl, 115–17; at Chavín de Huántar, 169; Chiripa, 163; cooking pots of, 197–98; and corn, 156–57 (*See also* corn; corn beer); Farfán, 154–55, 170, 178; of Moquegua Valley, 115; religious festivals, 166–67; shamanic practices, 168–69; of Upper Mantaro Valley, 125, 155–57
anemia, 111
Angola, 148
animal carcasses, 82; hominins and, 42–45; processing of, 46; in scavenging model, 43–45. *See also* burnt food, as ritual offering; butchering
animal sacrifice, 162, 175
Annapolis, Maryland, 2
antebellum South (US), 143–51; culinary creolization of, 151–54. *See also* enslaved people, in antebellum South; plantation diets
apex predators, Neandertals as, 72–77
apples, 163
aqllawasi, 124
Arctic societies, 8, 74, 82, 110, 195